D0207088

Ideologies and Technologies of Motherhood

Race

Class

Sexuality

Nationalism

EDITED BY

Heléna Ragoné and
France Winddance Twine

FOREWORD BY

Rayna Rapp

Routledge
New York and London

Published in 2000 by
Routledge
29 West 35th Street
New York, NY 10001

Published in Great Britain by
Routledge
11 New Fetter Lane
London EC4P 4EE

Routledge is an imprint of the Taylor & Francis Group.

Library of Congress Cataloging-in-Publication Data
Ideologies and technologies of motherhood : race, class, sexuality, nationalism / edited by Heléna Ragoné and France Winddance Twine ; foreword by Rayna Rapp.
    p.   cm.
    Includes bibliographical references and index.
    ISBN 0-415-92109-0 (hb) — ISBN 0-415-92110-4 (cloth)
    1. Motherhood.   2. Mothers—Social conditions.   3. Human reproduction—Social aspects.   4. Human reproductive technology—Social aspects.   5. Minority women.   6. Socially handicapped women.   I. Ragoné, Heléna.
II. Twine, France Winddance, 1960–
HQ759.I33 2000
306.874'3—dc21   99-054216

Contents

For my mother, Mamie Lois Twine
—*France Winddance Twine*

For Barbara
—*Heléna Ragoné*

About the Contributors

Deborah Connolly is an assistant professor of cultural anthropology and women's studies in the Sociology Department at the University of Missouri, Kansas City. Her forthcoming book, *Mothering on the Margins: An Ethnography of Homeless Mothers,* will be published by the University of Minnesota Press.

Susan Dalton earned her Ph.D. in sociology at the University of California at Santa Barbara in 1999. She is an assistant professor of sociology at Chico State University. Her areas of specialization include gay and lesbian studies, gender studies, and sociology of law.

Christine Ward Gailey is chair of the Department of Women's Studies and professor of anthropology at the University of California, Riverside. Professor Gailey is the author of *Kinship to Kingship: Gender Hierarchy and State Formation in the Tongan Islands* (University of Texas Press, 1987) and editor of *Civilization in Crisis: Anthropological Perspectives and State Formation* (Sheffield, 1992). Her research focuses on cultural forms of resistance to gender hierarchy and other conditions of domination. Among her articles are studies of gender and colonialism, changing kinship in international migration, and perceptions of race in foster care and adoption. Her forthcoming book is *Blue Ribbon Babies and Labors of Love: Class, Race and Gender in U.S. Adoption* (University of Texas Press).

Marcia Claire Inhorn is associate professor of anthropology at Emory University. A medical anthropologist, she specializes in gender and health, international health and infectious disease, and feminist-informed anthropological epidemiology. Her major research projects focus upon the problem of infertility among Egyptian women; her two previous books are *Quest for Conception: Gender, Infertility, and Egyptian Medical Traditions* (University of Pennsylvania Press, 1994; winner of the Society for Medical Anthropology's Eileen Basker Prize) and *Infertility and Patriarchy: The Cultural Politics of Gender and Family Life in Egypt* (University of Pennsylvania Press, 1995). She is also coeditor, with Peter J. Brown, of *The Anthropology of Infectious Disease: International Health Perspectives* (Gordon and Breach, 1997).

Gail Landsman is associate professor of anthropology at the State University of New York at Albany. She is the author of *Sovereignty and Symbol: Indian/White Conflict at Ganienkeh* (University of New Mexico Press); in addition to work on Iroquois Indian activism she has done research on efforts to pass family and medical leave legislation, and on issues related to reproduction, disability, and nurturance. Her article "Reconstructing Motherhood in the Age of 'Perfect' Babies: Mothers of Infants and Toddlers with Disabilities" appeared in the journal *Signs* (1998); her piece "Does God Give Special Kids to Special Parents?: Personhood and the Child with Disabilities as Gift and as Giver" is a chapter in Linda Layne's edited volume *Transformative Motherhood*. She serves on local and statewide committees promoting parental activism in the Early Intervention System, and is currently preparing a book for Routledge based on a three-year research project on mothers of infants and young children with disabilities.

Linda L. Layne is Hale Professor of Humanities and Social Sciences and associate professor of anthropology in the Department of Science and Technology Studies at Rensselaer Polytechnic Institute. She has edited two volumes on anthropological approaches in science and technology studies and *The Rhetoric of the Gift: Transformative Motherhood in a Consumer Culture* (New York University Press, 1999). Her book *Motherhood Lost: Cultural Con-*

structions of Pregnancy Loss in the United States will be published by Routledge. She is currently investigating the experience of loss in toxically assaulted communities.

Diana Mulinari teaches in the Department of Sociology at Lunds University in Sweden. Mulinari, a native of Buenos Aires, has lived in political exile in Sweden for two decades. She is currently working on a research project that explores the notion of home and the politics of exile for Latin American women.

Heléna Ragoné is the author of numerous publications: *Surrogate Motherhood: Conception in the Heart* (Westview, 1994); "Chasing the Blood Tie: Surrogate Mothers, Adoptive Mothers and Fathers," *American Ethnologist* 23, 2 (1996): 352–65; *Situated Lives: Gender and Culture in Everyday Life,* coedited with Louise Lamphere and Patricia Zavella (Routledge, 1997); and *Reproducing Reproduction: Kinship, Power and Technological Innovation,* coedited with Sarah Franklin (University of Pennsylvania Press, 1997). She has consulted for the CBS television program *48 Hours,* the NBC television program *Turning Point,* Radio-Television Luxembourg, the German television channel Sat 1, and for stories on paternity and ovum donation for the *Cleveland Plain Dealer,* the *New Yorker,* and the *Wall Street Journal.* She is currently completing *Distant Kin: Gestational Surrogacy and Gamete Donation,* an ethnography that will explore the meteoric rise in the rates of gestational surrogacy and ovum donation in the United States. She is also completing *Riding Danger: Women in Horse Culture,* an ethnography of equestrianism that highlights how and why women negotiate the risk of death and serious physical injury in the highly gendered sport.

France Winddance Twine, an enrolled member of the Creek Nation of Oklahoma, is an associate professor in the Henry M. Jackson School of International Studies at the University of Washington, Seattle, and associate professor of sociology at the University of California, Santa Barbara. She is the author of *Racism in a Racial Democracy: The Maintenance of White Supremacy* *in Brazil* (Rutgers University Press, 1997) and coeditor, with Jonathan Warren, of *Racing Research, Researching Race: Methodological Dilemmas in Critical Race Studies* (New York University Press, 2000) and, with Kathleen Blee, *Feminism and Anti-racism: International Struggles* (New York University Press, forthcoming). She is completing a critical ethnography that explores the meaning of race and racism for the white birth mothers of African-descent children in Britain.

Foreword

Rayna Rapp

New School for Social Research

The essays you are about to read use the qualitative methods of anthropology and sociology to illuminate the underbelly of motherhood. In describing, interrogating, and analyzing how the aspirations and labors of some mothers are silenced, scorned, belittled, and trivialized, these authors deserve our attention. In these chapters, the boundaries of normative maternity are powerfully shown to be shaped in part by mothering relationships that fall outside or contradict those norms. Heléna Ragoné and France Winddance Twine have used the theoretical tools of critical race feminism to nurture and present these essays. Here, the politics of motherhood plays out across fault lines that any generalizing notions of women's shared experiences must interrogate.

In the field of feminist anthropology, from which the majority of these chapters are drawn, analyses of the politics of reproduction have a hybridized theoretical genealogy. Feminist anthropologists were quick to link the study of kinship to the analysis of gender (see, e.g., Collier and Yanagisako 1987), and vigorous crossovers occurred with medical anthropology and health politics (Lewin and Olesen 1985). Volumes investigating the female reproductive life cycle appeared (Buckley and Gottlieb 1988; Kerns and Brown 1992), and the study of childbirth—medicalized and otherwise—became something of a cottage industry (Davis-Floyd 1992; Davis-Floyd and Sargent 1997; Ginsburg and Rapp 1991). The importance of racial formations and class locations were recognized in the medicalization of U.S. women's reproductive lives (Martin 1987; Michaelson 1988), and the international politics of the subject were dragged to the center of social theory

(Ginsburg and Rapp 1995b). The survival of children and the mothering work entailed in it were brought under analytic scrutiny (Scheper-Hughes 1992; Scheper-Hughes and Sargent 1998; Stephens 1996). Feminist scholars who focused on communities of color in the United States highlighted state surveillance, eugenics, and commodification as central issues for the analysis of motherhood (Collins 1990, 1994; Glenn, Chang, and Forcey 1994).

Building on David Schneider's insights into how U.S. kinship uses metaphors of blood and contract to condense and naturalize the biological and social bases of relationships, anthropological feminists also took on the new reproductive technologies (Casper 1998; Franklin 1997; Ragoné 1994; Strathern 1992a, 1992b), attacking their reductive foundationalism. This work crisply intersected feminist science studies (Haraway 1989a, 1989b, 1991, 1997; Franklin 1995), where contemporary biomedical rationality has been analyzed as operating to reproduce older forms of gender, ethnoracial, class, and national stratification, even (or perhaps especially) on its technologically "revolutionary" edges (Michaels and Morgan 1999; Rapp 1999; Stolcke 1986).

These multiple theoretical strands can be used as a sort of scaffold for an analysis of what several of us have elsewhere labeled "stratified reproduction"—the hierarchical organization of reproductive health, fecundity, birth experiences, children, and child rearing that supports and rewards the maternity of some women while despising or outlawing the motherwork of others (Colen 1986, 1990, 1995; Ginsburg and Rapp 1995b). The idea of stratified reproduction helps us to make sense of the rich and troubling case studies to which you are about to turn.

Most obviously, essays in this book reveal the overt biases whose everyday practices stratify some children and mothers as more culturally "real" and worthy than others. Christine Gailey's analysis of adoption shows how this expanding practice of making kinship across differences—of class, and sometimes racial category or nation—might provide a subversive lens through which to view the social naturalization of parents and children, and the denaturalized ranking of "good" adoptive mothers over "bad" birth ones. Instead, hierarchies of ideological value are quickly resolidified, usually to the detriment of adopted children. Gail Landsman's discussion of "real motherhood" explores emotional and cultural trajectories of women raising disabled children. Their children are clearly ranked as "defective," a classification that they learn to challenge and resist while remaking what Erving Goffman would have labeled their own "spoiled identities" as mothers operating under the courtesy stigmas attached to their offspring's disabilities (Goffman 1963). One strength of this volume lies in its display of the analytics of race: Heléna Ragoné's account of gestational surrogacy, in distinction to "traditional" surrogacy (surely a plausible oxymoron), demonstrates how racial difference is used to denaturalize one mother's rented womb and naturalize the powers of the adopting mother. In France Winndance Twine's contribution, we learn that white mothers bearing and raising African-descent children in Britain are often cut off from their original, more racially privileged communities of kinship and only problematically integrated into the communities of color in which they most often raise their offspring.

Class hierarchy, too, must be factored into an understanding of reproductive stratification: Those poor white women whose lives are spent struggling with devastating loss of household stability in the United States are most likely to be scrutinized by the state as mothers. Sometimes their maternal practices are acts of symbolic and practical resistance, as described in Deborah Connolly's discussion of homeless mothers. And the symbolics of maternity are highly stratified: in U.S. culture, dominant Protestant and individualizing values sort those who "finish the jobs they start" from those who fail various tests of completion. As Linda Layne shows in her discussion of pregnancy loss, women who suffer the death of a child, whether as a fetus or shortly after birth, are culturally classified as failed mothers. They may keep, display, and memorialize "boundary objects" associated with the child they never got to take home because such residues provide material, quite literally, for resisting their own liminality and invisibilization as nonmothers or failed mothers. In Susan Dalton's analysis of how nonbiological mothers have fared in the California courts, it becomes evident that the social work of parenting is awarded legal value only when attached to fathers or their subsequent wives. It cannot be assigned to the women partners of lesbian biological mothers without overturning the naturalism that undergirds family law itself. In the courts, even "blended" families are renaturalized.

When we apply the analysis of stratified maternity internationally, global political economic relations and local reproductive practices come sharply into view. Marcia Inhorn's analysis of Egyptian women's struggles with infertility reveals that only elite women with access to the international medical-economic sector can seek in vitro treatments. Poor women may resist the eugenic labeling their circumstances call forth. But all women are vulnerable to an Islamic *fatwa* that makes a husband's fertility dilemmas soluble through his right to divorce and remarriage if his wife is sterile. Women do not have this right. National religious institutions here intersect globalizing medical technologies to reproduce gendered social hierarchies. In Nicaragua, the "mothers of the revolution" are at once romanticized for their Marian sacrifice of husbands and sons to battle and trivialized as political agents in their own right. Diana Mulinari shows us how the courageous work of many Nicaraguan women as makers of both war and peace disrupts the polarizing discourse of good and bad mothering in practice, even while it is reduced to cultural stereotypes in public political discourse.

Collectively, these essays invite the reader to examine powerful ideologies and practices of motherhood that segregate women across familiar and biased lines of privilege and disdain. Peering across the chasms that sort us all—mothers and nonmothers, the fertile and the less than fertile, sexual-preference outlaws, able-bodied or disabled, older or younger, bearers of despised racial, class, and ethnic/national markings—into stratified reproducers, we better understand the consequences of discrimination in the policing of normative womanhood. Take a good look.

Acknowledgments

In 1996 we organized a session entitled "Ideologies and Technologies of Motherhood" for the ninety-fifth annual meetings of the American Anthropological Association held in San Francisco. The session was co-invited by the Association for Feminist Anthropology and the Association of Black Anthropologists: a special thank you to both sessions, as well as to our original panel participants: Marcia Inhorn, Susan Kahn, Gail Landsman, Iris Lopez, and our discussants Emily Martin and Rayna Rapp for their insightful comments. We also want to thank Faye Ginsburg, who served as an outside reviewer for this volume.

An additional source of inspiration for this volume is a course that one of us (Winddance Twine) conceptualized in 1995 and taught for three years at the Univesrity of Washington in Seattle. Twine is particularly indebted to her undergraduate and graduate students who enrolled in "Ideologies and Technologies of Motherhood" during the winter of 1999: Laura Blackburn, Brenda Broussard, Sara Otto Chakwanda, Molly Jean Eitzen, Antoinette Guzzo, Karen K. Hannegan, Jennifer Johnson, Jennifer Kullberg, Beth Leder, Suzanne Powell, Laura Root, Pamela Talley, Montana Vonfliss, and Mary Wyninger.

A very special thanks is due to our contributors who have graciously and generously worked with us over the last four years to make this collection possible. And last, but certainly not least, a heartfelt thank you to our feminist colleagues/friends whose support both personally and professionally has proved invaluable.

Introduction

Motherhood on the
Fault Lines

Heléna Ragoné and
France Winddance Twine

Ideologies and Technologies of Motherhood is intended to expand our understanding of critical race feminisms as well as the field of reproduction by exploring women's efforts to resist what Angela Davis (1998) has called "alienated and fragmented maternities." Such maternal projects problematize hegemonic ideologies that posit the unquestioned existence of racial matching, exclusively heterosexual family formations, unassisted or "natural" reproduction, unequal economic privilege, and the idea of "perfect" babies. By bringing together in one volume analyses of reproductive self-determination, maternal rights, and family formations that challenge racial ideologies of difference, class inequality, biogenetic ownership, restrictive legal definitions of parenthood, and restrictive adoption mandates, this collection contributes to an understanding of what Patricia Hill Collins (1994) has referred to as "divergent" experiences of mothering. Drawing inspiration from U.S. black feminist theory, critical race feminisms, feminist anthropology, and feminist sociology, it analyzes the ways in which capitalism, cultural ideologies, religious imperatives, and material privilege reverberate cross-culturally in women's maternal life practices.[1] The idea that motherhood, womanhood, personhood, race, and class are contingent is neither new nor novel, but *Ideologies and Technologies of Motherhood* clarifies why reproduction as a field of inquiry and a site of contestation cannot be consigned to naturalized domains or idioms.

1

The contributors to this book are all actively engaged in qualitative anthropological and sociological research on the varied dimensions of contemporary motherhood (psychological, material, medical, legal, and racialized). They provide ethnographic case studies and theoretical analyses of a range of maternal practices and experiences, from those of infertile Egyptian women, Nicaraguan mothers, white lesbian co-mothers, surrogate mothers, British transracial mothers, and homeless mothers to those of mothers in mourning for lost children and the mothers of disabled children. This volume is concerned with four categories of motherhood that have not been central in previous edited volumes: (1) women who are presumed to be or who self-identify as racially distinct from their children, by birth, gestation, or adoption (Twine, Ragoné, Gailey), (2) women (and men) who experience fractured identities as a result of not having produced "perfect" babies or "perfect" pregnancies (Landsman, Layne, Inhorn), (3) women who are mothering under conditions of material deprivation and political uncertainty (Connolly, Mulinari), and (4) women who are attempting to achieve motherhood through the use of innovative medical technologies (Inhorn, Ragoné) or new legal possibilities (Dalton).[2]

This volume seeks to integrate the insights of black feminist theory, feminist anthropology, feminist sociology, and feminist legal theory in one volume. The case studies exemplify feminists' analyses of the global politics of reproduction, the legal regulation of mothering, and the racialization of reproduction. *Ideologies and Technologies of Motherhood* furthers earlier feminist analyses of reproduction by bringing black feminist theory to bear upon the maternal struggles of nonblack and non-U.S. women (including British, Egyptian, and Nicaraguan women), reprising many of the themes integral to black feminist theorizing about race, reproduction, and social inequality. In describing the maternal experiences of women of color, for example, Patricia Hill Collins has argued that "much of their experiences with motherhood, in fact, stem from the work they performed as children. The commodification of children of color, from the enslavement of African children, who were legally 'owned' as property, to the subsequent treatment of children as units in agricultural work, family business, and industry, has been a major theme shaping motherhood for women of color" (1994: 50). Collins's insights into the lives of U.S. women of color can be applied to the lives of poor, working-class, and immigrant women elsewhere (see the essays by Connolly and Mulinari in this volume). By providing historical, sociological, legal, autobiographical, and literary analyses of motherhood, black feminist theorists have reframed and shifted the theoretical questions and answers, including one of the issues central to black feminist theorizing, that of the commodification of maternal-child labor (Shaw 1994; King 1995).

Racial Ideologies, Racial Realities

Part I, "Racial Ideologies and Racial Realities," addresses the ideologies of racial difference for adoptive, gestational, and genetic birth mothers of children who are presumed to be racially different, or "split off," from them. It also explores how ideologies of racial difference presuppose the existence of various types of maternal-child disjunctures. Black feminist theorists working in the United States, as well as others, have transformed and expanded analyses of gender and racial inequality by generating integrated analyses of mothering that consider the intersections of race, class, gender, and criminalization.

Christine Ward Gailey's analysis of adoption reveals not only the highly contested, emotionally charged climate in which adoption takes place but also how current adoption practices fail to safeguard the needs of children and families. As Gailey reveals, adoption as it is presently practiced serves instead to reinforce existing cultural notions of racial difference. In racial and class-based systems rife with tensions, adoption both owes its existence to and reproduces deeply entrenched, culturally generated categories of meaning, such as nature/nurture and genetic/nongenetic. Paradigms such as good (adoptive) and bad (birth) mothers and natural and unnatural are, we learn, being routinely manipulated by adoption programs, although Gailey's study illustrates that kinship is essentially processual in nature.

Heléna Ragoné's chapter traces the changes produced by the meteoric rise in the rates of gestational surrogacy (which now represents more than 50 percent of all arrangements at the world's largest surrogate-mother program). A rapid shift from "traditional" to gestational surrogacy has been accompanied by profound changes in the ideology of surrogacy, most notably with respect to critical issues such as identity, race, and ethnicity. A salient category of meaning, race is routinely manipulated by participants in ways that reconceptualize their experiences of pregnancy. Focusing upon the 30 percent of gestational surrogacy arrangements that involve pairing up surrogates with couples from different racial, ethnic, and cultural backgrounds, Ragoné's research reveals that women who participate in gestational surrogacy embrace a more traditional rendering of kinship or relatedness than do other surrogates. In the interest of reinforcing biogenetically based perspectives of relatedness, gestational surrogates also conceptualize racial differences so as to create additional barriers between themselves and the children they gestate.

Ragoné's analysis reveals that gestational mothers use the category of race to distance themselves from children they intend to relinquish at birth. Their arguments about racial difference and biogenetic links suggest that they resist or counter the experience of maternal bonding by drawing upon cultural ideologies about racial difference. This form of emotional management uses racialized difference to enhance maternal-fetal bonds; the fetus can be understood to be "separate" from the surrogate, so that she can perceive herself as simply providing a service and/or a product.

France Winndance Twine's chapter provides a rare ethnographic analysis of how white mothers engaged in transracial caretaking alliances cope with their own racialization within multiracial families.[3] Drawing upon four years of field research and ninety-five focused life history interviews in Britain with white birth mothers of African-descent children and their black family members, Twine asks how white birth mothers experience and conceptualize the presumed racial gap between themselves and their children. Comparing the narratives of white and black mothers of children of multiracial heritage, Twine traces the racial logics and ideologies that naturalize and racialize a mother's ability to empathize with her children. Twine analyzes the logic of discourses employed by family members (sisters-in-law and male partners) to uncover how ideologies of racial difference attempt to naturalize maternal empathy. Furthermore, Twine also explores racial divisions within British multiracial families that presume that white birth mothers are unable to empathize with their African-descent children's experience of racism due to differences in their racial status. Finally, she uncovers a trope of maternal incompetence applied to white birth mothers by some of their black family members, which motivates some white mothers to work hard to acquire and perfect the racial literacy skills necessary to counter the racism that their children will face.

Narratives of Personhood

In Part II, "Narratives of Personhood," Linda Layne makes an important contribution to our understanding of the complex relationship among pregnancy loss, personhood, and liminality. By providing an analysis of women and men who have experienced pregnancy loss (miscarriage and stillbirth), Layne reveals how the various cultural directives that minimize the significance of such losses may intensify feelings of suffering and despair. Individuals undergoing such losses find themselves experiencing disruption and discontinuity in a cultural milieu that privileges predictability and linearity. Layne weaves together a number of poignant accounts that reveal just how loss permeates the worldview of those who have had this experience. In its exploration of the significance of material objects in mediating reproduction and personhood, Layne provides a much-needed analysis of the degree to which material consumption signifies and defends conceptions of parental personhood.

Marcia Inhorn's comparative cross-class analysis of contemporary Egyptian women in Cairo illuminates the centrality of motherhood to the Egyptian concept of personhood. Inhorn maps the struggles of infertile women who are "seeking children," that is, negotiating access to assistive reproductive technologies in a legal context that denies infertile married women rights equal to those of their husbands, who are permitted to divorce them if they fail to produce a child, and in a medical culture that grants access to safer and more effective reproductive technologies only to transnational, elite Egyptian women. Inhorn's analysis of this differential economic access to therapeutic infertility treatments suggests that ideologies that privilege elites can be considered neoeugenic to the extent that they privilege the reproduction of educated and upper-class women over that of other women.

Gail Landsman provides an analysis of the debates that surround reproductive technologies. While much has been written on what constitutes a "real mother" (genetics, gestation, social factors, or some combination), little has been written about what constitutes a "real child." Landsman inquires into the circumstances that determine how motherhood is defined and how it is experienced by women who are raising children who do not fulfill expectations about perfection in the contemporary United States. Mothers who give birth to disabled children routinely blame themselves for failing to reproduce a normal child; they attempt to make sense of this experience through the notion of causation—for example, having taken Tylenol or having drunk a glass of wine during their pregnancy.

Blurred Boundaries: Definitions of Motherhood

In Part III, "Blurred Boundaries: Legal, Political, and Economic Definitions of Motherhood," Susan Dalton provides an analysis of recent legal cases involving co-mother custody disputes in California. In this exemplary study of the courts' role in enforcing ideologies of genetic ownership as a component of state-sanctioned motherhood, Dalton illuminates a number of dilemmas encountered by mothers who may not share a genetic link with their children. She questions legal definitions of motherhood that require a genetic link and fail to recognize the social relationships and nurturance provided by women whose maternal claims do not include genetic relatedness. Her analysis further illuminates the legal vulnerabilities shared by lesbian and nonlesbian co-mothers who are assumed (and expected) to follow prescribed pathways to motherhood in order to obtain legal recognition.

Diana Mulinari's work on Nicaraguan women reveals the palpable tensions that have arisen between culturally reified images of women as powerful and autonomous and those that demand women be long-suffering and self-sacrificing. Her research on women's roles during the Nicaraguan revolution demonstrates that domestic roles traditionally associated with motherhood and mothering are in fact integral to public and political fields of action. This point has perhaps been made nowhere more apparent than in the well-known activities of the mothers of the Playa del Mayo, the female relatives of the disappeared. While typical gender ideology in Latin America continues to portray women as dutifully remaining in the private domain, Mulinari has revealed through the lens of ethnography that women's participation in the Nicaraguan revolution disrupted such dichotomous renderings. She contributes to a nascent body of literature on the gendered iconography of nationalist and revolutionary discourses by illuminating the varied and complex role that Nicaraguan mothers assumed during the Nicaraguan revolution.

Deborah Connolly's ethnographic study of white homeless mothers in the United States adds an important dimension to the literature on mothers receiving income support or other forms of state assistance due to material deprivation.[4] Connolly examines unhoused mothers whose material conditions prevent them from being able to achieve the standards of "good enough" mothering but who nevertheless challenge the stigma of poverty and surveillance of their mothering by reaffirming their right to parent their children. This chapter pays careful attention to the links between material privilege and maternal authority. Like U.S. black, American Indian, and Latina mothers in need of state support, these poor white mothers also find themselves under moral surveillance and suspicion because of their material circumstances.

The contributors to *Ideologies and Technologies of Motherhood* break new theoretical ground by offering richly crafted ethnographies that ask what it means to be a woman and a mother in variously circumscribed technological, legal, material, and religious contexts. By placing at the center the experiences of surrogate mothers, adoptive mothers, lesbian co-mothers, transracial mothers, mothers of children with disabilities, poor mothers, and would-have-been mothers, this volume seeks to illuminate the ways that matrices of power reverberate in the lives of women attempting to mother along a range of fault lines—economic, sexual, religious, and technological. Whether one examines the intersection of womanhood and motherhood within technologized cultures or within the shifting, culturally situated constructions of family, personhood, perfection, or race, there remains a preponderance of taken-for-granted assumptions that routinely conflate the complexity of women's roles. In anthropology and sociology there has been a formidable tradition of feminist theorizing. It is our hope that *Ideologies and Technologies of Motherhood* will contribute to and extend this theoretical tradition within feminist studies of the family.

Notes

We thank Faye Ginsburg for suggesting the use of the phrase "motherhood on the fault lines."

1. A number of recently published volumes on race and reproduction and feminist legal theory have expanded analyses of how U.S. black, American Indian, and Latina women, in particular, as well as white women negotiate motherhood in a context of social, economic, and racial inequality. Work by U.S. black and Chicana feminists also has implications for theorizing about the maternal experiences of white women. See, for example, Roberts 1997; Gomez 1997; Kline 1994.

2. For example, see two edited volumes that expanded feminist theorizing regarding maternal subjectivities and practices by providing analyses that included slave mothers, gay/lesbian families, paid caregivers, race, and poverty: Thorne and Yalom 1992 and Glenn, Chang, and Forcey 1994. However, neither includes a discussion of transracial adoption, transracial birth mothers parenting in multiracial families, mothers of disabled children, or surrogate mothers.

3. This issue has been addressed in several recently published feminist memoirs, including Lazarre 1996; Thompson 2000; and Reddy 1994.

4. Examples of recent work by sociologists on the historical and contemporary experiences of unmarried mothers and welfare mothers include Luker 1996; Kaplan 1997; Mink 1995; Edin and Lein 1997; and Solinger 1992.

Racial
Ideologies
and
Racial
Realities

Ideologies of Motherhood and Kinship in U.S. Adoption

Christine Ward Gailey

In the United States, family formation by adoption involves a growing but still very small fraction of the population.[1] It nonetheless is overrepresented in the media as an issue, because it stands as peculiar in a society where birth is the prevailing way that children enter families and where the dominant idiom of kinship is that "blood is thicker than water" (Schneider 1968). Adoption in the United States has become the focus of a range of questions about motherhood. On television talk shows, in the newspapers, and on radio, adoption is given a prominence far beyond the numbers of children adopted or those known to be legally available for adoption.

Background: Adoption and Dominant Beliefs about Kinship in a Racialized State

There are a number of controversies in the United States surrounding adoptive parenting, ones that show that there is what is sometimes called a "master narrative" of kinship, namely, the belief that kinship is strongest where there are genetic connections between parent and child. For example, when surrogate motherhood became technically possible, the media and legal furor pitted the "rights" of the sperm donor or adoptive father against those of the egg donor or gestator or birth mother (see Ragoné 1996). The Baby M case, where the birth mother had signed a surrogacy contract with an adoptive couple but then sought to rescind the contract once the child was born, resulted eventually in the courts upholding her claim, because a "bond" had developed between her and the child during the pregnancy (see Pollitt 1987). In that highly contested case, the class issues were prominent, as the surrogate mother was working-class and the adoptive parents were prosperous professionals. The only rationale the courts could invoke that was more powerful than class and sperm-connection claims of the adoptive couple was the notion of maternal bonding. Notably in this case and other surrogacy situations, the primary players were the two genetic parents, with the adoptive mother decidedly in the background. Indeed, in the Baby M case the adoptive mother was vilified for not having been proven infertile before deciding to adopt through surrogacy. So the dominant narrative was supported: (1) those with genetic ties have greater claims to a child than others (nature over nurture); (2) women who can bear children should try by all means financially possible to do so before "resorting" to adoption; and (3) in infancy, at least, maternal bonding is stronger than paternal bonding because of pregnancy and birth. Although this essay will not address gestational surrogacy, I would add only that in the cases where a woman contracts to carry a fertilized ovum from a couple, her legal claims to the child are much diminished, pointing out an inherent set of priorities to that "master narrative." The adoptive mother is foregrounded in these cases only because it is her egg involved along with her husband's sperm.

In addition to surrogacy cases, there have been a number of highly publicized custody cases in the United States involving adopted children and birth relatives (primarily birth fathers) who had been unnamed or had not been contacted at the time the birth mother relinquished her rights to the child, or birth mothers who felt they had been pressured to relinquish claims and whose circumstances had changed in the interim (see Maloney 1994; Cordes 1993). These cases have made agencies far more stringent in "nailing down," as one social worker put it, the termination of the birth parents' and birth relatives' claims, and these cases informed debate over the national adoption law reforms of 1996–97, which streamlined the process of terminating parental rights. In those custody cases, despite the length of time (in one case three years and another, five) that the child had lived as part of the adoptive family, the birth parent was granted custody. The bonding or attachment of the child to the adoptive family was deemed not to supersede the birth parents' claims.

What these cases show is that adoptive parenthood is seen as problematic in the United States, and adoptive mothering is viewed as inferior to genetically based mothering. Complicating this last statement, however, is the racialized nature of U.S. society. These cases involved all white people, albeit from different social classes (a situation distinct from gestational surrogacy). The issue of transracial adoption is even more complex, because it pits a cross-cutting "master narrative" of race against those of class and kinship.

Transracial adoption in the United States is a gloss for the adoption of black (African-American especially, but also Afro-Caribbean) children by whites. It should be noted that, although Native Americans are racialized in most parts of the United States, community objections to whites adopting Native American children can be argued on the grounds of national sovereignty, and so are governed by different legislation (Strong 1998). As a number of scholars have pointed out, during slavery, and subsequently as paid nannies, African-American women have long reared white children among wealthier segments of the U.S. urban population and in the U.S. South; however, these women never had legal rights to the children (Ladner 1977). The question of transracial adoption concerns the problematic legal status of community rights in a situation where a group (African Americans) lacks sovereignty. The objections to transracial adoption center on the question of appropriate identity formation in a racist society or the right of children to grow up among their own people, especially where that people is targeted in terms of discrimination. While this paper cannot delve into the nuances of what is a politically complex issue, the longitudinal studies of transracial adoption point to strategies that are associated with successful identity formation (Simon et al. 1994; Gaber and Aldridge 1994). These circumstances generally involve parents reorienting the family to include peers who are from the child's racial background, recognizing and problematizing difference and racism, providing a diverse daily environment through neighborhood, schools, and the like, and so on. As one adoptive mother put it, "People may see us a white family with black children, but I point out that we're a black family with white members."

Those who are in support of transracial adoption tend to argue from a needs basis—there are a disproportionate number of black children in foster care—or a "race-blind" position, that is, laws should not distinguish by race (see Bartholet 1993). The range of those objecting to transracial placement tend to argue convincingly that the very reasons for a dispro-portionate number of black children in foster care stems from racial dis-crimination or the effects of it in the form of poverty, and the lack of effective and widespread recruitment of prospective adopters within the communities. Moreover, critics argue that "race blind" policies ignore the persistence of racism and its effects and thereby support white privilege (e.g. Howe 1995, 1997). Despite these arguments, the national adoption reform laws of 1996–1997 make it a ground for rescinding federal funding for agencies to use race as a consideration in placement. The actual num-ber of transracial placements has never been great, but their existence at all becomes a ground for confronting or downplaying issues of race in the United States. Given the polarization that has ensued, and the rhetoric of the "child's best interest" that is involved, the complex problems con-fronted by both birth and adoptive families are generally backgrounded, except in memoirs (Bates 1993; Costin and Wattenberg 1979; Townsend and Perkins 1992; Waldron 1995).

But even where surrogacy, paternal rights, or transracial adoption are not involved, birth mothers, adult adoptees, and adoptive parents form an arena where several ideologies of motherhood are disputed. Often the questions include whether or not a unique connection is produced between a woman and a child she gestates, sometimes called a "birth bond." If a birth bond exits, then how can some mothers relinquish legal rights to their children? Are adoptive mothers "supermoms" because they are seeking to overcome a disrupted "birth bond"? Are they "failed women" because so many in the United States adopt for reasons of infertility? Should open adoptions—where there is some kind of connection between birth parent(s) and adoptive family—be encouraged, or does this interfere with the children's attachment? These questions are provocative, certain to spark a lively, if not heated, discussion.

Adoption, one might think, poses a direct challenge to notions that mothering grows out of a genetic or birth connection between a woman and a child. Because most adoptions in the United States are not open— that is, the adoption records are sealed and the child no longer sees or has other contact with the birth parents at least until age eighteen—adoption either severs the connection between the birth mother and the child, or sometimes, if the child has been living in a loving foster care situation since infancy, severs the connection between foster parent(s) and child. Adoption involves created commitment. Anthropologist Judith Modell (1994) has argued that adoption provides a lens through which we can see that all kinship is made or constructed, rather than being the unfolding of a natural reproductive imperative. By *kinship* I mean the process of claiming people as belonging to a group that sees itself as connected in a fundamental way—a group that cares for its members through life transitions and crises as well as on an everyday basis, rears children, shares resources in an understood manner, and maintains often unspoken boundaries and rules for inclusion and expulsion.[2]

Whether or not to adopt invokes a range of concerns: what does infertility mean for a person or a couple? What does it mean if a child looks different from the parents? How important is genetic composition? Environment? Is genetic connection crucial to one of the partners? Both? Neither? How are the children's ethnic and familial identities formed? In the process of addressing or evading these questions, particularly among middle-income and wealthy sectors where there are more options—privately arranged adoption, international adoption, a plethora of infertility treatments and alternatives—we see beliefs regarding race, gender, heredity, and kinship at play. For those who have adopted, through public agencies, private agencies, lawyers, or internationally, adoption provides us with a way of seeing how the major vectors of difference in the society—class, race, and gender—affect the meaning of motherhood.

To understand the ways in which motherhood is contested in adoption, I interviewed a sample of adoptive parents from 1991 to 1998, attended several adoption conferences, observed preadoption training sessions in two adoption agencies, and participated and observed postadoption support groups. In listening to the parents' stories—how they spoke about their child and their child's birth parent(s), the circumstances that brought them to adopt, and their reactions to legally mandated home study by adoption social workers—it became clear that although adoptive parents do not hold uniform views regarding motherhood or uniform attitudes toward their children's birth mothers, there were some patterns. In this essay, I will focus on how mothering and mother-child relationships are conceptualized by adopters across the class, race, and gender divides in the United States.

This research is based on participant observation of preadoption parental training sessions, postadoption parental support groups, and interviews with a snowball sample of ninety-three parents of sixty-one children adopted between 1991 and 1997 and six adoption social workers active during that period, as well as five birth mothers considered at risk of relinquishing or being forced to relinquish their children and three relatives of these at-risk birth mothers. The adopter sample included single mothers, heterosexual married couples, lesbian couples, and a gay couple. Among these adopters were six African-American couples, twenty-nine European-American couples, four African-American single mothers, eighteen European-American single mothers, and one single European-American father. Among the unmarried parents, who had to adopt legally as individuals, there was one gay white couple and three lesbian couples: one African-American, one European-American, and one African-American and European-American. Of the sixty-one children adopted by these families, thirty-six adoptions were accomplished through public agencies, nineteen were through private agencies, and six were privately arranged; there were forty-seven domestic adoptions and fourteen international adoptions.[3] Of the domestic adoptions, twenty-five children were over three years old when adopted; of the international adoptions, all but two were infants or toddlers when adopted.[4] Each of these families was interviewed at least once; I interviewed couples together. In addition, the research included participant observation of two preadoption parent training programs run by agencies, several adoption conferences, and several postadoption support groups.

Based on this research, I will outline first the race, class, and gendered contours of the dominant images of motherhood in the United States. Following that, I will discuss how adoptive motherhood is shaped by these dominant images colliding with the ideologies of "natural" kinship in the United States, the subversive moment adoption provides to these dominant images, and the ensuing medicalization and marginalization of adoption. From there, I consider why the "natural motherhood" image is not extended to give status to the birth mother in adoption. How are birth mothers transformed ideologically into "bad mothers," and how are these images reproduced in the adoption process? Then I will discuss the adopter narratives and circumstances of three categories of adoptive families: single-mother adoptions, public agency adoptions, and international adoptions. Finally, I will discuss what these narratives reveal about motherhood and adoptive parenting in practice in a context of race, class, and gender hierarchy.

Dominant Images of Maternity: Mothers as White and Middle-Class

David Schneider argued that the dominant ideology of kinship in the United States, that "blood is thicker than water," stresses that normal kinship is rooted in genetic connections between parents and children they conceive (Schneider 1968). Dominant ideologies of maternity in the United States hold that a woman's natural role is that of mother, even if women today also are workers; a related belief is that a special connection exists between mothers and the children they bear, what one set of authors has called a "birthbond" (Gediman and Brown 1989). A number of anthropologists and historians have argued that these kinds of beliefs are part of patriarchally shaped ideologies of family and are far from universal (see, e.g., Collier and Yanagisako 1987).

There are two aspects of the dominant notion of women as mothers that enter into the adoption picture. One is biological determinism, the notion that women are predestined by nature to be mothers by virtue of having uteruses and ovaries; motherhood is created by women's role in biological reproduction. The second, related aspect is gender essentialism, namely, that across cultures and time periods, women and men have basically different natures, temperaments, and predispositions; women are inherently more maternal than men, and maternal behavior is marked by nurturing. Alongside these beliefs about women, and as a correlate of what Jonathan Marks (1995) calls the "hereditarian bias" of highly stratified societies such as the United States, are beliefs in genetic determinism: it is widely assumed, although not demonstrated, that genetics plays a determining role in the social potential of an individual, focused variously on criminality, intelligence, or personality, depending on the context. Together, these beliefs forge an ideology that "real" kinship is based on genetic connection, and that childbearing and child rearing are women's natural role, whatever else they may do in a society.

Consequently, adoption becomes conceived as what Judith Modell terms "kinship with strangers" (1994), a tie seen as inherently weaker than what Margery Wolf called in the Taiwanese case "uterine ties" (Wolf 1972). It might be added that other forms of kinship—fostering, marriage/life partnerships—also are viewed as weaker than the links between birth parents and their children and between siblings born of the same parents. This is focused in the U.S. adoption scene as a belief that attachment through caregiving cannot substitute for the connection created in giving birth; adoption cannot heal what Michael Dorris and Louise Erdrich have called "the broken cord" (Dorris 1989; Erdrich 1995; but see Jewett 1982 for a sense of adoption as involving a similar kind of separation and loss as other disruptions). Birth connections are viewed either fearfully or hopefully as persisting in the face of separation and loss (Gediman and Brown 1989).

Behind this assumption, or fear, is that "normal" motherhood is somewhat instinctual and that mothers who give children up are somehow "bad" mothers—or even bad women, particularly if they are single or have drug or alcohol addictions. Adoptive mothers, by extension, are seen as striving to be good mothers, although it is assumed that unless they are proven to be fertile either before or after the adoption, they are somehow compensating for failed womanhood. "Natural" motherhood is thus assumed to be biological motherhood, that is, motherhood through pregnancy and birth. Adoptive mothers become unnatural in this sense, even as birth mothers who relinquish their children voluntarily are also viewed as unnatural. The stage is set for both ends of the adoption continuum to be portrayed negatively in the media, although the class (and often race) imagery tilts the competency and compassion scales in favor of the adoptive mother.

Given this emphasis on birthing, the position of fathers is inherently problematic. In the dominant ideology of family, fathers are accorded a social construction of closeness based on the notion of genetic similarity, but this assumption of interest is negated when the crosscutting ideology of race comes into play. As such, black birth fathers and adoptive fathers, as well as stepfathers of all colors, are viewed with suspicion, or portrayed as needing either persuasion or tutelage by wives if they are to bond with children. This belief is played out in the ways parents come to adopt: studies have shown that usually wives persuade husbands to adopt, following an extended period of unsuccessfully attempting to conceive or a series of miscarriages or stillbirths. The husband enters into the adoption scenario, in these cases, as motivated in part to help the wife fulfill her desire to have children. To the extent that any of these beliefs is internalized in a population, it will seem natural or commonsensical to the participants. Practices may come to resemble the expectations, and in turn will underscore the seeming naturalness of the belief. People practicing kinship that is even superficially at odds with the dominant model will feel or be made to feel different, and adoption in the United States is accordingly seen or treated as a stigma to the extent that some adoptees and adopters have begun to describe the prejudice as "adoptism" (see March 1995b; Martinson 1993).

There were no uniform models of motherhood emerging from the interviews I conducted, taken as a whole. But if we take into account class, race, marital status, and gender, there were patterns in how the adoptive mothers viewed motherhood—their own and that of their child's birth mother. In their talk and their reflections, various degrees and forms of the dominant ideology of motherhood outlined above can be glimpsed. Alongside and often in opposition to these are practices and beliefs that reflect the dimensions of social hierarchy among these adults.

Conceiving Adoptive Motherhood

The prevailing model of kinship in the literature is one of "naturalness" as the "normal" situation. That is, adoption is considered to be problematic where kinship is seen as something that should develop from biological connections between mothers and offspring. The "normal" or "intact" family in the literature is a married, heterosexual couple with their birth children (see, e.g., Kirk 1982; Feigelman 1997). Other forms are deviant and prone to difficulty unless adoptive parents—and here the term *parents* is often a code word for *mother*—are trained especially to "cope," "manage," or "heal" the disrupted link of child and birth mother.

If people believe that the womb environment and birth experience are formative for mother-child attachment—and in many societies there are no such beliefs—then adoption is slated to be traumatic for children and parents. It is asserted in one study, for instance, that "every adopted child" asks the question "Why didn't she keep me?" (Burlingham-Brown 1994). But in cultures where adoption is more frequent or even normative (see Carroll 1970), children do not ask that question. In such societies kinship is seen as a cumulative process—an individual's life is conceived as a process of adding people, not separating from or losing people (see Terrell and Modell 1994). So adoption does not entail severing connections, but extending the sphere of sharing, caregiving, and caretaking (Etienne 1979). This is to a certain extent the case in some communities in the United States (Stack 1974), but it is crosscut by notions of exclusive kinship received via the airwaves, television, schools, and state ideological apparatus. Moreover, in societies such as the Baulé of Côte d'Ivoire, communities view certain women as particularly skilled in rearing children, and these women may be given children by birth mothers in recognition of their skill (Etienne 1979). In other places, such as the Tongan Islands of the southern Pacific, a childless woman may be given a child by her sister out of compassion and love; the child grows up in close contact with both women, the adoptive woman being the closest "mother."

But in the United States such practices are rare. Although it is not explicitly discussed as such, adoption is depicted as deriving from two failures or betrayals of a supposed "natural order." First is the failure of the birth mother to care for the child, presumably by being mature enough, married enough, sober or sane enough, or economically secure enough to permit "natural" mothering to occur. Thus mothering is viewed as natural, and non-nurturing women are viewed as aberrant. If we look at the statistics regarding women placing children for adoption with state agencies (the figures are not available for private agencies or for women working to arrange independent adoptions, that is, private adoptions mediated through lawyers), we can see that these images are highly misleading.

Only about 2 percent of all premarital births in the United States result in a child being relinquished for adoption (NAIC 1998). Proportionately more white women place children for adoption than African-American or Latina/Chicana women. The Alan Guttmacher Institute states that fewer than 2 percent of black unmarried women place children for adoption; the figure is fewer than 1 percent for Hispanic women (some of whom presumably also are black, but the research does not specify). Fewer than 3 percent of unmarried white women place children for adoption. Moreover, unmarried women who place children for adoption are more likely to have higher educational and career goals than those who keep children. Teenage mothers who place children for adoption tend to come from two-parent families that support the woman's decision to relinquish, and the pregnancy in question is usually the first among teenage family members (Stolley 1993).

The model of the nurturing or natural mother in the United States has embedded in it assumptions regarding class, marital status, sexual orientation, and race. The "good mother" image promoted in the mass media, from 1950s television sitcoms to the present, is that of a middle-class, married, heterosexual woman who, because middle-class status is glossed with images of suburban whiteness, is imagined as white.

Second, adoption is attributed on the receiving end to a childless couple's inability to procreate by normal means. The language used in the literature to describe infertility and efforts made to conceive through technological interventions overwhelmingly treats infertility as the wife's issue. The class issues are unmistakable as well. Several of the professional couples in my sample reported that they had been expected by their private adoption agency to have pursued all financially available means of treating infertility before their application to adopt would be treated seriously. The ethical or emotional objections two of the women had to these expectations fell on deaf ears. Public agency adopters I interviewed, who tended to be working-class or from lower-middle-income sectors, did not experience this kind of expectation, but were asked instead how they had "come to terms" with infertility. In either case, however, infertility was viewed by the agency personnel conducting the home studies as the most compelling reason to adopt, because as one social worker put it, "The adopted child won't risk facing parents' preferring a kid who may be born later." Another said, "It's a waste of time for people who only think they're infertile. I can't tell you how many times the couple comes in or calls and says to stop the process because they just found out the wife is pregnant."

Coming back to the dominant gender ideology in the United States, then, adoption is the result of two violations of natural motherhood: procreation without marriage and nonprocreation within marriage. So the U.S. adoption triad has two failed mothers and a rejected or substitute child as the major players.

In other words, although all kinship is socially constructed, the fiction of naturalness is stripped from adoptive kinship. In the media it is held up as a laudable curiosity, a rearguard action, courageous because it is fragile without the genetic infrastructure. The bonds of attachment must be built carefully, painstakingly, and in some media portrayals, by close mother-child interactions from infancy (Talbot 1998). The child's grief and loss over the birth parent must be addressed, lest their personalities be permanently damaged (Smith and Sherwen 1983). My argument here is not that there isn't grief and loss—even babies can sense a change in personnel holding or feeding them—but that the source of the grief and loss isn't seen as due to disruption per se, but an exile from the natural way of things. Grief and loss are experienced by many children under many disruptive circumstances: a child disrupted from a violent but long-term foster setting will exhibit symptoms of grief and loss, regardless of the trauma received, merely because it is—dare we say—familiar?

Similarly, attachment—the building of trust and knowledge that one belongs to a group of people and they belong to you—is a long-term process in birth families as well as adoptive ones. Attachment in any family can be disrupted or terminated by a range of traumas—illness, death, physical or sexual abuse, psychological betrayal, war, or emotional abandonment (Cline 1979; Jewett 1982). Associating attachment problems with adoption—rather than, for instance, with the range of traumas kids may experience in birth or foster homes, which may turn children into survivors akin to refugees—does not facilitate bonding. Attachment in birth families can be assisted through the promotion of family mythologies—why "we" are special—and the same is true of adoptive families. The difference lies in the societal boost given birth families by presenting the family unit as rooted in nature: the myth that genetic connection makes attachment expected or even automatic. The failure to be "natural kin," then, appears as a contributing factor in what gets called attachment disorder. But because women are seen as primarily responsible for what Micaela di Leonardo has termed "kin work" (di Leonardo 1987), we can see that adoptive mothers will be held most accountable for their children's attachment or lack of bonding.

Popular media depict "successful" adoptive families as heterosexual couples: the parents often as heroic, risk-taking, saving children through not giving up on them, helping "problem children" through their identity crises, which are depicted as qualitatively different from other U.S. adolescent identity crises. The reality of their parental tie is demonstrated through commitment through difficulties: the harder the child rearing, the more they become "real parents." Another reason successful adoptive families are portrayed in the media as supermoms and superdads (the children are not depicted as having a positive involvement in making themselves) is perhaps because the prevailing image of adopters in the literature is tragically infertile but otherwise successful, heterosexual, middle-class, white couples adopting healthy little white or ambiguously or acceptably tan babies. Such people are permissible heroes in a racist society. In addition to the class and race bias of this imagery, it should be noted that few successful adoption stories are told that emphasize the primary caregiving and resource- mobilizing role of the mother in those couples, or, even rarer, the successful single-mother adoption.

When an adoption by anyone not matching the rather archaic nuclear family imagery is deemed successful, the social work literature discusses the success as resulting not only from parental (erasing the demographic fact that most single adoptions are by women) commitment to the child, but also from the "parent's" (that is, mother's) perception of the need for substantial and long-term social services and her efforts to obtain kin and community support (Groze 1996; Mansfield and Waldman 1994). Memoirs and related writings by adoptive parents, both mothers and fathers, eschew any parental heroism and focus instead on what was needed to take care of the child and to build and bolster family ties (Wadia-Ells, 1995; Burlingham-Brown 1994; Martinson 1993), although many also emphasize the need for social services and long-term community support (Bates 1993; Riggs 1995; Pohl and Harris 1993). One theme in the adopters' writings, as well as adult adoptee literature, is the range of ignorant and prejudicial attitudes by educators, counselors, and community members regarding adoption. This has been labeled as "adoptism" in one set of essays (Martinson 1993).

Birth Mothers as Bad Mothers: Class and Race Issues

In the adoption literature and among the adopters and prospective adopters I interviewed, a range of attitudes are expressed toward birth mothers. In the literature, the most positive images can be found in the letters between birth and adoptive parents collected in one volume (Silber and Speedlin 1991) and Karen March's study of adult adoptee interactions with their birth mothers (1995a). Other works are highly ambivalent or condemnatory, particularly when the child's health has been affected by the birth mother's unsafe sexual practices, or drug or alcohol abuse (e.g., Erdrich 1995: 102–3; Dorris 1989).

In the training session for prospective adopters I observed, the prevalent attitude was negative. Birth mothers were spoken of as irresponsible teenagers—confused, immature, foolish. More compassionate positions, taken by women in the group, painted birth mothers as victims—"Do I know if she was raped?" "Maybe she wanted to have a kid because kids are your hope for the future." The overarching picture was of a poor, promiscuous, addicted, unthinking, or self-destructive young woman. The birth mother became the bad mother: sexually active, able to procreate, but unable or unwilling to nurture. For the married couples the absence of marriage became the indication of irresponsible sexuality and abnormal motherhood. The presence of three single-parent adopters, plus three single-parent social workers in the room, prevented none of these comments from being made.

By far the most negative statements came from a working-class white couple who were adopting three abused sisters. They spoke of what the birth mother "let happen" to her daughters, holding the mother accountable for sexual and physical abuse perpetrated by her boyfriend. "I don't care how often he beat her up," said the foster-to-adoptive mother, "I would never let anyone do that to my kids. I'd have killed him." "I can't help it," said her husband, "Capital punishment is too good for people like that." But the wife's condemnation was not from a distance: her comments implied to me that she was on some level identifying herself with the birth mother. She could picture herself to an extent as at least potentially in an abusive situation, but handling it differently. The husband seemed more abstract in his judgment.

The single black woman seeking to adopt an abused older girl was silent during this venting session; so was an older black couple seeking to adopt an abused sibling pair. During the coffee break, I said to the single black woman that I've been so angry I could have attacked the foster-to-adopt couple who injured my adopted child, but that my daughter's birth mother probably had been trying to do the best possible thing for her baby. She looked somewhat surprised—perhaps she expected the white mother of a black child to be negative toward the birth mother—and said with some bitterness, "Where do they get off putting down the woman who's giving them their child?"

After the session, I was walking with the young woman when the black couple joined us. We began to talk about the dynamics in the room during the birth mother discussion. The wife commented, "Don't ask me to judge those girls [young birth mothers]. I don't have to live their lives. We just don't know, do we?" Her husband added, "I condemn what they did, but not the girls themselves. If they're messed up, it isn't all their fault. Look at what they have to live in every day. They probably didn't have a decent upbringing. I think it's up to us to help our people out, to give the generation coming up a better chance." The children the single black woman and the black couple were seeking to adopt had been abused in foster homes.

Many of the international adopters I interviewed characterized the birth mothers as irresponsible in giving birth to children they couldn't afford, but responsible enough to give them people who could. I found this attitude among a few of the white single adopters as well. Several of the international adopters clung to the belief that their child was somehow an orphan, relying on the legal designation of children available for adoption in many countries, the category "orphan" including anyone who had been abandoned or legally relinquished (see Gailey 1998b). The private domestic adopters were even more ambivalent, expressing some fear that the birth mothers or the birth fathers would not really be absent, or might change their minds later on and search for the child or bring legal suit to reclaim the child.

Such attitudes make open adoption unusual; few states routinely arrange open adoptions, and what is considered to be "open" is generally restricted to periodic letters and photographs, rather than ongoing personal contact (Ninivaggi 1997; Etter 1993). In societies where adoption is not rare, as in the Afro-Caribbean, a number of Pacific societies, and parts of West Africa, forms of open adoption are commonplace, and the adoptive mother or parents have multidimensional, long-term relationships with the birth mother or birth parents (see Etienne 1979; Brady 1976; Carroll 1970). Among those adopters I interviewed, the people most receptive to forms of open adoptions were the single mothers and the working-class African-American adopters.

Shadowboxing with Nuclear Family Ideology: Single-Parent Adopters

There is little in the literature on single-parent adoptions, partly because it was rare twenty years ago, when many of the longitudinal studies began (Shireman and Johnson 1986). Indeed, the term *single-parent adoption* disguises the fact that the overwhelming number are single mothers. Many of these women adopt through private agencies. Some agencies are known to cater to this clientele; a very few use openness to single-parent adopters as an access code for lesbian couples as well, although it is extremely rare for an agency to encourage a woman to attend preadoption training sessions with her partner. In any case, private agency adoptions are hard to monitor before or after placement.

Another reason so little data are available may be that public agency single-parent adoptions involve mother and child in a myriad of difficulties, even though the vast majority are deemed successful (Shireman and Johnson 1986; Groze and Rosenthal 1991a). Rather than evade that issue, I think we need to acknowledge it and ask why. I propose that it has little to do with being single and much to do with social conditions and the paucity of support services (see Shireman and Johnson 1985). The situation for single-parent adopters, thus, parallels that of many single birth mothers, although single adopters generally are older, are better educated, have higher incomes, and are more stably employed at the time of the home study than were the birth mothers at the time of relinquishment. Moreover, they have access because of these other class- and maturity-related advantages to more social resources they can bring to bear on problems they encounter. This parallel to many of the birth mothers, and the perceived precariousness of their own financial and employment situations, make the single adoptive mothers more attentive to the issues facing a pregnant single woman. These adoptive mothers were far more forthright in addressing the problems they faced in parenting than were the couples interviewed together.

Another reason these adoptive families might have to confront more problems stems from the position single women have in the adoption process. Bluntly, they are not the preferred clientele, which remains married couples in their thirties. Single women seeking to adopt through public channels were matched with categories of children who also were less desirable in the adoption scheme: older, survivors of physical or sexual abuse, having developmental delays or physical disabilities, and so on.

I interviewed eighteen women who had adopted domestically through public or subcontracted private agencies (four African-American women, the rest European-American); their children ranged in age from five to fourteen years old, and virtually all had been adopted at age four or older. Most of these mothers had been given children labeled as "hard to place" or "older" or "special-needs." Indeed, the only infant or toddler adoption among these single mothers adopting domestically was a child with developmental delays who had tested positive for the presence of drugs at birth. The single adoptive mothers, being on all levels except age, education, and income in the same category ideologically as young birth mothers, were actively recruited by agencies only if they were women of color, and there, too, the women were given children who had experienced considerable brutality in their lives. The two-parent, heterosexual family, where at least one parent can stay home during the first few months after the adoption, remains the ideal, even though the social workers involved understood one of the frequent repercussions of special-needs adoption: divorce or separation within six years. In one private agency that conducts a lot of subcontracting work in adoption for one state agency, the adoption case workers were almost uniquely single parents. The reason for this, I was told by one worker, was simple:

> When you work in adoption, you end up adopting. You see so many
> kids who are hard to place, you end up taking one of them, or two

of them. Your husband is okay with this for awhile, but they just aren't cute and cuddly and they're *real* hard to show off to the folks, so you end up divorced. I tell my friends that if you want to avoid a custody battle, do a special-needs adoption [laughs].

Most of the social workers were not single when they undertook to adopt and experienced a rapid decline in their standard of living when they were divorced. "Frankly, I try to warn off most single clients—it's just too hard," one worker stated. For those who are persistent enough to gain approval, however, this same social worker said, "I try to give them the biggest post-adoption subsidy they can get, because they're going to need it." The particular need for postadoption subsidies to facilitate successful special-needs adoptions—by far the largest category of public agency single-parent adoptions—is borne out by research (Barth 1993).

Another reason single women are not high on the recruitment priority list is because their sexual orientation or sexual practices may be questionable. Ironically, because of the reluctance of most agencies to place children with lesbian couples, closeted single women may be the front for a two-parent family closer to the ideal nuclear arrangement in all ways other than gender and sexual orientation. Another adoption social worker I interviewed said she tried to point out to her agency supervisor that they could recruit a lot more two-parent families if they permitted lesbian couples to apply, but it was not a welcome suggestion.

While transracial placements have been done very carelessly in the past, strongly favoring white clients seeking healthy infants (see Ladner 1977; Gaber and Aldridge 1994), in my study I found that transracial placement seemed to have been done as a "last resort" for children whom the social workers feared would continue to be shunted from foster home to foster home. The transracially adopted black children in my sample were all older, previously traumatized children who had already been in an average of three foster homes at the time of adoptive placement. Moreover, all of the children at one time or another—generally in infancy or toddlerhood—had been considered and rejected by prospective adopter black couples:

one child had been rejected by four couples in the first eleven months of her life. The children adopted by the single African-American women in the sample also had been buffeted in the foster care system and had been considered and rejected by black couples. One of the African-American adopters put it succinctly: "My girl was 'too dark' and had 'bad' [very kinky] hair so they didn't want her. Well, I did and I do."

In other words, single mother adopters—at greater risk for disruption because of more limited finances than two-parent adopters, and more constrained by the need to work full time unless they are in a disguised partnership—are given the children demanding the most specialized care and therapeutic parenting. Despite the obstacles, it is notable that single-parent adoptions do not result in any greater rate of "disruption"—return of a child to foster care—than do comparable dual-parent adoptions.

How these single women adopters spoke of kinship shows a pattern of highly conscious social construction of kinship as daily practices of survival:

> We're a team more than a family. We have to work together or we'll all go down the toilet. I grew up in a family where my parents never talked money around the kids. My son has seen me cry over unpaid bills, we've been near bankruptcy a hundred times. I've told him I just can't afford for him to fail in school—he just has to do his part. We've just go to make it work. We may not have much, but we're in it together.

> I've always said Nick will either end up on Wall Street or Sing Sing. I never realized before he came home how useful husbands might really be. Oh, not for helping with Nick—I'm no fool—but just for unloading at the end of a rotten day, to keep you from killing him or yourself. I guess we bottomed out when I had to go bankrupt this year and we lost the condo. But when we were packing he put his arm around me—he hates displays of affection—and said "Wherever we go will be home, Ma."

We all have chores. We all contribute. We keep the place running somehow. I feel like a dictator sometimes, and sometimes like an older sister, but Jessica and I manage somehow.[5] I just love her and she knows it, even when I yell at her. She's been home now for five years. I guess the first two years were horrible, but it's like labor, I guess you forget how awful it was once things get better. She's four-teen now—it's such a hard time for girls—and I know now that she'll let me know if something's really bothering here. We've worked out so many problems over the years. Really, adolescence isn't that different, knock on wood!

The theme that runs through these narratives is struggle and expecta-tions of helping one another out. The risks involved are acknowledged but are seen as deliberately taken by both mother and child(ren) (see Zwimpfer 1983). Boundaries between mother and child are not always clear, but the sense of belonging and building something together is unmistakable. Most of the women I interviewed expressed a longing for financial assistance or spiritual support from another adult—a husband, a sugar daddy, a rich aunt or fairy godmother, a boyfriend. Most also qualified that wish almost imme-diately with something like, "Of course, only if he was a good guy" or "Only if he were as committed to Jay as I am" and the like. There is an imagined nuclear family behind these narratives, but it is rejected as unworkable, unrealistic, or undesirable in the long run. It should be noted that the two single-parent adopters I interviewed who went through international chan-nels did not share these expectations, probably because they had greater financial resources and so greater access to privately arranged (paid) sup-port services.

Family formation among single-mother adopters was a conscious process for the most part, with the women drawing in support people from natal and created kin networks. For the transracial adopters—in this case four white mothers who had worked through public agencies or subcontracted private agencies to adopt four black children—the mother did extra kin work, extending patterns of sharing, exchange labor, carpooling, gifting, socializing, holiday festivities, and the like to include black godparents, grandparents, aunts and uncles, and what a range of black feminist scholars have called "othermothers"—experienced women who provide advice regarding child rearing, counsel children, and act as role models and mentors:

> Some of the African Americans in [this urban neighborhood] don't approve of our family; some of the whites don't either. They stay away from us and we stay away from them. But I've learned so much from the women who *have* taken a positive interest in Kenya. Ms. Wells has taught me how to grease and braid her hair, my neighbor Angela showed me the best lotions for her skin, Mrs. Hicks told me which schools were better for "our children," and on and on. I really feel supported, and believe me, I listen when they tell me something. They know what it's like to be black in America—I don't. It really does "take a village to raise a child," even if that sounds hokey.

Other mothers explained,

> Whenever there's an incident at school or in the park, I call up my friend Barbara [an African-American woman]—I work with her and like her kids—and ask her what she would do. I make up my own mind, but I weigh her words a lot.

> Hey, if I don't give Monique examples of all different kinds of black people, she'll take the stuff on TV as reality. What's out there on TV for black women? Hookers, addicts, or rich housewives, plus the talk shows and a few athletes. Well, where we live, there are all kinds of black women—secretaries, teachers, day care people, even an apprentice electrician. There are jerks, too. But I want her to grow up knowing the good people, so she has some real choices.

The fourth mother said,

> You give up some control to do transracial adoption right. You need
> people from the community involved with your kid, and that means
> you have to be involved in your community. You also have to be will-
> ing to admit your limitations, to learn and be taught, and that's not
> always easy. But sometimes you have to draw the line, like when one
> mother said a little physical discipline would teach Lee Ann a les-
> son. I thanked her for her advice. No way will I do it, but I'm not
> going to tell her that either. And I do feel great when Lee Ann gets
> compliments on her hair or skin, because it means I've learned a
> thing or two.

One of the mothers summed it up this way:

> When you're the white mother of a black child, there are many eyes
> watching you and your kid. If the kid makes a mistake, some white
> folks will think, "See, even in a good environment, 'they' mess up,"
> while some of the black folks will think, "Look at that poor kid with
> a white mother—no wonder he's a mess." I figure he'll be fine, and
> it'll be everyone's "fault"—mine, his, our crazy, mixed-up family,
> the people who helped—everyone's.

Two of these adoptive mothers had sought the support of Big Brother/
Big Sister programs to provide their sons and daughters with mentors from
black or West Indian communities; others used recreational programs
known to have diverse staff and participants for sports, after-school activities, and summer day camps. In other words, the mothers in this sample
were not isolating their children in all-white surroundings. For all of these
mothers, the arrival of the children and the concomitant, consciously
undertaken shifts in family orientation toward African-American or other
communities of color created rifts in their birth families. As one mother put

it, "Taisha's coming home sure brought out my sister's true colors!" Interestingly, the structure of single-parent adoption, coupled with the awareness most of the women had about the controversies surrounding transracial adoption, led to a situation where the women had constructed networks of support and strategies of survival reminiscent of Carol Stack's account of life in an urban black community (Stack 1974). One of the mothers said,

> I can tell now when white people are treating me different from Rashad, better. I want him to be aware of that, and I don't want to "use" my being white to get things, because he won't be able to when he grows up. I have to be real careful about it. It's made me much more aware of racism that I ever was before.

Considerable realignment of kin patterns seemed to accompany single adopters of black children. This was far less so for those adopting children from so-called buffer races—East and South Asians, and Latinos. When asked, these mothers of black children said that the stakes were very high for their children in a racist society; they expressed a sense that they could not on their own provide the child with ways of negotiating racism, and that they needed and sought community support. After acknowledging this, they then adopted many of the strategies taken by African-American parents (see Hopson and Hopson 1990). Some mothers of internationally adopted Asian and Latino children claimed color blindness, a situation that most researchers argue is not healthy for the child's identity formation. A few expressed concern that their children might be hurt by prejudicial comments or have difficulties with dating in adolescence. Issues of survival, however, were not present in the way they were for the single-mother adopters of black children, especially African-American boys.

What the single-mother adopters shared was a sense that motherhood is learned, not natural. They differed regarding whether or not wanting a child was natural for a woman, but they all thought no one was automatically good at it. One mother put it this way:

I had no idea older-kid adoption would be this rough or this costly. [She lost her job because of time spent taking care of her nine-year-old in his first year with her.] It's such a crap shoot. I live day to day now. I can see how much better he is now, but if anybody says it's because of my maternal instinct, I'll bite their face.

Many of these mothers seemed keenly aware that they were "an upbringing and a paycheck and maybe ten years" away from their child's birth mother. None of these women condemned the birth mothers, having veered close to or fallen into bankruptcy or temporary unemployment within a few years of adopting. None of the women in the sample had an open adoption, although several expressed that they would welcome it. One of the women commented,

I wasn't able to get an open adoption—the agency just doesn't do them. . . . I actually hope my kid wants to search, because I'd like to thank her [the birth mother] for giving me her daughter. I don't know what my life would be like without her [her adopted daughter] and well, whatever her reasons were, she had it in her heart to give up that precious little girl. She made my becoming a mother possible, see?

Another said,

I knew about open adoption and asked about it, but the social worker said my daughter's mother didn't want it. I didn't pursue it, because I didn't want the agency to think I was a crazy.

Like public agency adopters in general, the single mothers whose children had tested positive for the presence of drugs at birth or who had been injured by one or both birth parents were adamantly opposed to the notion of open adoption:

Are you nuts? They tried to kill my kid. No way! I hope they rot in hell.

I hope she's gotten her act together over the years, but I'd be pretty afraid to risk having a connection with a druggie. . . . I guess open adoption could work where there hasn't been a lot of problems like drugs or abuse.

Among the public agency adopters and the single mothers, however, several stayed in contact with the foster family if they had been particularly close to the child. One mother explained,

They're a positive link to the past, and believe me, we need all the positive links we can get! They were really the first family he had, and I don't want him to lose them. They've given me some useful information, too, and besides, they're really warm and caring folks.

When asked, none of the international adopters thought open adoption would work, citing "confusion" for the child about "who his real parents were." One woman said, "Open adoption? Too risky." When probed, she said, "Would you want people from a whole different lifestyle like that in your life? It just wouldn't work. We were getting her out of that."

"Kids Need Families to Turn Out Right": Public Agency Adopters

Public agencies in the northeastern United States have stepped up efforts to move children in foster care toward what is called "permanency planning," which includes adoption. Agencies continue to recruit married couples far more than others, although they have increased efforts to recruit working-class families (NAIC 1998), as middle-class ones have moved toward private agencies and "independent" adoption, as well as the rapidly expanding new reproductive technologies, as alternatives. One reason for this move concerns the search for healthy (white) infants, the long wait that often ensues for those not willing to take a special-needs or hard-to-place child, and the thoroughgoing scrutiny that public agency home studies entail. In private agencies, the prospective adopter is the client, who pays hefty fees for a more streamlined process. In public agencies, the client is the child.

Over the last ten years some states have increased efforts to recruit families of color, especially African-American couples, to facilitate in-race placements for thousands of black children in foster care; while most of this recruitment increased what is called kin adoption or placement with relatives of a birth parent, it also increased the number of couples adopting unrelated children. Under the 1996–97 adoption reform legislation, however, agencies are pointedly barred from making same-race placement a consideration in adoption, and no increase in federal funding can be expected to allay the impact of this ban by facilitating greater recruitment of families of color. Moreover, in my observations, screening procedures and training sessions still form barriers to effective recruitment of African-American adopters, by not affirming at strategic moments the actual parenting experience of so many of the people recruited. Again, although single-mother adopters in general are not a preferred category for adopting, there was in at least one case an active effort to recruit single African-American women as adopters for older black girls.

The sixteen couples I interviewed who had adopted or were seeking to adopt through public agencies, whether through a private subcontractor or directly through the particular state's "Department of Social Services," shared certain characteristics. In keeping with national patterns,[6] the ones who went through the entire process tended to be less well-off than those who were seeking private or international adoptions; the couple who stayed for a home study but then opted for international adoption expressed a fear that they would never get a healthy infant going through public channels. In most cases these couples' (self-reported) incomes seemed similar to those of the single professional women (white and African-American) seeking to adopt through public channels; most of the couples were working-class, but because of the typical dual-earner strategy, they had a comparable household income.

The white couples in the sample tended to be younger (in their thirties), and seven were adopting because of infertility; the one middle-class African-American couple (also in their thirties) was adopting for infertility reasons, too. The other five African-American couples in the sample (working-class, or the wife was white-collar and the husband blue-collar) were seeking to add to their family, as were three working-class white couples. Two of the latter were adopting because they were starting a second family as a result of remarriage; in both cases the husband had nonresident children from a former marriage and did not wish to sire any more children. The remaining middle-class white couple expressed a belief in zero population growth as their motivation to adopt.

The couples who had adopted because of infertility did not seem to harbor unresolved feelings about it. One mother said, "Sure, it's sad [not to be able to get pregnant]. You cry, and try and try, but, hey, it's either fate or God's will, whatever you believe in." Another woman explained, "I didn't want to have the doctors do all those things to me, just on the off chance I could get pregnant. It just didn't seem natural to me." Her husband said, "Besides being, well, demeaning, like, you could go bankrupt from all those in vitro this, implant that! Well, we still wanted children, so, well, we adopted." Another of the adopters said, "The miscarriage really did it for me. I was willing to try again, but this guy [elbows her husband, who smiles] said he didn't want me to risk it." Her husband added, "I didn't want to lose her, you know? She's my best friend."

The working class African-American couples tended to be older than the other couples by a decade—in their mid-forties. Two of these couples were starting second families, not because of remarriage, but because their first set of children had grown and moved out of the house. As one wife put it, "We have room in our home and hearts, now that the kids are grown, for another family." Her husband added, "Children need families and we did a fine job with our other ones." When asked what their older daughter thought of their adopting, the husband laughed and said, "Well, at first she was jealous that they were going to eat up her inheritance, but she came around." The wife added, "I took her to look at that notebook [a state adoption resources book with descriptions and pictures of children available for adoption]. When she saw all those kids just waiting, she just had to agree with us. It just is the right thing to do." The other working-class black woman in the session murmured, "Mmm-hmmm. You said it." Her husband patted her hand, perhaps in affirmation and perhaps to remind her it was such a white setting—in this group there were only three African-American people out of fifteen, and the three social workers were white (see Hairston and Williams 1989).

Among the families who adopted through public agencies, a theme of working hard to win over a child to the family way runs through the stories. One husband said,

> I wouldn't have made it through that first year without Michelle [his wife]. She kept saying, "Don't give up on him, he just has to learn he's one of us. Don't let him win and keep being a loner." We just kept showing him our ways and expecting him to live up to them. Then, one day almost—[turns towards his wife] after that horrible birthday, remember?—he just sort of came around. Since then, he's done better in school, made friends, shown us more respect. We still have our ups and downs, but it's like he decided we were really going to be his family, that he was one of us.

His wife added, "I thought I would melt the first time he hugged me without wanting something from me except a hug in return. That's when I knew we'd won, we'd won him over."

Another woman described how their adoption came about:

> We set out to adopt a baby and one day [the social worker] just called us up and said, "We have three girls who've been through a lot. They've been physically and sexually abused. One doesn't talk and one sets fires. They aren't legally free yet. Can you take them?" I looked at Sam [her husband] and said, "Are you ready for this?" He said, "Hell, no! Are you?" So, crazy fools that we are, we got in

the car and went to get them. It sure was a roller coaster at first, but each of them had strengths that helped the other ones along, and we could build them up that way. My mother helped out a lot, and I practically moved my sister in with us. Now it's four years later, and they're doing fine. It made me and Sam feel real good about ourselves—we did it, we made it work. What's funny is that each of the girls is like me and Sam but in different ways.

One African-American mother—herself reared in a loving foster home—laughed about why she and her husband adopted a toddler they knew two other black couples had rejected because of her appearance: "She has bad hair and is too dark, but then, look at our family—we're all a mess!" More seriously, she added, "The real work with that child had to be done on the inside and that's where we got down to business. She needed to know that she belonged somewhere, and that somewhere was us."

In these narratives there is a strong sense that adoption meant bringing a child into an ongoing family system, and a belief that the values of the family are solid, good for the child and everyone else. The parents do not neatly fit notions of gender role segregation in the analytical literature on the working class (Rubin 1976, 1995), although husbands deferred to wives for child-rearing calls and there seemed to be more reliance on kin from the mother's side during critical periods. Both husband and wife express strong support of each other and stress the strength and endurance of the other in periods of difficulty. Parental authority is unquestioned by either husband or wife.

Given the profiles of children—particularly the ones over age eighteen months—awaiting placement in public agencies, adopters openly talked about the risk they saw themselves taking (Barth 1988; Cahn and Johnson 1993). The white couples spoke of potential risks that the children would not "turn out right." What was absent from their discussion of risk was attributing failure to the children themselves, that is, to purported innate qualities. The risk was that the couples would "not have enough time" with the kids "to turn them around." I asked if they considered that the child's problems might be genetic. One wife said, "Well, maybe so, but there's nothing you can do about that, right? You gotta do what you can." Her husband said, "There are no guarantees that come with biological kids either, so what's the difference?" The wife of another couple said, "You know, you gotta be careful with those labels. A lot of people put a label on something they just don't understand." Her husband added,

> Yeah, when our son was in first grade, they had him labeled every way but the right way. We went along with it for awhile, they being the experts and all, but when he was gettin' worse, not better, we put our foot down and took him off the pills and made them try him out in a regular classroom. He still needs discipline sometimes, but basically he's OK.

The working-class African-American couples also did not attribute possible problems to the innate qualities of the child. Indeed, they framed the discussion of risk for adopted kids within one for all African-American children, and especially boys. "It's genocide out there, and you don't know from one day to the next if the kids are going to make it," summarized one father. The wife of another couple added, "This place just eats some people up alive. We just hope we can give the children enough strength to get through it in one piece." Another mother said,

> I tell her [adopted daughter who had been physically and sexually abused] that a lot of good people had a hard time coming up. Sure she's had a hard time of it, but she's not the only one. It don't mean she got to shrivel up and die.

Kinship, then, is conceived by these mostly working-class adopters as a process of claiming and fitting in: changes can be traced in someone's behavior, approach to life, and even personality (see Loehlin, Willerman, and Horn 1987). Parenting was a combination of modeling, counseling, discipline, and acceptance. These parents seemed willing to deal with the children where they were, without major expectations in terms of societal measures of success. Instead, their hopes and expectations centered on the child's becoming a "good person." Responsibility for outcome, however, was allocated between social conditions—over which these working-class couples expressed little sense of control—and familial grappling with the effects of the child's history.

Although most of the parents said they had come to the adoption process at the suggestion of the wife (which is typical of U.S. adoption), the adoptive fathers seemed active in the lives of the children and, in the context of an interview, highly supportive of things the mothers were saying. In general, the working-class adoptive couples presented a unified front in the interview—perhaps because of the status issues involved—yet both fathers and mothers seemed attuned to the children's personalities, changes, and ways of interacting with the other parent and any siblings.

"A Child of Our Very Own": International and Private Adopters

In this sample of fourteen families who had chosen to pursue international or private adoptions, ten had gone through the adoption process as married couples and four as single women. Two couples had adopted through private, lawyer-mediated channels internationally and eight couples had adopted internationally through private agencies. Among the couples, I found a strong commitment to nuclear families, albeit one with dual earners; a strong belief in genetics as having lasting consequences for children's outcomes; and the most discomfort and personal pain expressed about infertility. The four single women who adopted internationally had worked through private agencies; they did not share the commitment to nuclear families, but one expressed a regret that she had been unable to give that to her son. Two of the single women adopting from East Asia had long-term, stable lesbian partnerships and were co-mothering the children.

I should note from the outset that this group of international adopters contrasted markedly with the many international adopters I knew already, the vast majority of whom were middle-income academics and teachers or military families. In addition, several people I knew had worked with inter-national relief or related organizations and had been urged by their local counterparts to adopt war orphans or homeless and abandoned street children; in one case the mother had been given a child by one of her consultants, in the kind of open adoption that brought the two women into a long-term friendship. These international adopters had attempted to locate relatives of their children (sometimes finding them and keeping contact thereafter between the child and the relatives), visited the child's country of origin with the child periodically for research and vacations, often spoke the local language and used it at home, and seemed keenly attuned to issues of cultural identity, desiring their children to have positive images of their national heritage and culture (see also Register 1991; Bartholet 1993).

The adopters in the sample fit the financial profile of the "new" interna-tional adopters—wealthier, nonacademic professionals working through private agencies specializing in international adoption, or lawyers with simi-larly focused practices. This group was all white and had the highest income levels of any the people I interviewed. The average cost of adopting interna-tionally for these people was $42,000, ranging from a low of $25,000 to a high of $63,000 (due to major legal complications). When I asked an inter-national adoption lawyer about the fees, he quipped, "Well, our clients place a lot of value on these children. And we're honest about our fee structure."

The couples all had issues of infertility. Indeed, these couples, far more than other adopters in the sample, had been expected by the agencies through which they worked to have gone through extensive infertility treat-ment prior to being approved for adoption. Infertility treatment, presented in the media as a benefit, was experienced by at least some of the adopters as an expectation, and by one as a punitive demand: "They [the agency] wouldn't consider us for adoption unless we'd been through the gamut of treatments."

In talking about infertility, several of the women became tearful or showed other signs of distress, sometimes as much about the pain of the infertility treatments as about the infertility itself. I found an intriguing pattern indicating that responsibility, verging on blame, for infertility was gendered: in the three cases where infertility was associated with the husband, the husband spoke of the difficulties "they" had "getting pregnant," while in the other seven cases, when the wife assumed responsibility for infertility, she spoke of the problems as her own. In three cases, emotional response also emerged when they spoke of holding their infant for the first time, and when the topic of lawyers came up. Indeed, most of the internationals adopters became animated as they spoke of the local lawyers' expense or corruption, but, curiously, not when they spoke of their own U.S.-based lawyer.

The concern with infertility may underlie the reluctance most of the couples showed when asked to talk about their child's birth parents. One couple explained that the parents were "too poor" to care for the child adequately, and so had turned the child over to an orphanage. "They had so many children to feed; they wanted this one to have a chance in life," the wife said. Her having realized that her child had living birth parents was unusual in this international adopter sample: most assumed their child was an orphan or had been born to an unmarried mother and abandoned (but see Fonseca 1986).

One prevailing motivation for "going private" as one husband termed it, is "to avoid the hassle and the wait" involved in going through a public or regular adoption agency. Race was a submerged motive for most of the couples. One woman said international adoption was a way of "making sure you get a blue-ribbon baby." When I asked what a blue-ribbon baby was, she laughed a bit self-consciously and said, "Oh, you know, smart, blond, blue-eyed ... [a pause while she looked at brown-haired me] ... Well, I mean looking like us as much as possible."

One couple had planned to go to Romania and use some of the husband's business contacts to obtain a child, but when reports started coming in about psychological problems of post-institutionalized children (see Johnson and Groze 1993; Groze and Ileana 1996), they decided to adopt in Colombia. "They've been at it longer and the procedures are more straightforward," the father explained, "and the orphanages are clean and well-run." "They do much with so little," the mother went on, "Our little girl was well taken care of, you could just tell from her alertness."

Another white couple, each a professional who had lost a child in a court battle over custody, stressed their need to establish secure legal rights to the intended infant. Their "going international" with the search was connected with seeking to minimize any subsequent claims by birth parents. "Of course, we intend to bring up our daughter with a sense of her cultural heritage," the mother added. When I asked how they wanted to do that, she said, "Oh, books and music, special foods, that sort of thing." I asked if they planned to visit the child's country of origin. She said that they had carefully considered that. "It really depends on the child, doesn't it? Some might need to, some might not. We'd do it if it really mattered to her."

Literature on international adoption points out that visiting the country of origin is far more important to some children than others. But children harboring deeply negative images of natal countries may be glossing personal identity issues with condemnation (see Bagley et al. 1993). Few of the adopters, however, mentioned ways they might change or had changed their cultural engagements, attitudes, and so on, due to their children. One mother addressed the issue of cultural identity through the purchases of services for her child:

> We hired a gem of a nanny from the same country of origin as our daughter. [Our daughter] gets to play with [the nanny's] little nephew once a week, too. This way she feels connected to her heritage. We're hoping she grows up bilingual.

When asked if she or the father spoke to the child in that language, she said, "Not really. We just don't have the time to take the courses." An international adoption lawyer responded to a question about the cultural impact of international adoption this way:

> I think we're doing our part to give these kids a break. No one asks to be poor. No one wants their kids to be poor. We get approached

all the time by parents wanting to give us kids, because they know we'll do right by them. . . . [W]e started a support group in this part of [location] for people who've adopted kids from Latin America through us. We have parties a few times a year. We celebrate these kids' heritage. It's fun and it's a service.

The issue of control over the infant's physical and mental condition was a theme through these narratives. According to a social worker in the agency involved, a couple received an infant from India that they returned after a week, because—contrary to the way the child had been presented to them by the agency—it seemed to have marked developmental delays. The agency returned the child to the orphanage and no longer worked with that local institution. According to the international adoption lawyer I interviewed (who had adopted, with his wife, two children from Latin America), returns are known, but infrequent:

Occasionally an orphanage or local agency tried to switch children from the ones we've identified, but that doesn't happen twice. Every once in a while, a couple, having adopted, discovers that the wife is pregnant, but we've never had a problem with anyone deciding not to keep the adopted baby as well. [Even though the agency in question has a return clause], I always tell my clients that there are no return policies for birth kids, but you know, these people are usually so traumatized by their own infertility issues that they just want everything to be predictable.

More typical is a pattern, once the child is in the U.S. home, of addressing, managing, or coping with whatever issues came up. There are class dimensions to coping: personal engagement was typical of less affluent parents, and seemed apparent in the single-parent and working-class adopters particularly, although some had the child in psychotherapy despite the expense (not covered by medical insurance or the post-adoption subsidies). With the exception of two couples who seemed very engaged with their children (who had significant behavioral or cognitive problems) the more affluent adopters—especially the international adopters—seemed to use more professional intervention regardless of the children's state of health: nannies, extensive day care, supervised play groups, lessons, tutors. Where the children did seem to have problems, there was even more intervention—psychotherapy especially—but not more parental engagement on a personal level. At least one couple had tried to return their child when an infant, when she showed signs of developmental delays; among this group the terms *attention deficit disorder, attachment disorder,* and *hyperactivity* were sprinkled thoughout the discussions of their children. The question of how attached these parents were to their children cropped up among these parents more than in any other group of adopters, a situation that mirrors media representations of the affluent parents of children adopted from Eastern European institutions (Talbot 1998). There was considerable ambivalence when the children showed signs of not "ironing out" their cognitive, developmental, or behavioral issues in the first two years after adoption. One mother said quietly, "It's just hard to love someone who doesn't seem able or willing to love back." Another mother confessed, "It hurts me to realize, and I'm being honest with myself here, that although I love her [her daughter]—and I do, believe me—I probably would feel closer to her if she did well in school, or even if she was really great at something—anything."

One woman, who had adopted internationally because fifteen years ago it was virtually impossible for even a middle-class white woman to adopt domestically if she had never been married, said in an interview for a documentary,

> My kid was a bright eyed, alert little baby. I got him at eleven days old—an empty slate, I thought. Only later did the learning disabilities emerge, probably due to prenatal malnutrition. Would I have taken him if I knew all that ahead of time? Much as I love him, heart and soul, in all honestly I can't say definitively yes. (WGBH 1994)

The people I interviewed talked more than other couples or single parents about the "risks you take," and had all questioned carefully the agencies or lawyers through whom they were working about return policies. Another couple stated, "Life is so unpredictable—we never imagined [her husband] would be sterile. We just want to start out with as healthy a baby as possible." She added, "You know, as close to the real thing as possible."

With few exceptions, family in this group seemed to be associated with essentialist notions of kinship as well as race. There was more concern expressed in this group about "matching"—looking similar to the parents or sharing an ethnic heritage—than in other couples interviewed. (The exceptions were the single women adopters, who seemed less concerned with appearances; one of these had adopted transracially with an awareness that her lifestyle would have to accommodate the child's need for role models and community.) Some couples "didn't care" about the appearance of the child—so long as it was not "black" (meaning of African heritage), which at least one woman said she was "not prepared to handle." Almost all had deep concerns that the child show signs of intelligence and physical health.

Fears about unanticipated genetic disorders or organic problems were pronounced in this group. The session at the conference about AIDS testing in international adoption was packed with women and a few men, to my classed eye, who seemed like professionals. Many were taking notes. Most showed signs of distress when the speaker, a pediatrician treating many international adoption children, said AIDS testing was notoriously unreliable in children.

The possibility of psychological distress in even infant adoptees was not considered (see Cline 1979). In the one case where such distress seemed possible to me, the situation was viewed as intrinsic to the child rather than a result of her early history (see Bagley, Young, and Scully 1993). One of the fathers in my sample, half joking, expressed his anxiety about his four-year-old daughter, adopted in infancy from Korea, this way:

> Our daughter is overly friendly, even seductive, if you want my opinion, and I don't appreciate the way she tries to manipulate my wife.

When she acts that way, she reminds me of an old movie from the fifties—maybe you saw it if you're my age—"The Bad Seed." But then, I've always seen this nature/nurture bit as more weighted toward the nature end of things.

When I asked him later why he thought more girls than boys were adopted, he said, "Well, if they don't turn out right, at least they change their names when they marry."

In the absence of her husband, the mother of a toddler adopted from Ecuador responded to the same question this way:

He would never have gone for a boy. It's like, a man has to have a son that carries his sperm in him. It's a male bonding thing, I think. It doesn't seem to matter so much with girls. But don't tell [him] I said so [giggling self-consciously].

There was an assumption underlying the international adopter couples' narratives that marriages have stages and that in the long run married people were incomplete without children: "We wanted a child of our very own. My parents were getting older and it was time, you know, and then we had trouble getting pregnant." One couple expressed that one of their motivations to adopt was their being "isolated" at company get-togethers when the other couples their age were discussing their children. Adoption was clearly seen as an inferior substitute for childbirth, but if undertaken, it was pursued with a clear agenda: a healthy, intelligent child as near to new-born as possible. The goal these parents expressed, in one way or another, was minimizing the effects of early environment on the child. So, the targeted child was as young an infant as possible, from as stable a back-ground as possible, and being cared for in a setting that was as controlled as possible (agency-mediated, well-run, and sanitary orphanages; affec-tionate foster families, etc.). None of the sample would have considered adopting an older child or one considered to have "special needs." One husband explained,

> I admire people who do that, I really do, I'm glad someone's doing
> it, but it just wouldn't work for us. We just couldn't devote the time.
> Given our schedules, we need to have things as much like normal
> around here as possible.

For both international and domestic private adopters (excepting one single woman adopter), unambiguous rights to the child also mattered a great deal. This contrasted markedly to the months- or sometimes years-long ambiguity that characterized the public adopters' experiences with foster-to-adopt programs (Lee and Hall 1983), or the willingness stated by most of the single parents who adopted through public agencies to enter open adoption arrangements. As one international adopter put it, "We discussed the possibility of surrogate parenthood, but the Baby M case scared us" (see Pollittt 1987). Another mother said, "Once the child is out of the country, you can relax—no custody fights years later." At the time of these interviews, it should be noted, gestational surrogacy was not well known and did not enter into the discussions these couples had about reproduction.

Many children adopted internationally have birth parents who are still living, but many private agencies brokering international adoptions discuss the child in the legal terms prominent among the sending countries, that is, as "orphans." The illusion of kinlessness this term connotes seems to appeal to some of the parents I interviewed. The image created minimized their concerns about exclusive possession and fed a sense that the adopters had that the children would have been "lost souls," as one mother put it, without adoption. The unwillingness during or after the adoption process to delve into the actual status and origins of the child, other than the medical history, underscored many of the parents' discomfort with knowing the child had relatives in the sending country. This, coupled with the adoptive parents' often unresolved feelings surrounding infertility made it difficult for these parents to discuss their children's histories on any other than a very general or health-related level. The curiosity or serious concern so many adoptive children in the United States have about their origins and especially about why their birth mothers gave them up (see Burlingham-Brown

1994)—questions usually beginning around age eight—is a sort of time bomb for parents who have until then been comfortable considering the child as an "orphan."

Parenting at the Intersections of Class, Race, and Gender

What do these adoption narratives tell us about parenting and mother-hood? First and foremost, there is no single maternal or parenting nar-rative. The lines of class and race intersect and sometimes subvert both the "blood is thicker than water" ideology and that of "natural" mothering. The adoptive mothers all seemed aware that adoption was seen as an oddity, although many said that it was becoming more common than before. What makes adoption odd, however, is precisely the ideology of "blood is thicker than water" or genetic connection as the preferred means of developing closeness.

The most prominent theme that distinguished the different narratives were underlying questions: What role do class and race play in parental expectations of the child? Who is seen as responsible for the child's out-come? The single mothers felt extremely responsible for the outcome, regardless of the child's initial issues; in part to address what they viewed as problems with single parenting, they also created wider networks of support based on sharing than did most of the married middle-class or affluent adopters. Their notion of "being a team" came through again and again, as did their deep identification—not altogether unproblematic—with their children and their issues. The irony of single-mother transracial and same-race adoptions lay in the parallels between these mothers and many of their children's birth mothers. As one mother put it, "I can't help but realize that if this country had decent social supports, my kid probably could have grown up with her birth mother." The awareness of similarities to birth par-ents and the role of social services in family preservation was shared by working-class African-American adopter couples as well, but by very few of the other adopters.

Where the issue cropped up in the interviews, international adopters seemed to assume that the poor in another country were healthier or more morally upright than the poor of their own country. If they talked about their children's birth mothers—and some simply talked about their children as orphans—the picture was presented of an unmarried woman with few options in a "traditional" society. While this is doubtless true of many of the children, only two of the couples realized that some of these children's birth mothers were married women. Although some of the academic international adopters raised the problematic issue, which is not easily addressed, of whether or not the children would be better off if the $25,000 or more being paid for the child were simply donated to the birth parent(s), none of the international adopters spoke of it. They assumed the child was better off with them because of their nuclear family status (which may or may not have been true of their children's birth parents) and affluence.

Among the adopters in my larger sample, I found the greatest emotional distancing in the couples who adopted internationally, and emotional distancing or parental noninvolvement is one of the major risk factors in what is called adoption disruption, or rejection of a child (Barth and Berry 1988). This may be an artifact of their assumptions about how human relationships should work; I got the sense that their own relationships were somewhat contractual, and that affection was granted or withheld—consciously or unconsciously—depending on the performance of the other party. In keeping with the ways that class reproduction operates, these parents thought encouraging a child's independence was of major value in their upbringing. These manifestations of a consistent commitment to individualism have consequences for children who may see themselves as survivors or as unable to trust other people. Such children may act very independent, but this behavior grows not out of basic security but out of fear and mistrust, out of feeling alone in the world. In short, the style of parenting in all but two of the couples is consistent with the role the adults play in the society, but would not necessarily help a child grappling with attachment issues.

The emphasis many of the international adopters gave to spending "quality time" with their children echoed the frustration that all the adopters experienced in one way or another with the conflicts inevitable in a capitalist society between demands of work versus family life. The differences lay in what "quality time" meant in cases where the children in question required firm boundaries and highly structured interactions to feel safe or to be able to focus; the interactions among the international adopters, as presented by themselves rather than through observation, rarely approached the idea of "playing and having a good time with your kid," expressed by one of the mothers. According to the parents, most of the discipline and teaching was left to hired professionals, and at least one couple felt their child was "getting too close" to the nanny. These patterns, again, are consistent with class reproduction, but do not address the specific issues that many adopted children in the United States face.

The public agency adopters (single and married) seemed more consistently engaged with their children than did most of the international adopters. Mothering was caregiving and providing, but also building an expectation of belonging, of mutual obligation and support, as was demonstrated amply in the interviews with the couples. There were performance expectations, but they were not geared towards societal measures of success; rather, they were in keeping with a moral order centered on an extended family. One problematic arena for many of the working-class adopters in particular was corporal punishment, which is discouraged in preadoption training sessions in public agencies and their subcontracting agencies in favor of logical and natural consequences as disciplinary measures. Like any birth kids in these families, the adoptive kids were spanked when their behavior went beyond the parents' endurance. For children who have been physically abused previously, corporal punishment is confirmation that the previous treatment was normal.

The most poignant observations about birth mothers came from the African-American adopters who went through public agencies and the single adoptive mothers. In most cases there was a recognition that circumstances often beyond their control limited the birth mothers' choices and left them with a painful decision. Building on their compassion for the women whose decision made them parents, we can move toward a practice of adoptive parenting that helps our children appreciate the complex circumstances—international, national, familial, and personal—that brought them home to us. We also can work ourselves to remedy the economic and political inequities that made the birth mother's decision to relinquish the child a terribly constrained type of "choice." In the literature, adoption is assumed largely to be the search by an infertile woman for a way of becoming a mother, and it is rendered "second best" or different by beliefs and practices that help reproduce genetic similarity as "real kinship." How women and men respond to those scripts reveal how class and race as well as gender hierarchies, in shaping the lives of the adopters, alter or underscore their adherence to dominant ideologies.

Notes

Portions of this paper were presented in the 1996 Robert D. Klein University Lecture at Northeastern University. Other parts of the argument, related to international adoption, were developed for the Wenner-Gren symposium on kinship held in 1998. I want to thank Jennifer Wells and Tricia Caputo-Wells for our discussions of transracial adoption issues and Barbara Schram for our conversations about single motherhood in adoption. I thank all of the people interviewed for their generosity in sharing their insights and stories, and Heléna Ragoné for her patience, encouragement, and insightful conversations.

1.   The estimates are that between 2 percent and 4 percent of U.S. families include an adopted child (Stolley 1993; see also NAIC 1998). About half of these adoptions are said to be by relatives or stepparents.

2.   The argument made in this essay is elaborated in a book that I am preparing, *Blue Ribbon Babies and Labors of Love: Class, Race, and Gender in U.S. Adoption,* to be published by University of Texas Press.

3.   The sample was somewhat skewed toward older-child adoptions, because public agency adoptions are better documented and most older-child adoptions are through public agencies (the media imagery of Eastern European adoptions aside). Most estimates claim that privately arranged and private agency adoptions now outstrip public agency adoptions, although there are no national data on the numbers of nonpublic domestic adoptions or the demographic profiles of these adopters. I think it is a safe assumption, in keeping with my sample, that most private agency and privately arranged adoptions are by white upper-middle-income people.

4.   The international adopters were a snowball sample of fourteen families, twelve of whom had worked through private agencies and two through individual adoption lawyers to locate children. They had each adopted one child. The children included eight from China, Korea, or India, and six from Colombia, Guatemala, and Brazil.

The international adopter group had annual incomes ranging from about $65,000 per year plus significant family rental property for one single woman adopter, to a dual earner couple with an income close to a million per year. Without the wealthiest couple, the average declared salary was approximately $120,000 per year; for the single women adopting internationally the average was about $75,000 per year, putting them in upper income brackets. All of the international adopters were professionals with at least four years of college education. Many of the women and men also held post-graduate degrees. Four of these adopters were single mothers as far as the adoption agencies or lawyers were concerned, although two were in long-term lesbian relationships before, during, and after the adoption took place.

5.   All names have been changed to ensure anonymity.

6.   Although there is a national database documenting the number of public agency adoptions, only the data from twenty-one states are considered reliable for comparative purposes. The patchy state of affairs has been discussed by Vick (1995) and Stolley (1993). Studies by a range of adoption advocacy groups argue that privately arranged (lawyer-mediated) and international adoptions are the most rapidly growing forms of adoption in the United States (see Meezan 1978; Taylor 1995). These are the domain almost exclusively of higher-income white clients, who are working through lawyers, doctors, and private agencies. Data on the number of these adoptions become nebulous because of the privacy involved. Because of the reporting issues, more attention within the social science literature has been paid to public agency adoptions.

Of Likeness and Difference

How Race Is Being Transfigured by Gestational Surrogacy

Heléna Ragoné

Gestational surrogacy (where a surrogate gestates a couple's embryos) was developed in response to greatly accelerated advances in reproductive medicine and increased consumer demand. Together, these two factors have contributed to a redefinition of reproduction as a field of technological possibility and consumer choice. This technology now permits a woman who is unable to sustain a pregnancy (for example, who is lacking a uterus, prone to miscarriages, or affected by a preexisting medical condition that might be exacerbated by pregnancy) to have her ova fertilized with her partner's sperm and then have the resulting embryos transferred to a gestational surrogate. Technology also allows a woman who either has no ovaries (for example, who has had them removed for medical reasons) or who has experienced premature ovarian failure but who still retains a uterus to sustain a pregnancy through the use of donor ova.

When I began my research in 1988, gestational surrogacy was a relatively uncommon practice. The cost of procedures such as in vitro fertilization (IVF), zygote interfallopian transfer (ZIFT), and gamete interfallopian transfer (GIFT) was high, and their relatively low success rates made them a poor choice.[1] However, during the six-year period that followed, the practice of gestational surrogacy in the United States increased at a rather remarkable rate, from less than 5 percent of all surrogate arrangements to 50 percent as of 1994 (Ragoné 1998). As of 1997–98 more than 50 percent of all surrogate arrangements at the largest surrogate mother program are now gestational, and that number is continuing to increase. Couples who could not reproduce are now, with advances in reproductive medicine, able to have children who are completely or partially genetically related.

However, prior to the introduction of IVF, ZIFT, and GIFT, which have increasingly begun to routinize and naturalize the removal and fertilization of gametes (in this case, ova), surrogates were required to contribute their own ova toward the creation of the child. Before the advent of gestational surrogacy, surrogate motherhood was utilized primarily by Euro-American couples who were most often matched with Euro-American surrogates.

This type of surrogacy was not without its complications, since it, like all other forms of third-party reproduction, required individuals to reconceptualize procreation, reproduction, and family. In that arrangement, only the father was able to attain the highly desired genetic link to the child, and, as a consequence, both the intending/adoptive mother and the surrogate mother tended to emphasize the importance of nurturance and social motherhood in order to offset that imbalance (Ragoné 1994, 1996).

Alternatives to Surrogacy: Adoption?

Approximately 35 percent of couples who choose surrogacy have either attempted or considered adoption (Ragoné 1994). The majority of those who do eventually turn to surrogacy view the adoption process as one that is riddled with problems and that has been, in most cases, unable to provide them with a suitable child. For example, in 1983, fifty thousand adoptions were completed in the United States, but there were an estimated two million other couples seeking to adopt (OTA 1988: 1).

Of the major obstacles encountered by couples seeking to adopt, the first is the length of the waiting period, which can be as much as five to six years (Kadushin 1980). Because couples usually become aware of their infertility only later in life, their age often constitutes a major barrier to "agency-defined desirable limits" (Kuchner and Procino 1988: 25; Deutsch 1983). Many couples also spend years undergoing infertility treatments, attempting cycle after cycle to achieve an ever elusive pregnancy (Sandelowski 1993; Modell 1989). The quest for a biological child can also mean that couples finally decide to pursue adoption at a later age. This factor, along with new patterns of delayed childbearing (because many individuals now prefer to focus on their careers in their twenties and thirties, postponing children until later in life, when they have achieved a degree of economic and/or professional success), has also increased the number of individuals whose age exceeds agency-defined limits.

An additional barrier is posed by the discriminatory practices of some private adoption agencies. Many private adoption agencies, for example, are affiliated with the Catholic Church (which expressly opposes the use of all forms of contraception as well as abortion), and these agencies prohibit non-Catholic couples from adopting. Another difficulty related to adoption is the financial expense. In states that permit private adoption—California, for instance, allows only private adoption—expenses can be as high as $50,000 (Blank 1990: 75), as much as or higher than the cost of traditional surrogacy. And one of the most emotionally difficult aspects of private adoption is that after a couple has negotiated with the birth mother, and in some cases paid her living expenses for nine months,[2] birth mothers often change their minds, sometimes at the last minute, and decide to keep the child.

Efforts to keep Euro-American families intact are not new; the results of this policy are that these children often spend time in and out of institutions and foster care for years until they are too old to be successfully adopted (Tizard 1977).[3] The next obstacle with adoption is the shortage of healthy white infants, a shortage that was created by the legalization of abortion, the reduction in social stigma associated with single motherhood (Solinger 1992; Tizard 1977; Snowden, Mitchell, and Snowden 1983), and the availability of more effective birth control methods.

It is important to note here how children born to single mothers during the post–World War II years became racialized. Specifically, children born to Euro-American single mothers were viewed as "highly valuable," whereas children of color were not (Solinger 1992: 9), a perspective that regrettably has not significantly changed. The complexity of race in the context of adoption is suggested in the position statement of the National Association of Black Social Workers (NABSW), in which it is recommended that children of color not be placed with Euro-American couples or individuals (NABSW 1991, 1994). NABSW's critique, however, is not limited only to transracial adoption but rather addresses the "deplorable child welfare system" (1991: 1), a system that places undue emphasis upon the child rather than upon the family. The removal of African-American children from their biological and/or extended families is, according to NABSW, in the "vast majority" of cases a response to "neglect" rather than "abuse." The association argues that neglect results from poverty and cannot be easily ameliorated by the child's family (1994: 1–5). If, and only if, all reasonable efforts have been made to keep the child and family together, "then, and only then, should we seek adoption" (NABSW 1994: 6). Transracial adoption should not be considered until "clearly documented evidence of unsuccessful same race adoption" has been presented (NABSW 1994: 6). In addition, they reason that the adoption process has in fact been biased against African-Americans as a result of its undue emphasis on "high income, educational acheivement, residential status, [and] high fees" (NABSW 1994: 6).

Questioned as to whether or not couples who insist on adopting only a white infant are practicing a form of racism, surrogate-program directors often point out, as one did at an American Civil Liberties Union (ACLU) meeting, that this is a social problem for which everyone in society shares responsibility: "It is not, nor should it be, the sole responsibility of the infertile to remedy this particular problem. Every one of you in the audience should ask yourselves why you haven't adopted one of these children. You don't have to be infertile to adopt."

As a society, we claim to place "great value on children," but "we accept very limited responsibility for any but our [own] biological children" (Tizard 1977: 2). Regrettably, biological children continue to be considered preferable to adopted children, since adoption is most often understood as a last resort for those who are unable to fulfill a genetic dictum. Whatever the validity of adoption agency policies, there are many more couples attempting to adopt than there are available white infants, and agencies are therefore able to select couples they consider most suitable, based upon their own criteria. As a consequence, adoption remains a domain where existing misconceptions, complexities, and contradictions about race, class, and cultural politics are routinely played out.

Gestational Surrogacy

The growing prevalence of gestational surrogacy is, in part, guided by recent legal precedents in which a surrogate who does not contribute an ovum toward the creation of a child has a significantly reduced possibility of being awarded custody in the event that she reneges on her contract and attempts to retain custody of the child. However, while legal factors have certainly contributed to the meteoric rise in the rate of gestational surrogacy, it should be remembered that for couples the ability to create a child who is genetically related to both parents is the primary reason that gestational surrogacy continues to grow in popularity.

But not all gestational surrogate arrangements involve the couple's embryos; numerous cases involve the combination of donor ova and the intending father's semen. Why, then, do couples pursue gestational surrogacy when traditional surrogacy (with the surrogate providing the ova) provides them with the same degree of genetic linkage to the child, has a higher likelihood of being successful, and costs less. Several reasons are cited by the staff of the largest surrogate mother program, the primary one being that many more women are willing to donate ova than are willing to serve as traditional surrogate mothers.[4]

The second reason, as previously mentioned, is that the U.S. courts would, in theory, be less likely to award custody to a gestational surrogate than to a surrogate who contributed her own ovum to the creation of the child. In June 1993 the California Supreme Court upheld lower- and appelate-court decisions with respect to gestational surrogacy contracts. In

Anna Johnson v. Mark and Crispina Calvert (SO 23721), a case involving an African-American gestational surrogate, a Filipina-American mother, and a Euro-American father, the gestational surrogate and commissioning couple both filed custody suits. Under California law, both of the women could, however, claim maternal rights: Johnson, by virtue of being the woman who gave birth to the child, and Calvert, who donated the ovum, because she is the child's genetic mother. In rendering their decision, however, the court circumvented the issue of relatedness, instead emphasizing the "intent" of the parties as the ultimate and decisive factor in any determination of parenthood. The court concluded that if the genetic and birth mother are not one and the same person, then "she who intended to procreate the child— that is, she who intended to bring about the birth of a child that she intended to raise as her own—is the natural mother under California law."[5]

A third reason cited is consumer choice, specifically, that couples who choose the route of donor ova plus gestational surrogacy rather then traditional surrogacy have a significantly greater number of ovum donors to choose from.

Perhaps most important, when commissioning couples choose donor ova and gestational surrogacy, they sever the surrogate's genetic link to and/or claim to the child, whereas with traditional surrogacy the adoptive mother must emphasize the importance of nurturance and social parenthood, while the surrogate mother deemphasizes her biological and genetic ties to the child.

An additional reason, and one of critical importance, is that couples from certain racial, ethnic, and religious groups (such as Japanese, Taiwanese, and Jewish) were rarely able to locate women from these groups who were willing to serve in the capacity of surrogate; they were able to find women who were willing to donate their ova, however. Thus, couples from particular ethnic, racial, or religious groups who are seeking donors from those groups often pursue ovum donation and gestational surrogacy.[6]

It is not surprising that the shift from traditional to gestational surrogacy has attracted a different population of women. Specifically, gestational surrogacy has appealed to women who would not, under most circumstances, consider participating in traditional surrogacy. They are uncomfortable with the idea of contributing an ovum to the creation of the child, but are nonetheless interested in participating in gestational surrogacy because it provides them with access to the world of surrogacy.[7] This often includes, interestingly enough, women who have been voluntarily sterilized (tubal ligations).

Overall, the women interviewed who elect to become gestational surrogates tend to articulate the belief that traditional surrogacy, even though it is less medically complicated, is not an acceptable option for them because they are uncomfortable with the prospect of contributing their ovum to the creation of a child. They also cannot readily accept the idea that a child who is genetically related to them would be raised by someone else. In other words, they explicitly articulate the position that in traditional surrogacy (where the surrogate contributes an ovum) the surrogate is the mother of the child, whereas in gestational surrogacy (where she does not contribute an ovum) she is not. For example, Barbara, age thirty, married with three children, a Mormon, and a two-time gestational surrogate (now planning a third pregnancy), stated, "The baby is never mine. I am providing a needed environment for it to be born and go back to Mom and Dad. It's the easy kind of baby-sitting."

Oddly enough, IVF surrogates' beliefs run contrary to current legal opinion as expressed in the findings of both Britain's Warnock Report and the Australian Waller Commission's report that "when a child is born to a woman following the donation of another's egg the women giving birth should, for all purposes, be regarded in law as the mother of that child" (Shalev 1989: 117). It should be noted that the opinions of both the Warnock Report and the Waller Commission not only contradict the views expressed by IVF surrogates as well as commissioning couples who choose gestational surrogacy precisely because it eliminates the issue of genetic relatedness for them, but also contradict Euro-American kinship ideology, specifically, the continued emphasis on the importance of genetic relatedness.[8] This fragmentation or dispersal of parenthood, a by-product of reproductive technologies, has resulted in what Strathern has described as the "claims of one kind of biological mother against other kinds of biological and nonbiological mothers" (1991: 32) and fathers.

How, then, to account for the gestational surrogate's motivations? Should a gestational surrogate's maternal rights be "modeled on the law of paternity, where proof of genetic parentage establishes . . . parentage, or . . . on the nine month experience of pregnancy as establishing the preponderant interest of . . . parentage" (Hull 1990: 152)? It is of fundamental importance to gestational surrogates to circumvent the genetic tie to the child, and they do so in spite of the greatly increased degree of physical discomfort and medical risk they face in IVF procedures (as compared to risks associated with traditional surrogacy, which are the same as those faced in traditional pregnancy).[9] Any effort, legal or ethical, to argue that pregnancy is a determining factor in parenthood not only fails to consider Euro-American kinship ideology but, perhaps most important, neglects to consider the position of the gestational surrogate and commissioning couple.

As previously mentioned for gestational surrogates, circumventing the genetic tie to the child is of critical importance. The medical procedures commonly encountered by gestational surrogates (including the self-administration of hormonal medications) can cause quite of bit of discomfort, as they did for Barbara:

> After a while you dread having to do it; I had lumps from all those injections. Two times a day, and twice a week, three injections a day. If you don't do it, the pregnancy would be lost. . . . You are just [as] concerned with the pregnancy as if it's your own, sometimes more.

Linda, age thirty, Mexican-American, married with three children, and six months pregnant with a child for a couple from Japan, described her feelings about the physical discomfort in this way:

> At first . . . I broke out. [But] I got past the lumps in my thigh and butt. It was uncomfortable, but it's worth it.

Vicky, age thirty-three, Euro-American, married with three children, who had given birth three weeks earlier, explained how she was able to sustain her motivation and commitment throughout the difficult medical procedures:

> It was hard, but it needed to be done for the baby's sake. All the shots [were] on a daily basis. I didn't mind it at all, but it had to be at a certain time. It was like a curfew. Sure, it was painful, but it does go away.

The sentiments expressed by Barbara, Linda, and Vicky are similar to those expressed by traditional surrogates who have experienced difficult, sometimes life-threatening pregnancies and deliveries. Both cast these experiences in terms of meaningful or heroic suffering (Ragoné 1996). The vastly increased physical discomfort and scheduling difficulties are, however, a price that gestational surrogates are willing to endure in order to circumvent what they regard as the problematic genetic tie. Barbara expressed a belief shared by many gestational surrogates about their pregnancies when she stated:

> I separate AI [artificial insemination] and IVF completely, almost to the point I don't agree with AI. I feel like that person is entering into an agreement to produce a child to give to someone else. I feel it is *her baby* she is giving away. [Emphasis added]

In a similar fashion, Lee, age thirty-one, married with two children, Euro-American, who was waiting for an embryo transfer, discussed the differences between traditional (AI) and gestational surrogacy:

> Yes, it's [the fetus] inside my body, but as far as I am concerned, I don't have any biological tie. The other way [AI], I would feel that there is some part of me out there.

This view of surrogacy differs in several important ways from the one expressed by traditional surrogates, who advance the idea that the term *parent* should be applied only to individuals who actually choose to become engaged in the process of raising a child, regardless of the degree of relatedness. They achieve this perspective in part by separating motherhood into two components: biological motherhood and social motherhood. Only social motherhood is viewed by traditional surrogates as "real motherhood"; in other words, nurturance is held to be of greater importance than biological relatedness. In this respect, it is the gestational surrogate, not the traditional surrogate, who tends to subscribe to a decidedly more traditional rendering of relatedness.

Race and Ethnicity

The gestational surrogate's articulated ideas about relatedness (or more accurately, the presumed lack thereof) also produces a shift in emphasis away from potentially problematic aspects of gestational surrogacy, such as race and ethnicity. Unlike traditional surrogate arrangements in which the majority of couples and surrogates are Euro-American, it is not unusual for gestational surrogates and commissioning couples to come from diverse racial, ethnic, religious, and cultural backgrounds. In fact, approximately 30 percent of all gestational surrogacy arrangements at the largest program now involve surrogates and couples matched from different racial, ethnic, and cultural backgrounds. I have, over the last four years, interviewed a Mexican-American gestational surrogate who was carrying a child for a Japanese couple; an African-American gestational surrogate who had attempted several embryo transfers unsuccessfully for both a Japanese couple and a Euro-American couple; a Euro-American gestational surrogate who had delivered twins for a Japanese couple; and a Taiwanese couple looking for an Asian-American egg donor and gestational surrogate.

During the course of those interviews, I discovered that the issue of race, like that of class among traditional surrogates, is deemphasized by all the parties involved. Since surrogacy challenges so many of our shared cultural ideas about the "naturalness" of reproduction, it may be that other differences are consequently of diminished significance to participants. Differences such as class, race, and ethnicity appear to be set aside when infertility and childlessness are at issue. As I discovered in my previous research on traditional surrogacy, when questioned about class inequities between themselves and their couples, traditional surrogates also tend to describe their own fertility indirectly as a leveling device, because they reason that couples' financial success and privilege cannot provide them with happiness; only children can give them that (Ragoné 1994). When I questioned gestational surrogates whose racial backgrounds were different from those of their couples about the issue of racial differences, they responded much as traditional surrogates respond to questions about class. On one occasion, for example, when I questioned Carole, an African-American gestational surrogate (who at twenty-nine was single, with one child, and had yet to sustain a gestational pregnancy) about the issue of racial difference (between herself and her couple), she stated:

> I had friends who had a problem because [they thought] I should
> help blacks. And I told them, "Don't look at the color issue. If a
> white person offered to help you, you wouldn't turn them down."

However, the following statement by Carole reveals that the issue of racial difference is further nuanced as a positive factor, one that actually facilitates the process of separation between surrogate and child:

> My mom is happy the couple is not black because she was worried I
> would want to to keep it [the baby]. The first couple I was going to
> go with was black. I don't want to raise another kid.

When I questioned Linda (the thirty-year-old Mexican-American woman pregnant with a child for a couple from Japan) about this issue, her reasoning illustrated how beliefs concerning racial difference can be used by surrogates (and couples) to resolve any conflicting feelings about the child being related to a surrogate by virtue of having been carried in her body:

> No, I haven't [thought of the child as mine], because she's not
> mine, she never has been. For one thing, she is totally Japanese. It's

a little hard for me. In a way she will always be my Japanese girl; but she is theirs.

In this quote, we can see how Linda recapitulates one of the initial motivations cited by gestational surrogates—the desire to bear a child for an infertile couple—while highlighting the lack of physical and racial resemblance, or genetic tie.

If I was to have a child, it would only be from my husband and me. With AI [traditional surrogacy], the baby would be a part of me. I don't know if I could let a part of me.... AI was never for me; I never considered it.

Carole and Linda are aware, of course, that they do not share a genetic tie with the children they produce as gestational surrogates. But remarks such as Carole's about her concerns about raising an African-American couple's child reveal how racial resemblance raises certain questions about relatedness even where there is no genetic tie.[10] Cultural conceptions such as this about the connection between race and genetics deserve further exploration. Although she knows that the child is not genetically hers, certain boundaries become blurred for her when an African-American couple is involved, whereas with a Euro-American couple the distinction between genetic/nongenetic or self/other is made more clear.

Here we can see that the issue of likeness and difference is being played out in unique configurations, similar to those expressed by social fathers in a longitudinal study on donor insemination (DI), in which the social fathers theorized that "the role of genitor is unimportant compared with that of the nurturing father" (Snowden et al. 1983: 119). By stressing the social aspect of parenthood, fathers minimize the genetic "facts" (Snowden et al. 1983: 141), a strategy that is remarkably similar to that adopted by AI (traditional) surrogates and adoptive mothers. Once DI children are old enough to exhibit gestures, mannerisms, and characteristics similar to their father's, it is not unheard-of for a father to speculate that perhaps the child is after all his own biological child—to say, for example, as one father did, "I keep thinking perhaps he [the child] is mine" (Snowden et al. 1983: 141). In traditional surrogacy arrangements as well, a statement such as the following made by a father illustrates that perceived likeness may play as strong a role as it does in other families: "Seeing Jane [the surrogate mother] in him [my son], it's literally a part of herself she gave."

It is not surprising, then, that surrogate programs no longer seek to find gestational surrogates who bear a strong physical resemblance to the intending mother, as they once did with traditional surrogates (Ragoné 1994, 1996). But this should not be interpreted to mean that gestational surrogacy arrangements are in any way less complicated than traditional surrogacy arrangements, since they too involve third-party reproduction and as such partake of all the attendant issues and areas of potential conflict, including cultural differences.

With traditional surrogacy the matching of a commissioning couple with a surrogate was (and is) predicated upon finding a surrogate who not only physically resembles the intending mother but also is personally compatible with the couple. For example, it is considered ideal if surrogate and couple have similar personalities—for example, outgoing couples are matched with an extroverted surrogate. And it is considered to be of particular importance that they share similar views on contested topics such as abortion, although as paying clients, couples are privy to a great deal more information than are surrogates (Ragoné 1994). For example, if a surrogate is opposed to abortion and a couple is prochoice, a psychologist may conclude that aside from this area of disagreement, the surrogate and couple have a high likelihood of compatibility; the couple would be given this information about the surrogate and offered a chance to either accept or reject her.[11]

The issue of abortion is an obvious area of overlap between traditional and gestational surrogacy, since couples and surrogates still have to agree upon whether or not they believe in the practice of abortion. With gestational surrogacy, however, the surrogate and couple must agree upon the practice of "selective reduction." With IVF, it is common practice for several embryos to be implanted into the uterus and in the event that two or more embryos begin to develop, the attending physician often recommends that the embryos be selectively reduced—for example, from triplets to twins, or twins to a single fetus, in order to reduce the risk of complications to both the fetus(es) and the pregnant woman. The decision to implant several embryos (four to six is common) is determined by a number of considerations, including the number of ova retrieved and fertilized and the quality of the resulting embryos.[12] The practice (routine by now) of implanting multiple embryos frequently results in multiple births, a rate that is higher among surrogates than for the general IVF population, since surrogates are young, healthy, and not infertile, and have not previously taken fertility drugs. Further complicating the practice of implanting multiple embryos is the belief on the part of some surrogates and couples that selective reduction is a form of abortion.

While conducting research on traditional surrogacy, I discovered that although many surrogates are personally opposed to abortion, they are nonetheless often willing to defer to their couple's wishes, since they do not consider the child (or children) their own. They believe that the couple should make the final decision as to whether or not to terminate a pregnancy (Ragoné 1994). This is also true for gestational surrogates, and it is not surprising, since gestational surrogates do not perceive the children they are producing as their own. Thus far, I have found that gestational surrogates uniformly defer to their couple's wishes when and if both the physician and the couple conclude that the pregnancy should be reduced. However, problems sometimes arise if both the surrogate and the couple are opposed to abortion and to selective reduction. I learned, for example, of a case in which both the gestational surrogate who was pregnant with triplets and her couple were opposed to abortion and selective reduction. Typically, physicians recommend that a multiple pregnancy be reduced to twins since each additional fetus increases the risk to both the fetuses and the woman carrying them.[13]

Of Likeness and Difference

Individuals who participate in collaborative reproduction routinely manipulate categories of meaning as they pertain to issues of relatedness (Ragoné 1994, 1996, 1998). For example, in traditional surrogacy arrangements, the question of the importance of the blood tie, with all of its attendant symbolic meanings, cannot be completely resolved, particularly as it pertains to the adoptive mother, since she does not share in the genetic tie. One adoptive mother stated the problem in this way: "I think of him [the child] as Joe's side of the family. I wish he had some traits of my family. I'll always feel that way."

The fact that this adoptive mother is not able to see herself in the child but is able to identify her husband's and his family's "traits" there intensifies her feelings of exclusion and separation; it reminds her that she is not biologically connected to the child. Another adoptive mother expressed her feelings in this way: "There are times when I see my husband with him and I'm a little sad because they are carbon copies and I know he [her husband] can't see me in him [the child]."

Again, as the above quotes demonstrate, in Euro-American kinship ideology the child continues to represent the symbolic fusion or unity of the couple. Thus a surrogate child, if not reconceptualized (by the surrogate and her husband, and by the biological father and intending/adoptive mother), can come to represent symbolic disunity (Ragoné 1994, 1996).

During a gestational surrogate's initial in-person screening at a surrogate program, the resident program psychologist asks her whether a commissioning couple's racial or cultural background is of concern to her. The psychologist also asks the same question of the commissioning couple.[14] My preliminary findings suggest that the majority of gestational surrogates do not object to being matched with a couple from a different racial background, and may actually find it desirable.[15] One of the stated reasons for this preference, as mentioned earlier, is that racial or ethnic difference provides "more distance" between them, a degree of separation that the gestational surrogate is able to place between herself and the child (or children) she is producing for her couple through her manipulation of existing cultural ideation about racial difference.

In this way we can see that a decision that initially appears to be uninflected by racial difference is, upon closer examination, a means by which surrogates and couples establish or reinforce distance and emotional boundaries between themselves.

Likeness or resemblance as a symbolic feature signifies more than just biological resemblance. In both of the aforementioned cases in which adoptive mothers expressed a sense of sadness that they (or their husbands) could not "see themselves" in the child, the child was a son. I offer the following example of a couple who was able to achieve a pregnancy through donor ova and the husband's semen with the intending mother carrying the fetus to term. Prior to this couple's decision to embark upon ovum donation and IVF, they decided that they would employ sex selection to get a daughter, inspired by the "special" relationship between the intending mother and her mother. Both wife and husband agreed that having a daughter was a way to extend the specialness of her relationship with her mother. It is also possible that this couple's decision to select the sex of their child was related to the issue of identity, specifically, the intending mother's ability to imagine feelings for a daughter. Chodorow, in her pathbreaking work, advanced the theory that mothers "identified more with their girl children than with boy children" (Chodorow 1974: 47). Her conclusion is that "a mother is more likely to identify with a daughter than with a son, to experience her daughter (or parts of her daughter's life) as herself" (Chodorow 1974: 47), a view that has not been studied in the context of reproductive technologies, especially sex selection. The decision to select for a daughter may represent an acknowledgment that the husband rather than his wife will achieve a genetic tie to the child and that sex selection will provide her with a modicum of control over the process as well as an engendered link to the child. I would like to suggest tentatively that perhaps this issue of likeness and identification extends to gender in the same way that it extends to race.

The Next Frontier?

For the first time in the history of human reproduction, both phenotypic and genotypic traits of surrogates are, in the context of gestational surrogacy, understood to be irrelevant. On the one hand, gestational surrogacy forces the surrogate and commissioning couple to reconceptualize relatedness and pregnancy, but genetic relatedness remains a core issue for both. The couple is able to reproduce themselves as they would with "traditional" reproduction, while the surrogate is able to dismiss her connection to the child. What constitutes relatedness in Euro-American kinship ideology (at least as we have defined it until now) is understood to be the contribution of genetic material, whether ova or spermatazoa.[16]

Adding to the complexity of this issue are arrangements in which the intending mother has no viable ova, so that the services of an ovum donor are enlisted. When individuals and couples pursue this remedy to their childlessness, they are essentially returning to a model identical to that in traditional surrogacy, and as such they must search for an ovum donor who shares both phenotypic and genotypic traits with the intending mother.

Stories of third-party reproduction are routinely found in the media nowadays, and it is fast becoming a familiar and even naturalized aspect of American culture. But with the manipulation of categories such as family, race, class, gender, and ethnicity, the categories undergo redefinition as individuals who avail themselves of these technologies make increasingly difficult decisions concerning the nature of desirability, agency, and choice, for example, through processes such as selective reduction, sex selection, suitability of donors, and so on.

Many of the early theories about the future of surrogacy focused at times exclusively upon its potential for exploitation, but they failed to take into consideration the fact that both fertility and infertility are embedded in a series of personal, social, historical, and cultural processes. Understanding the complexities of reproductive technologies, in particular those that involve third-party reproduction, requires that critical attention be paid to the individuals whose lives are most intimately affected by these technologies, and how their experiences interface with culturally produced models of meaning. I hope that this essay has begun the process of exploring some of these relationships.

Acknowledgments

I owe a very special thank-you to Dr. Sydel Silverman, of the Wenner Gren Foundation for Anthropological Research, for her support. An additional thank-you is also owed to the University of Massachusetts, Boston, for ongoing support in the form of Faculty Development Grants. I am especially indebted to the women and men who have shared their experiences with me over the last ten years; their belief and commitment to this research has made it an engaging and rewarding experience. I would also like to extend a very special and heartfelt thank-you to the directors, psychologists, and surrogate-program staff who have over the years generously given of their time and their expertise.

Notes

1. IVF is a process whereby ova are fertilized outside the female body and the resulting embryo(s) are implanted either into the womb of the ovum donor or into a host womb. ZIFT involves the placement of an embryo in the fallopian tube, where it can descend and implant in the uterus in a manner that imitates "nature." With GIFT, which approximates "natural" fertilization more closely than either IVF or ZIFT, an unfertilized ovum is mixed with semen and then placed in the fallopian tube. The current cost for one IVF cycle is between $5,000 and $9,000. The issue of cost is of critical importance since it limits couples' and individuals' ability to avail themselves of these technologies. A handful of states require health insurance to cover infertility treatments, but for the vast majority of people infertility treatments are an out-of-pocket expense. I have discussed elsewhere that while the majority of couples participating in surrogacy are upper-middle-class, many middle-class individuals take out second mortgages on their homes or borrow money to pay for surrogacy. With gestational surrogacy, however, many more individuals appear to be advertising in newspapers or on the Internet for their own surrogate, to avoid the $15,000 agency fee. However, this practice is not without risk.

2. The amount paid is determined by the individual woman's circumstances and the standard of living to which she is accustomed. It is not unusual for a couple or individual to pay anywhere from $1,500 to $3,000 per month to the birth mother. Elsewhere I have discussed the fact that a state may ban commercial surrogacy (where the surrogate receives payment) but nonetheless permit couples and individuals to pay the living expenses of a birth mother who is allowing them to adopt her child.

3. Researchers have concluded that there is an underlying assumption held by many social workers that the biological mother should, irrespective of her actual chances for successful parenting, raise the child (Tizard 1977: 238), a belief that may influence the outcome of such cases. For an account of the intricacies of open adoption, see

Yngvesson 1997.

4.   This surrogate program is now also the largest ovum donation program in the United States, with over three hundred screened donors on file. Ovum donors are medically, genetically, and psychologically screened and come from various racial, ethnic, cultural, and religious backgrounds.

5.   For a critique of the court's decision, see Grayson 1998.

6.   Why women from certain cultural groups are willing to donate ova but not serve as surrogates is a subject of considerable interest. Since gestational surrogates reason that they (unlike traditional surrogates and ovum donors) do not part with any genetic material, they are thus able to deny that the child(ren) they produce are related to them. Given the parameters of Euro-American kinship ideology, additional research will be required to ascertain why ovum donors do not perceive their donation of genetic material as unproblematic.

7.   I have discussed elsewhere in great detail the system of rewards that makes surrogate motherhood attractive to this group of women (Ragoné 1994, 1996); those same rewards prevail for gestational surrogacy as well.

8.   While there are in fact observable differences in family patterns within the United States, most notably among poor and working-poor African-American communities whose alternative models of mothering/parenting may stem from "West African cultural values" as well as "functional adaptations to race and gender oppression" (Collins 1990: 119; Stack 1974), we should not be tempted to lose sight of the fact that such perceived differences in family patterns do not necessarily weaken Euro-American kinship ideology, which continues to privilege the genetic model of family.

9.   Aside from studies of the increased rate of multiple births, there are few longitudinal studies on the effects of infertility treatments. Research does, however, suggest that infertility patients have an increased risk of ovarian cancer (Jensen et al. 1987). Although an infertile woman knowingly accepts the risks associated with infertility treatments, the question remains whether surrogacy and ovum donation programs provide their populations with adequate information about the possibility of long-term risk.

10.   During the course of the interview, I specifically asked her what her feelings and ideas were about having a child for a couple from another racial background. (I asked this question of all the surrogates who were matched with couples from different racial backgrounds.)

11.   It was not unusual for a program to match couples with surrogates who did not share their views on abortion.

12.   Ova and the embryos from older women are often of inferior quality.

13.   There is little doubt that the recent case involving septuplets in Iowa will reinforce

the belief that multiple births can have successful outcomes even though, from a medical standpoint, multiple births pose a high risk not only to the mother but to the fetuses as well.

14. I have observed numerous consultations between program staff and prospective commissioning couples and surrogates at the largest of the surrogacy programs, and the resident psychologist routinely asks gestational surrogates and couples if the race and ethnicity of their future couple or surrogate matter to them. Although the program does not compile statistics on this issue, the majority of individuals (both surrogates and couples) appear to be unconcerned about race and ethnicity. However, it is important to note that many surrogates and commissioning couples reject the prospect of being matched with an individual from a different racial background when pursuing gestational surrogacy.

15. I have formally interviewed twenty-six gestational surrogates and twelve individual members of couples.

16. With the advent of assisted reproductive technologies, in particular gestational surrogacy, will we, as a culture, be forced to make a distinction between biological and genetic relatedness? Will Euro-American cultural definitions of relatedness be modified by the phenomenon of gestational surrogacy? Specifically, will we as a society come to emphasize biological relatedness over genetic relatedness so as to account for the fact that the gestational surrogate provides the physiological environment for the developing fetus? Or will we instead circumvent this issue by continuing to emphasize the genetic component of parenthood, characterizing the gestational surrogacy as the vessel through which another couple's child (or children) is born, as is currently the case amongst gestational surrogates and couples who employ their services? As AI and IVF surrogates' and commissioning couples' responses indicate, nearly everyone involved in these processes appears to experience some degree of ambivalence about the relationships created by these technologies.

3

Bearing Blackness in Britain

The Meaning of Racial Difference for White Birth Mothers of African-Descent Children

France Winddance Twine

Is there not something unseemly, in our society, about the spectacle of a white woman mothering a black child? A white woman giving totally to a black child; a black child totally and demandingly dependent for everything, sustenance itself from a white woman. The image of a white woman suckling a black child ... such a picture says there is no difference.

—Patricia Williams

Thus, although there are limits to the experience of many "white" people when compared to "black" people, there is no single truth about racism which only "blacks" can know. To assert that the latter is so is, in fact, to condemn "white" people to a universal condition which implies possession of a permanent essence which inevitably sets them apart.

—Robert Miles

On August 30, 1998, the British Broadcasting Corporation (BBC) aired a documentary entitled *Love in Black and White* as part of the Windrush series, acknowledging the achievements and experiences of British blacks and celebrating the anniversary of the landing of the S.S. *Empire Windrush*. A little over fifty years earlier the *Windrush* had landed at Tillbury Dock in London, filled with 492 migrants from Jamaica, many of them ex-servicemen who had served in the war in Britain and had then returned to the West Indies to receive their discharges and war benefits (Scobie 1972: 194).

Love in Black and White represents a significant departure from mainstream representations of the black British experience in that it privileges the experiences of five white women (and their adult children) who had married and established families with black Caribbean men. The inclusion of white mothers of African-descent children in a documentary series celebrating black Caribbeans and how they have transformed British culture signals a growing public recognition of the part that white mothers play in the "reproduction" of the black British community. However, despite their presence in this documentary, they have typically been invisible in media and government reports concerned with racism and antiracism in contemporary Britain.[1] White mothers of African-descent children appear to occupy a paradoxical and pivotal role in the reproduction of black Britishness. Thus, if we are to understand contested meanings of transatlantic blackness, Britishness, racism, and antiracism, then an analysis of the experiences of white mothers in black British families is of critical importance.

Until now the degree to which white mothers located in multiracial families experience forms of racial abuse and racial exclusion has received little attention, although according to the 1997 annual report of the Commission for Racial Equality, sixty-four white English women and fifteen Irish women filed applications for assistance in racial discrimination cases in the United Kingdom.[2] There is now a growing body of feminist scholarship on racism and antiracism among white women in organized racist and antiracist movements (Ware 1992; Blee 1991, 1997); however, with a few notable exceptions, there has been little sustained theoretical or empirical analysis of the ways in which racism and antiracism structure the maternal experiences of white women of African-descent children (Frankenberg 1993; Luke 1994; Twine 1998).

Foundational analyses of gender inequality and motherhood (de Beauvoir 1952; Rich 1976; Chodorow 1978; Ruddick 1989) among white middle-class women in the United States and Western Europe have not explored the degree to which transracial mothers—that is, white mothers who are socially defined as belonging to a racial group presumed to be distinct from that of their birth children—conceptualize and experience race and motherhood. White women who give birth to African-descent children in contexts of white supremacy and racial disparities provide an innovative theoretical lens through which to examine the multiple meanings of maternal competence. Their experiences also illuminate the limits of racial privilege for those whose families of reproduction transgress the prescribed ideals of their local communities. An analysis of the racialized experiences of white mothers of African-descent children provides a necessary corrective to earlier literature that conflated various forms of discrimination and assumed racially unified and monoethnic family formations. Elizabeth Spellman has undertaken a critical analysis of feminist scholars who did not theoretically account for the intersections of race, class, and gender hierarchies: "Women mother in societies that may be racist and classist as well as sexist and heterosexist. Are we to believe that a woman's mothering is informed only by her relationship to a husband or a male lover and her experience of living in a male-dominated society, but not by her relation to people of other classes and races and her experience of living in a society in which there are race and class hierarchies?" (Spellman 1988: 85).

How, then, in view of these more nuanced analyses of intersecting forms of discrimination, do we evaluate the impact of racism on white women parenting children who are socially classified as "black" or "mixed-race"? Does transracial motherhood transform the racial consciousness of white women? Several recently published memoirs by U.S. white feminist mothers (Reddy 1994; Lazarre 1996) have begun to illuminate some of the ways that racial hierarchies structure the emotional experience of mothering for white women and generated what Sara Ruddick (1989) has called "disciplined reflection" in the context of long-term domestic partnerships with black men. However, with the notable exception of these memoirs by U.S. feminist scholars, ethnographic analyses of racism have not yet offered empirical explorations of white parents' experience of negotiating racism and acquiring an antiracist consciousness as they parent African-descent children.

In 1995, when I initially began to explore the impact of racism upon white birth mothers parenting their children of African descent in England, I sought to understand how white mothers (and their black partners) mediate, interpret, and respond to white supremacist ideologies.[3] As a black feminist theorist and ethnographer concerned with the contingent nature of white racial privilege for women whose relationships with black men constitute a transgression of orthodox ideologies of social respectability, I found that critical race theorists or feminist theorists had focused little attention on a growing population of white mothers of African-descent children in Britain. If we are to develop a sophisticated understanding of transformations in the meaning of Britishness, blackness, and contemporary racisms, then an analysis of the consciousness and practices of white women who are members of black British families is invaluable.

In this essay, drawing upon both public discussions and private focused life history interviews with white women and their black Caribbean family members in the East Midlands of Britain, I will examine one of the paradoxes that emerged when I asked black women and men to consider the impact of racism upon the white birth mothers of African-descent children in their families. By exploring the perceptions and expectations that black family members have of white mothers of African-descent children, my aim is to illuminate how some white women contend with their own "racialization" by black family members.[4] I will then examine the racial literacy skills that some mothers acquire in their efforts to counter the racism that their children encounter. I end with an analysis of why the trope of maternal incompetence is invoked by some black family members as multiracial families' households bear the burden of producing black subjectivities out of multiracial lives.

When I began to pursue these questions with black family members of white women, I found that black Caribbean women and men typically perceived their white relatives as unable to "equip" their children to cope with racism because, as whites who had not experienced racism, they could not "empathize" with the children. White mothers, in particular, were described as racially disadvantaged because they are perceived as being incapable of feeling racism. In other words, the black family members interviewed distinguished between racial "empathy" and "sympathy," arguing that while white mothers could sympathize with their children, they did not typically possess racial *empathy*, the ability to experience the pain of racism, and thus could not really understand the impact of racism upon their children.

In addition to this paradoxical discourse, I found that because white mothers must often manage the presumed "racial" divide between themselves and their children, they may sometimes work hard to acquire an understanding of how racism impacts their children. In other words, if they are conscious of the assumptions made about their maternal competence (and if their children report racism to them), they may be more likely than some of their African-Caribbean counterparts to develop proactive antiracist parental strategies.[5] In other words, the presumed racial differences between themselves and their African-descent children may advantage them by calling to their attention the cultural work that must be done in order to prepare their children to negotiate racist ideologies and racist structures in contemporary Britain.

Research Methods

Between 1995 and 1998 I conducted eight months of field research in London and the East Midlands of Britain.[6] I also interviewed white and black parents who were members of interracial families. This essay draws upon data from this research and focuses upon the life histories of ninety-five parents of African-descent children in Britain. I interviewed a snowball sample of ninety-five black and white parents that included sixty-five white birth mothers and their black family members between the ages of twenty-eight and seventy years. The white women interviewed were the birth mothers of children whose fathers were African-Caribbean, African-American, or black British[7] men; the women had been in relationships with these men that ranged from a period of several months to more than thirty years.[8] In order to evaluate how gender structures the dynamics of transracial motherhood, I also interviewed a comparable group of fourteen white English fathers of African-descent children who resided in the same communities as the white mothers interviewed.

During my field research I lived in the home of an African-Caribbean education officer employed by the Leicestershire City Council, who was also actively involved with the African Caribbean Education Working Group and was thus linked to virtually all of the recognized local African-Caribbean community members and leaders. I also attended and participated in private family events and African-Caribbean cultural events, interviewing residents who self-identified as either West Indian, black, African-Caribbean, or mixed-race with origins in Antigua, Barbados, Dominica, Guyana, Jamaica, Montserrat, St. Kitts–Nevis, Trinidad and Tobago, and the United States. The families interviewed reported that their parents had immigrated to England between 1955 and 1965.

The Local Context: The East Midlands

Leicester, which is known as a hosiery manufacturing city, is located ninety-nine miles north of London, in the East Midlands of England. Leicester's textiles continue to constitute a major segment of its economic base, and it is a principal supplier of the British knitwear industry. Approximately 30 percent of the local adult population works in the industry, and according to a recently published City Council report, Leicestershire "has the largest number of people employed in the manufacture of hosiery, knitwear and fabrics in the United Kingdom" (Leicester City Council 1993: 42; see also Leicester City Council 1995).

During the 1970s Leicester served as the national headquarters of the National Front, a right-wing political party that represented the unification of the League of Empire Loyalists, the British National Party, and the Racial Preservation Society. [9] John Solomos has described the political aims of the

National Front as "to provide a new arena for the far right activism, outside the Conservative Party and as an independent organization" (1993: 188).[10] As the site of an organized racist political party, Leicester also became a logical political organizing base for antiracist organizers. As John Solomos notes, "Between 1977 and 1979 the activities of the National Front also became the focus for anti-racist political mobilisation orchestrated by the Anti-Nazi League and Rock Against Racism" (1993: 190). Leicester became a national testing ground for racist and antiracist political organizing. For example, a 1990 report notes that "the Leicester Racial Attacks Monitoring Project, better known as RAMP, was set up at the end of 1986. This was a direct response to the high level of racist incidents being reported to the Highfields and Belgrave Law Centre" (RAMP 1991). Some of the local white antiracist activists became the parents of African-descent children and members of black Caribbean extended families.

Another distinctive aspect of Leicester is the size of its ethnic minority population. Outside of London, it is the local authority with the highest percentage of all ethnic minorities, and it has one of the largest Asian populations with origins in East Africa (Kenya, Malawi, Tanzania, and Uganda) (Leicester City Council 1993). In 1994 the total population of Leicester was 293,400, with whites constituting 71.5 percent of the population.[11] South Asians are 23.7 percent of the local population, making it second only to Birmingham.[12] Leicester ranks fifth in the total number of all ethnic minorities (76,991) and second in the absolute number of Asians (63,994). It ranks first in the absolute number of its population of Indian origin, while Birmingham is second. The Indian population of 60,297 constitutes 22.3 percent of Leicester's population, making it a national cultural and shopping center for the Asian diaspora in Britain (Leicester City Council 1996). In striking contrast, the local black population, which is subdivided on the census into black Caribbean, black African, and black other, makes up only 2.4 percent of the local population (it is ranked thirty-fifth in size for the United Kingdom). The African-Caribbean population, a segment of the larger black population, is only 1.5 percent of the total local population.

The size of Leicester's Asian Indian population is relevant to this study because Indians constitute 78 percent of the ethnic population, and thus ethnics of Asian origin outnumber those of African-Caribbean origin by nearly ten to one.[13] In a context in which African Caribbeans tend to view themselves as the older and more established ethnic community, the African Caribbeans often argued that the more recently settled Asian Indian population has secured control over many of the local community resources targeted for ethnic minorities. Religious, linguistic, and other cultural differences between the black Caribbean and Asian (Indian, Pakistani, Bangledeshi, and East African Asian) communities appear to have generated tensions between the African-Caribbean and Asian ethnic communities. Consequently, there appears to be some shared resentment by both the indigenous white population and the black Caribbean community toward the Asian community, which is perceived to be experiencing rapid upward mobility.[14] This phenomenon poses particular problems for the white working-class mothers of African-descent children, who tend to reside in communities where the dominant ethnic minority population is Asian (typically Bangladeshi or Indian) because their children are sometimes mistaken for Asian and consequently discriminated against as Asian [differently than Caribbean].

Racial Logic and Racial Empathy

In my conversations with the black relatives (including sisters-in-law, domestic partners or spouses, and adult children) of white mothers parenting birth children of African descent, I uncovered a racial logic that can best be understood as characterized by doubts concerning a white mother's ability to properly parent a child of African descent. It was assumed that some white mothers were in fact both "racist" toward their own children as well as racially "disadvantaged" because of their social experience as white persons.[15] For example, as I previously mentioned, I was informed that white mothers of children categorized as black were unable to empathize with the racism that their children experience because they cannot personally experience racism. Black women whose brothers had established domestic partnerships with white women argued that white women were not adequately prepared to raise black children because they could not understand or "feel" racism the way a black mother could.

The differences in racial logics that I detected in the families I interviewed appear to be further exacerbated by traditional gender ideologies that dictated that children be given what Sharon Hays (1996) has described as "intensive mothering" and that place primary responsibility on mothers alone for the transference to children of a black identity and African-Caribbean culture. My research suggests that white women who are the birth mothers of African-descent children may be parenting in a familial context in which racial empathy is assumed to follow naturally from racial resemblance. In other words, black family members often perceive white mothers as lacking racial empathy because they do not share their children's racial location. Thus it is typically assumed that they do not have a proper understanding of racism and thus cannot feel (or respond appropriately) to their children's pain as black mothers would. In spite of this widely held view, I found that some white mothers had acquired a range of sophisticated skills in coping with racism.

The skepticism regarding white mothers' ability to empathize with their children is illustrated by the comments of Camille, a recognized black leader in the local African-Caribbean community. Like many of the U.K.-born black women I interviewed, Camille opposed interracial relationships, but because two of her brothers had established domestic partnerships with local white women, she had reluctantly become part of a multiracial extended family.[16] When I asked her to share her views on white women parenting African-descent children, she argued that white mothers are typically ill prepared to deal with racism.

> I don't think white mothers have that understanding of what it means to be black. . . . Sometimes they haven't dealt with their own racism. They meet a system that's racist and they don't know how to deal with it. I don't think they're always ready . . . in terms of being prepared for racism—they haven't dealt with their own racism. I think a lot of time [white mothers] aren't prepared mentally, aren't

emotionally prepared—just don't know what they're dealing with. They haven't had the sociological discussions around racism. What it is, how it affects people, that kind of thing. . . . Somehow the forums aren't there to discuss it.

Camille's comments must be understood in the context of her ongoing personal and professional experiences with antiblack racism. As a social worker, she had acquired extensive experience providing supervision and treatment for African-Caribbean children who have been placed in foster care, often in response to neglect, abuse, or family disintegration. She reported to me that the majority of her cases involved children of dual heritage who had one white parent and one black Caribbean or black British parent. Her experiences led her to conclude that due to antiblack racism in British society, black children are at risk, and this risk is heightened when there is a white mother parenting.

However, when I asked Camille to elaborate on how her own parents (Jamaican blacks) had helped her to cope with racism as a child, she began to contradict herself. She had suggested, for example, that only black parents know how to prepare their children, but it soon became clear that her parents had not provided her with the very preparation she described. For example, because her parents had grown up in Jamaica, they did not appear to have had an understanding of the particular kind of racism that their children encountered in England. Alluding perhaps to her own parents, she said,

Some black parents feel they need to fit into society and that they're guests within this society and therefore have to behave that way. I think that, in some respects, we were protected [from racism] because we had black parents. I don't think they were always aware of the level of racism. I don't know that we even got into any discussions about it. I don't know that they had particularly good strategies for dealing with it, either, because I can remember when I was at school I had tremendous problems—it really affected my education—in terms of levels of racism. . . . It wasn't something that I

discussed openly [with my parents] at the time. I just felt—you
needed to get on with it.

Fiona, the thirty-six-year-old mother of a four-year-old daughter, also described coping with racism alone with no effective guidance from her parents. Her parents immigrated from Antigua in the 1960s, and she described
them as lacking a vocabulary for discussing race or racism in Britain. When
asked how her Antiguan parents helped her to cope with the racism she
encountered as a child, she described her mother's failure to understand
the racism that she encountered routinely at school.

> We very rarely discussed [racism], you know. From my parents—
> nothing. For example, I came home one day from school and said
> to my mother that a teacher told me that I had rubber lips, and all
> she said is, "Don't take any notice." She appeared not to recognize
> my pain, appeared not to want to talk about it in any further detail,
> and the sad fact is that I think my parents were internalized racists.
> I'll give you an example of why. My mother once said to me, when I
> was seventeen, that if I ever brought an African home that I could
> walk out the back door straightaway because she didn't want a blue-
> black African in her home.

When I asked whether her parents had actively discussed racism with her or
tried to prepare her for racism, she said:

> No, they didn't. No. A lot of what I've learned and what I've been
> able to articulate and what I've been able to discuss came once I left
> home. . . . Even when I married a white man, there was never any
> discussion about how we would cope or what problems we might
> face or how they felt about it.

Fiona's experience is not unrepresentative of the childhood experiences
described to me by other black Caribbean women I interviewed. Although

black women tended to argue that black parents could better understand their children because they had personally encountered racism, their descriptions often contradicted this theory. While Fiona did not argue that white women were not prepared to parent, she did express skepticism about her white husband's ability to comprehend the impact of racism on his daughter. Fiona's and Camille's attitudes illustrate a pattern that I found in interviews with black women, in which black women applied a different maternal standard to white mothers of black children than they did to their own mothers.

In cases in which black women view white women as a threat to the reproduction of black families that consist of two black parents, they may be highly critical of their own white sisters-in-law who are parenting their nieces and nephews. In response to the growing numbers of interracial families, some black women invoke a maternal hierarchy in which they called into question the emotional and cultural competence of white mothers of African-descent children.

Carmen, another black woman of Jamaican origin, whose white sister-in-law was parenting Carmen's nieces and nephews, provided an analysis that paralleled that of Camille. A thirty-three-year-old university student, Carmen had two siblings (a brother and a sister) who had established families with white English partners. When asked to compare her own situation as a black mother (whose youngest daughter has a white father) to that of a white mother of black children, she replied:

> Who you are, your culture, your identity ... comes through the mother. And so therefore your cultural awareness, your ability to deal with racism—as we've been discussing—and a lot of other things will be defined by your mother. And that doesn't matter whether you're African-Caribbean, European, Asian, whatever. It's the mother who brings the children up. And so I think that where the mother is black and the father is white ... the children will stand a better chance of being more culturally rooted than when the mother is white because the [white] mother will pass on her

own traditions, sometimes will stifle the tradition of her kids, will actively tell them that they're not black.

Like several other mothers interviewed, Carmen placed the primary responsibility for parenting upon the mothers and did not appear to hold fathers accountable or responsible to the same degree as mothers. While few black mothers presented critiques of patriarchal arrangements that required women to bear the primary burden, occasionally a black mother would challenge this assumption and offer a more critical analysis of traditional gender roles. For example, Jamilha, a thirty-nine-year-old mother of two sons who self-identifies as a feminist, identified patriarchy and traditional gender roles as a serious problem for both married and single white mothers of African-descent children. She agreed with other black mothers that "it's not that their white parents don't love them, but they don't know what it's like and so children in that position do need black input. And a lot of them don't get that much [black cultural knowledge] if they happen to be with a white mother." She also argued that the African-descent children of white mothers who lived with their black fathers did not necessarily have more access to support in preparing the children to cope with racism.

> Even if the black father has been around, they still treat the child as if, well, the child is the child of the mother. The child is seen [by the father] as within the sphere of the mother for the nurturing and all of that, you know, patriarchy. You know, what women's roles are, what men's roles are. So I'm not quite sure whether there is a black influence even when black men are around. [Black fathers] will still very much feel that they need to be letting the mother bring up the children.

With few exceptions, the view that white mothers are expected to take the primary role in socializing and caring for children seemed to be shared by black Caribbean men and women in the extended family. Carmen, who had nieces and nephews who were being parented by a white mother, described her brother's parenting responsibilities in this way: "A lot of the black men tend to take a backseat rather than actually doing anything about their partners' understanding of being black, about black culture, about community."[17]

As I became more familiar with Leicestershire and spent more time living in this community, I became interested in exploring further these patterns of contradictory racial logic. I also wanted to compare black and white mothers parenting children of African-Caribbean and Anglo-English heritage in the same extended families. Although the black women interviewed had typically been parented by two black Caribbean parents, who they reported rarely addressed the topic of discrimination, they continued to insist that white mothers were less adequately prepared than black Caribbean women to parent African-descent children. Such beliefs persisted in spite of their acknowledgment that they themselves had rarely received explicit support when they shared stories of racist incidents with their parents. Moreover, according to their reports, many of their parents, like some white parents interviewed, seemed unaware of the kind and extent of the institutionalized racism their children were encountering in Britain. In fact, what I found striking about the narratives of the black professional mothers interviewed is how similar they are to those of the white mothers interviewed, in that none of the black women reported having received any explicit education or guidance about racism at home (with two black parents). However, several of the white parents of African-descent children described having formulated and implemented strategies on their own to teach their children to recognize and counter multiple forms of racism.

Black Fathers

David, a black father, had been in a committed relationship with his white wife, Simone, for more than sixteen years.[18] Childhood sweethearts, they had two sons who were four and eight. Asked to describe his relationship with his wife, David expressed admiration and respect for her "character" and remarked upon her "strength." However, when asked to compare his wife's experiences as a white mother with those of black mothers of African-descent children, he too employed the ideology of racial empathy, invoked by the black women I interviewed.

> My wife is always going to see things differently to a black mother anyway. Black mothers traditionally are very strong and very protective of their children, but when the ugly head of racism starts rearing its head, black mothers deal with it a lot. For example, they know—they can *feel* [racism]. They're doing it from an *empathetic* position. They [experience] the racism themselves, so they know how to challenge the racism. [Emphasis added]

Like many other black parents interviewed, David also assumed that if one has experienced racism firsthand, then one automatically knows how to challenge it. He did not consider the social ostracism, abuse, and exclusion that his wife had experienced (from her family and other whites) to be a form of racism. Although he acknowledged how much privilege she had "lost," for example, he did not consider that experience a parallel one that she could draw upon to empathize with their children's experience of racism. In other words, he appeared to consider her racial privilege contingent upon her willingness to form familial relationships exclusively with white men, even as he did not seem to recognize his wife's experiences as a form of racial abuse comparable to that of their children.

> She's classed as a second-class citizen. It's a deal [black men] can never pay back [to their white partners]. And the majority of them don't realize it. They don't realize how much their partners have lost—none of them. But I see what she's lost ... when I go to the family get-togethers and I look around the room and I'm the only black face and my children are the only black kids in that environment.

As another example of what she had lost, David revealed that Simone's brother, "who she looked up to," had not spoken to her since her marriage to him. They no longer had contact, and Simone had experienced considerable overt hostility from several other members of her family as well. Other white mothers I interviewed had also been expelled from their families for refusing to abort or to give their children up for adoption, yet this experience was rarely recognized or conceptualized by them or their black family as an experience with racial discrimination.

This view that white mothers are unable to "feel" racism or "equip" their children to address it was also extended to white fathers, who were described by their black partners as unprepared to cope with the racism their children were likely to encounter. For example, one black mother expressed the fear, not uncommon among the black mothers interviewed, that she might die before her children reached adulthood. She was especially concerned that her white husband would be unable to respond properly to racism on an emotional level.

> I don't think [their white father] could deal with [racism]. And I don't think he could very well *equip* them because, again, he doesn't have the understanding. I think he would deal with them in *sympathy*, but he couldn't deal with them as I would, in *empathy*. In some ways that's perhaps not a bad thing. The first time [my daughter] came home from school and said that she'd been subjected to racism I just sat on the bottom of the step and cried because I just felt it so personally. [Emphasis added]

However, because fathers are not expected to parent to the same degree as mothers, most of the focus was placed upon the mothers. Black women thus tended to interpret whiteness, in and of itself, as an undifferentiated marker of inexperience with racism, rarely acknowledging that gender, class inequality, and marital status mitigate the way that white women experience racial privileges. White mothers were typically described to me in terms that placed emphasis upon their "whiteness," without recognition of the ways in which their marital status, class, age, and tenure in the local community might hyperwhiten or unwhiten them. Their maternal and familial ties to blacks were deemphasized in these discourses.[19] A similar phenomenon has been explored by John Hartigan, Jr. (1997) in his analysis of U.S.

whites living in working-class and "underclass" communities. He emphasizes the "uneven reproduction and experience of whiteness" and provides
an example of a white woman whose grandchildren are of African descent.
Describing how ideologies of racial difference and racism rebounded upon
her as a member of a multiracial family, he notes:

> Relating to her grandchildren racialized her because it brought her
> into zones where only her racialness would be read; attending to
> her "black" grandchildren made her whiter even though she pro-
> moted no notion of racial superiority. It is notable that in such het-
> erogeneous family sites, race retained an indelible content, no
> more diluted than if these members were in homogeneous family
> groups.... For Esther, the complexity of their racialness (her, her
> daughters', their children's) had expanded exponentially. Whereas
> as an individual she could efface the significance of race with her
> friends ("we don't get into that stuff"), as a family member she had
> become racialized in a manner outside her control or will, both by
> her nurturing role and by the positions in which it placed her.
> (Hartigan 1997: 202)

Like Hartigan, I found that white parents, particularly mothers, were
racialized in this community in ways that they could not anticipate or
control. This had particular consequences for the white mothers who lacked
an education and had not been involved in organized antiracist politics.
Since they typically do not constitute an organized political constituency,
their concerns as white parents of African-descent children do not register
in public debates. Moreover, they were not recognized as having struggles
that parallel those of the black parents of African-descent children.

Thus far, I have explored the assumptions made by the black family
members of white mothers in order to highlight the discursive field that
white mothers negotiate without the benefit of formal channels and with
few, if any sources of antiracist support. In contrast to black mothers, who
are assumed to possess a sophisticated understanding of racism naturally,
white mothers are expected to acquire this type of understanding even

before having children. I have also analyzed how black family members tend to conceptualize white mothers' ability to cope with racism. Among the seventy families interviewed, both working-class and middle-class blacks exhibited a pattern of perceiving white women as less capable of relating to their children because their race renders them incapable of understanding racism. It was assumed that white mothers did not possess experiences with racism because they had not been the targets of racial abuse. Since they were assumed to have little knowledge of racism, it was assumed that they could not respond appropriately to their children's experiences. Such understandings assume that white mothers are a monolithic group and stand in direct contrast to the experiences of some of the white mothers interviewed. I now turn to a discussion of the racial consciousness and racial literacy of five white mothers who are representative of the white women who argued that they had experienced a transformation in their consciousness of racism.

Racial Consciousness, Racial Literacy: White Mothers' Analyses

In making the case for the "retention of racism as a key concept within the social sciences," Robert Miles provides a historical review and analysis of the use of the term *racism*. Miles argues against what he refers to as the "analytic inflation" of the concept of racism, and he critiques North American scholars who "enlarged the conceptual and explanatory scope of the concept":

> The concept of racism is used therefore to refer to a range of phenomena (beliefs as well as intended and unintended actions and processes) but with a specific emphasis upon their consequences for the domination of one group over another. These groups are defined, respectively, as "black" and "white," and consequently racism is conceived as something that "white" people think about and do to "black" people. This inflation of the meaning of racism is accompanied by a narrowing which defines racism as an exclusively white phenomenon. (Miles 1989: 3)

One can detect echoes of Miles's critique in the arguments made by a sub-set of white mothers interviewed. Women who self-identified as antiracists or who were attempting to raise their children as "black" argued against definitions of racism that did not consider the class exploitation and diversity within the "white" category. Several mothers argued that white women are not monolithic and that while some white mothers communicate racist ideologies to their children, others struggle to learn how to counter every-day racism (Twine 1999a).

An analysis of white mothers' own perceptions of how racism shapes their experiences as parents of children who may be classified as black or Asian in public spaces is useful when analyzing how racism impacts upon what Sara Ruddick (1989) calls "maternal thinking." Among the sixty-five white birth mothers interviewed, virtually all reported that they had been subjected to some form of racial harassment or racial abuse when their pregnancy was revealed and they decided not to sever their ties to their children through abortion or adoption. While not all mothers articulated an understanding of the forms of racism their children could encounter, mothers who had sustained relationships with black Caribbean women and men tended to give responses similar to those of black women to questions about the areas of discrimination that their children would face, identifying the same domains: education, employment, police harassment and surveillance, and routine racial abuse. And they developed various strategies for securing the networks of support that they anticipated their children would need (Twine 1998, Twine 1999a).

In the following section I draw on conversations with five white mothers who are representative of the working-class and middle-class mothers interviewed to explore their understanding of race and racism as mothers. These include two mothers raising their children without any assistance from their children's fathers, two mothers in long-term marriages, and one divorced mother.

Diana, a forty-nine-year-old mother, who described herself as a "white woman defending a black family," was representative of white parents who had previously been actively involved in antiracist and antifascist political work in London. Her involvement in antiracist work mediated her encounters with racism as a white member of a black family. As Diana said,

> I knew about institutional racism. I knew about racial harassment, so I knew that when I stepped out on the street with my black child, the chances were that I would get harassed in some way or another. And I was ready for that. I was ready for someone to call me a name. I was ready for somebody to throw something at me. . . . I had that in my head, that that could happen. I wasn't ready for somebody to doubt that he was mine. It just hadn't occurred to me at all. So it was a real shock the first time. After that I was ready for it [whenever I was questioned about my son's origins by a stranger] . . . my answer would just be straight: "No, he's mine. I bore him. He was in my womb. I carried him for nine months, just like any other child."

Diana's statement illustrates how the perceived racial difference between herself and her son undermines her experience of her maternal status in public spaces. In this case, she must negotiate doubts about her biological relatedness to her own child.[20] This aspect of discrimination was never reported or commented upon by black mothers whose children resembled their white fathers in skin color and phenotype.

Beverly, a forty-five-year-old mother of two young adults, argued that her husband does not recognize the forms of racialized exclusion that she experiences on a regular basis. She argues that racism has marginalized her from her children and husband. Her analysis of her situation provides another example of how she believes that racism affects her as a white mother when she is in public spaces. As she says:

> Well, I suffer from secondhand racism. [My husband] said, "You can't understand racism in the sense that a black person can understand racism because when you're out on your own in the street, you're the white person on your own." But I'll always say [to my family] . . . when my kids were small, say I was standing

in front of them, [the store clerk] would serve me—then they'd try to serve the kids because they didn't think we were a family ... and that even happens to me and [my husband] today when we're out shopping—people don't always associate that you're together.

In the above quote we can see that Beverly interprets the absence of recognition that she receives as a mother related to her children as a form of racism. While it may be problematic to inflate the concept of racism to include the experiences of white mothers, it is important to recognize the language that she employs to describe the challenge posed to her relatedness to her birth children. Her relation to her children is not visible, and she experiences this symbolic assault as a form of racism. Middle-class and working-class women identified this as a routine occurrence. However, black family members did not mention this kind of treatment when I asked them to evaluate the impact of racism on their white family members. Consequently, the white mothers interviewed reported that they seldom, if ever, received racial empathy from their children or other black family members when they encountered racial abuse because they were considered members of a racially privileged group. Their racialized experiences remained invisible to some family members.

Racial Literacy and Activist Mothers

Some of the university-educated mothers interviewed were conscious of and informed about multiple forms of racism. They related examples of working very hard to provide their children with social experiences and other resources that would counter the racism they might face in their lives (Twine 1999b). Several of the mothers interviewed were white women of working-class origin who met the fathers of their children while they were university students or white-collar workers in multiethnic community organizations. The following remarks made by Jennifer, a forty-six-year-old welfare rights activist who was raising her seven-year-old daughter alone, are typical of how these activist mothers tended to conceptualize racism.

Jennifer, who grew up in an exclusively white rural village, did not have any contact with nonwhites before she attended the University of Canterbury, but her awareness of racism had become acute, as her remarks illustrated:

> I think racism in this country is very insidious . . . compared to some European countries where it's very overt. You know, you'll go some-where and you'll see black people literally quite separate from white people. . . . They're not included by the white people as part of society. . . . Racist arguments are presented quite openly. I think here there is a traditional English hypocrisy that you don't actually say things openly. It's always . . . behind the scenes, and I realized how closely it's woven into the English psyche, both gender phobia and racism, I think particularly. . . . Where I work [in the Welfare Department] . . . has helped me to at least think about some of those things, as well as having [my daughter]. . . . I've learned about racism, that it's an insidious thing, that it's so much a part of all our traditions and our ways of thinking that it's something that you have to be aware all of the time. It's almost made me much more critical, I think, of white liberal thinking because . . . that can be in a sense a more dangerous racism. You know, the so-called color-blind approach to things.

In contrast to both working-class white women with less education and uni-versity-educated black women, Jennifer sought to employ her racial and class privilege (as a professional), taking an active role in the state school her daughter attended. As the white mother of a black child, she actively sought to mediate and minimize the effects of racism on her daughter. And here too she was fully conscious of how her racial privilege as a white woman operated to her advantage in her struggle to protect her daughter. As she described the position she found herself in:

> I've become involved in the school because I'm interested in sup-porting it anyway, but I realize that also I want to pave the way

for her. I'm also very conscious of the fact that if there is an issue that I take up, they will deal with me as a white person. And that's what I mean about the sort of ambiguity, that I may have access into . . . institutional society as a white person that a black person wouldn't have. . . . And, obviously, I will use that to her advantage. A black mother of a black child or mixed-race child would have a very different experience in that respect because if there was an issue at school . . . she wasn't happy with, then she will immediately encounter some sort of racial stereotyping . . . a list of cultural expectations.

In contrast to Jennifer, who lived in a predominantly black and Asian residential community, Claire's case illustrated the isolation that many such mothers feel, caught as they often are between racialized communities. Although Claire, the thirty-seven-year-old mother of a teenage son, was also a university-educated professional, she described the many difficulties that she has had in locating discursive spaces in which to discuss the struggles that she was experiencing as a transracial mother. "I don't have somebody at work that I feel that close to, that I can share those very specific issues with," she said. "I know there's lots of nice people around, but I don't know anyone else who is struggling to raise a black child and would be prepared to talk to me about it. Because even within the black community . . . they're seeing my son as white." She expressed the fear that some black people would suspect her of trying to use her black son to secure quick entry into and intimacy with the black community. So she avoided discussions of her African-descent son with black coworkers—even though most of them appeared to know that her son was of African descent, because they referred me to her when I asked to meet white parents of African-descent children.

Somewhat ironically, her reluctance to identify herself as the mother of an African-descent child placed her at risk of being perceived by some blacks as ashamed of that fact and thus keeping her son's existence in the closet. Her silence, born of her fear of offending black colleagues, was thus misinterpreted by them as shame or racism, as I discovered when one of her black colleagues confided that "she doesn't tell anyone that her son is black." This example illustrates how difficult it is for some middle-class white mothers to locate a forum in which they feel comfortable sharing their concerns and receiving support or advice from other parents of African-descent children. This issue seemed to be more problematic for women who were not natives of Leicestershire and thus had no organic networks of childhood or school friends in whom they could confide.

When asked how she thought black mothers perceived her, Claire offered the following analysis: "They make assumptions about your experiences and about what you know. I find it difficult to be articulate about my specific experiences because there is no one to talk to about it." As a white teacher in a school serving a predominantly Asian and African-Caribbean population, Claire had acquired a sophisticated understanding of how institutional racism operates to target black students for exclusion or expulsion from school at much higher rates than white students. She speculated that her son, for example, had been accused of being a drug dealer at school simply because he was black. While she acknowledged having been a bit "naive" in her twenties, when she first became a parent, Claire contended that she had since developed a more complex view of how racism operated in her son's life.

She made, for example, a concerted effort to deploy her racial privileges and university education to challenge the racist practices of school officials and police, as illustrated by the following remarks: "They were threatening to throw him out, so we had to go to the governors and defend him. . . . The other situations have been . . . more about trouble that his friends have got into. And because they're all white, somebody watching can't distinguish between the white kids, so they'll go, 'Oh, there was a black one with them.' And in the end, he gets into trouble when he might only have been sort of a bystander. . . . Because he's six foot two and he's the only black one in that particular group, he gets sort of fingered out for various things that he hasn't actually done. He has spent a night in a [prison] cell. He has been stopped on numerous occasions for, you know, standing on the street corner with a sports bag."

Like several other university-educated mothers interviewed, Claire was very conscious that the police responded to her differently than they would, for example, to a university-educated black woman or a working-class white mother who did not exhibit a similar understanding of her legal rights. Of a black mother she had witnessed in a similar situation, she said, "There was no politeness. There was no extra . . . leeway for her, and I felt I was given leeway in comparison to her. . . . [The police] don't deal with me like that."

Fighting back tears as she spoke of her most recent encounter with the police, Claire described constant fear for her son's well-being, acknowledging that her experience was nothing when compared to what black mothers must endure daily. Once when her son failed to return home after ten hours, she decided to phone the local police. As she described it:

> I've been really paranoid given what's been happening lately with him being stopped in the streets. . . . I thought the police had got him. So I rang the police station and said, "This is Claire Cunningham. Have you got my son in custody?" They tapped through [the computer] and said, "No, there's no Cunningham being held in Leicestershire." The police asked, "Why are you ringing at this point? He's not been missing that long." So I said, "My son is six foot three, black, and male. Your officers have been giving him a lot of hassle recently. They've stopped him on numerous occasions as he's got his key in this door coming into our home. Squad cars have stopped him and asked, 'What are you doing?' because this is not a black area. What's a six-foot-three black male doing entering a house in a white middle-class area?" So I said to this chap on the phone, "I'm really sorry and I know that I'm going to offend you personally but your officers have been spending far too much attention on my son. I have to eliminate this as a possibility."

Claire's experiences are the type of racism that members of the black community routinely manage; it has become associated almost exclusively with blacks (and the Irish). It is precisely these "limits" on white racial privilege that white mothers engaged in transracial caretaking alliances encounter. The fact that white privilege has limits is not always recognized by black family members when they calculate the impact of racism on their white family members, a perspective undercuts the amount of racial "empathy" that white women can expect to receive from their families and friends. Although the white mothers interviewed held a broad range of understandings about how racial privilege intersects with gender, age, and class hierarchies, most argued that their "suffering" and "abuse" as members of black families is not recognized and had consequences for them as mothers.

Another white mother, Britney, who was less educated than Claire, had arrived at the same analysis. While Britney was divorced, she had been married for more than ten years and raised her children with episodic support from her former husband, a Jamaican black. She described her daughters as "an extension of me" and did not differ from the university-educated mothers in her analysis of her children's hypervisibility (and thus vulnerability) to school administrators and the police because of their skin color. "When my children were in school, there were very few what we called in the old days 'half-castes.' Now today they would be called 'black.' . . . But I always did say to them that if ever they were out in a group, if there was anybody doing anything wrong, they would be the ones to be singled out [by the police] because they were different. They stuck out [from whites] . . . which they understood [was a problem]."

While parents expressed concern for their daughters' self-esteem because they were sometimes subjected to racial abuse, they argued that racism was gendered and that teenage girls were less likely to be racially harassed by the police on a regular basis. And because parents assumed that their sons would experience more frequent and vulgar forms of racial abuse in public spaces, they seemed to develop a more heightened and proactive perspective about sons' needs (rather than a reactive antiracist consciousness). Proactive strategies included things such as teaching their sons how to respond to the police politely and to document instances of racial harassment or police abuse, asking their white peers to report incidents and act collectively as witnesses.

Conclusion: The Racial Gaps within
Multiracial Families

I have traced racial logics and ideologies circulating within interracial families that "naturalize" and "racialize" a mother's ability to empathize with her
children. In my field research and focused interviews I identified a discourse of maternal incompetence in which black family members assumed
white birth mothers' inability to mother properly. Thus maternal incompetence is racialized. White mothers may find themselves parenting children
in a familial context in which their black family members suspect them of
not possessing racial "empathy." They are assumed to be less prepared to
parent their children because of their "whiteness" and have to manage the
presumed "racial gap" between themselves and their children.

This raises the question of why black women typically invoke the trope of
maternal incompetence as a code for white women's (and perhaps their
own) vulnerabilities. In a context in which two-parent black heterosexual
families are idealized but increasingly less common as a family form, the
trope of maternal incompetence registers larger anxieties about antiblack
racism, educational disparities, and aesthetic hierarchies that privilege
white and light-skinned women in a range of ethnic communities in
Britain.[21] The dearth of two-parent black families was interpreted by local
black women as a rejection of black women, who they argued were disadvantaged because they tended to come from more religious families than
white women. I was repeatedly told that black teenage girls from Caribbean
families, unlike white girls, are not typically allowed to date or go out at
night unsupervised, while their brothers are given these liberties. Consequently, they argued, their white female peers were less restricted by their
parents and so were able to frequent the same nightclubs and leisure places
that the young black men in their age cohort frequented. The black men
paired up with white girls as teenagers before their black female peers
acquired this freedom of movement. This was confirmed in interviews with
the white women who had been in long-term relationships.

White mothers who were attempting to transfer a black identity to their children perceived access to black Caribbean social networks as desirable because they believed that such networks were a reliable source of emotional and social support for their children if they experienced racism. However, these same mothers expressed apprehension that their children would be rejected by the black community if they did not display specific cultural behaviors or traits defined as "black" by some segments of that community. In some families these cultural traits were explicitly class-linked and reflective of immigration and educational histories. They included an ability to display certain culinary preferences, musical tastes, hair care and hygiene practices, clothing styles, humor, and patois-speaking skills. The black women interviewed confirmed that the black community evaluates the children of white women on the basis of these learned cultural behaviors. For example, Camille, the black social worker mentioned earlier, perceived differences in the way such children were viewed by the black community: "I don't think they [black children with one white parent] are necessarily accepted by the black community. They are treated differently from black children [with two black parents]." This issue of acceptable "black" cultural behavior is complicated by the absence of a unitary and fixed conception of what constitutes black British or African-Caribbean cultural traits among the various African-Caribbean diasporic communities in Leicester.

When compared to the black mothers who had children of multiracial ancestry, white mothers of children of African ancestry expressed the same fears that their children might be distinguished from black children with two black parents. However, black mothers reasoned that since they shared the same "racial" identity as their children, they were prepared to empathize with their pain and respond appropriately. As members of the black community, black mothers felt equipped to compensate for the "horizontal hostility" their children might experience within that community. Both middle-class black and white mothers who lived in professional enclaves feared that their children might be excluded from certain black social circles because of their more privileged lifestyles. They feared that their children's greater access to material resources and social experiences could generate tensions and class-based cultural differences between them and the children of working-class or low-income blacks, depriving them of the emotional and social support of that segment of the community.

While some white mothers expressed concerns that racial difference and racism were strong enough to disrupt their maternal bond with their children, others expressed the belief that the mother-child bond transcends race, so their children's experience of being labeled racially "other" would not threaten that primary intimacy. Others expressed both the fear of losing that bond and the fear that they wouldn't know how to comfort their children. Several white mothers, for example, expressed concerns about being eventually rejected by their children because they had not said the "right things" or known how to respond when issues of racial difference and racism emerged. But in spite of the numerous examples given of black parental failure (for example, failure to empathize or to teach about racism), none of the black parents interviewed expressed fears of being rejected by their children. Thus, regardless of how they responded to racism and assumed racial difference, white mothers were assumed to lack the social experiences (including racial discrimination) black family members considered necessary to ensure maternal competence, whereas all black mothers were believed to possess maternal competence by virtue of belonging to the same race as their children.

Black mothers of very light or white-skinned children argued that their children did not need to physically resemble them because no matter how closely they resembled their white fathers, they still shared their mother's racial status. In this way, they deemphasized physical resemblance while arguing that racial sameness and thus racial resemblance is a consequence of the way that the white Anglo-British population responds to anyone who possesses visible traces of African ancestry. An assumed absence of racial differences between black mothers and their children reaffirmed black mothers' belief that they possessed the adequate racial empathy and maternal competence. The inability of white mothers, however, to claim membership in the same racial category as their children, combined with cultural beliefs about racial difference, appeared to undermine their maternal compe-

tence (and authority) even when they had acquired sophisticated understandings of racism.

As we have seen, black mothers were not required by the black women
interviewed (or their families) to prove that they possessed the skills necessary to mediate racism, while white mothers experienced considerable
skepticism (and occasionally even intense criticism) about their maternal
abilities if they failed to demonstrate a sufficiently sophisticated understanding of everyday racism. White mothers who had children who were not
perceived as white had to continually strive to diminish the perceived
"racial" gap that prevailed between themselves and their children. It might
be argued that since white mothers who have African-descent children perceive them as not belonging to the same racial category (whatever the
degree of physical resemblance), they may have more motivation to develop
and/or articulate some forms of proactive antiracist strategies. In contrast,
due to a belief in a shared racial position, black mothers presumed their
own maternal competence, whereas white mothers were perceived by others as well as themselves as needing to earn competence in this area.

Acknowledgments

A version of this essay appeared in *Social Identities: Journal for the Study of Race, Nation and
Culture* 5, no. 2 (1999): 1–25. I am very grateful to David Theo Goldberg and Abebe
Zegeye, the coeditors of *Social Identities,* for their insightful comments on an earlier version
of this essay. While this work is the product of a single author, it would not have been possible without the insights and support of Nelista Cuffy, an African-Caribbean antiracist education officer, who facilitated this research by providing me with numerous referrals to
white mothers of African-descent children and to members of the African-Caribbean community in Leicestershire. I am very grateful to a number of antiracist activists and scholars
for their support of my research. In this vein I thank the following African-Caribbean
antiracist community activists in Leicestershire: Nelista Cuffy, Amelia Dowdye, Rachel
Hunte, Bernice Bennett, Owen Brown, and Gerry Burke. In the United States I wish to
thank my feminist friends and colleagues whose intellectual commitments and friendship
have sustained and nurtured me during the past years: Tani Barlow, Kathleen Blee, Karen
Brodkin, Jacqueline Nassy Brown, Margaret Conkey, Susan Dalton, Ruth Frankenberg,

Maria Franklin, Irma McClaurin, Carolyn Martin Shaw, Avery Gordon, Gail Hanlon, Kristin Luker, Sandra Morgen, Jodi O'Brien, Beth Schneider, Becky Thompson, Ara Wilson, and Jonathan Warren. This paper is based upon research that was funded by the Royalty Research Fund at the University of Washington, Seattle, and the University of California, Santa Barbara. I also benefited from the comments of the following audiences: the Stanford Humanities Center, the Department of Sociology at the University of Wisconsin-Madison, and the Northwestern University Gendered Politics of Reproduction session organized by Carole Browner and Caroline Bledsoe for the 1998 annual meetings of anthropology held in Philadelphia.

Notes

1.   For example, several reports published by the Commission for Racial Equality document the racial violence in housing and education. However, while these reports identify black and Asian families, they do not generally acknowledge multiracial families that include white parents or white women who are the lone parents of African-descent children. See Commission for Racial Equality 1981, 1986a, 1986b.

2.   The report did not state whether these applications involved white women who were members of multiracial families. The largest number of applications were filed by Caribbean women, who submitted 232 applications for assistance in racial discrimination cases to the Commission for Racial Equality in 1997.

3.   This line of inquiry represented an extension of my earlier research in the United States and Brazil (Twine et al. 1991; Twine 1996, 1999) and was also inspired by the work of feminist antiracist scholars such as Kathleen Blee (1991), Vron Ware (1992), and Ruth Frankenberg (1993).

4.   In contrast to previous British research on interraciality and transracial familial relations, which has typically focused upon interracial families in London (Benson 1981), the racial identity of children (Wilson 1987), or the racism that children encounter (Tizard and Phoenix 1993), my research is concerned with how white birth mothers mediate, interpret, and respond to antiblack racism as parents. Second, this study belongs to the nascent body of ethnographic research being conducted by U.S.-based "whiteness studies" scholars rather than to what are known as racial identity research studies.

5.   See Twine 1998 for a brief discussion of several of the specific strategies employed by white mothers to minimize the racism that their children will encounter.

6.   My original research design involved a comparative study of three different cities in England: London, Leicester, and Liverpool. After conducting pilot research in London and Leicester I decided to conduct a focused community study of an African-descent

community that, in contrast to London and Liverpool, has been neglected by researchers concerned with multiracial families. This enabled me to reside in one community for an extended period of time rather than dividing my time between three cities with very different histories of immigration and ethnic populations. It is my hope that this will generate a more richly textured ethnography that is sensitive to the uniqueness of this locale. I also selected Leicester because it has been an important site for organized racism.

7.   I am employing the term "black British" to refer to African-descent men who were born and grew up in Britain but whose families have origins in Africa, the Americas, or the Caribbean. They have no experience of immigration and consequently experienced a different socialization process than their peers who immigrated to Britain as children or adults. Few of the U.K.-born blacks of Caribbean heritage self-identified as "black British," preferring instead "African-Caribbean" or simply "black." Some employed a range of self-identity markers depending upon the social context.

8.   While marital status was not a criterion of inclusion, I did attempt to interview a greater number of individuals in the category of mothers who had sustained a domestic partnership or marriage for a minimum of ten years. Long-term relationships enabled me to explore in-depth changes in their racial consciousness and parenting practices. I also interviewed a comparable sample of white fathers with black female partners in order to evaluate how gender affected the experience of racism.

9.   For a discussion of the basis of support for the National Front, see Phizacklea and Miles 1980 and Cashmore 1987.

10.   The National Front reaped electoral rewards in local elections of 1976 and 1977, prior to the period when Margaret Thatcher served as prime minister (1979–91).

11.   The 1991 census was the first in the United Kingdom to include a question on ethnic origin.

12.   I am following the British use of the term *Asian*, which typically includes South Asians with origins in Bangladesh, India, Pakistan, and East Africa while excluding the Chinese and other East Asians. Chinese were counted as a separate category on the 1991 U.K. census and constitute 0.3 percent of the local population.

13.   Pakistanis and Bangladeshis constitute 1.0 percent and 0.4 percent, respectively, of the population.

14.   Tariq Modood and his research associates at the London Policy Institute have documented significant differences among Asian ethnic groups along axes of class, immigrant status, tenure in Britain, and religion. For example, there appear to be profound economic differences between Bangladeshis as a whole and Indians in some communities. The diversity of the Asian population and economic differences are not always accounted for in the evaluations by non-Asians of Asian upward mobility (Modood and Berthoud 1997).

15.   Black scholars examining the African diaspora in Britain have described the anger that some black women feel toward local black men for dating and desiring white women (Brown 1998). I encountered this same phenomenon in Leicester. In private and public discussions local black women expressed frustration over their unsuccessful attempts to establish long-term relationships with black men, who increasingly formed partnerships with white women. This reaction was sometimes articulated in their evaluations of the maternal competence and racial empathy of white women in their families.

16.   Black women described their unsuccessful struggles to establish long-term monogamous relationships with local black men. Several women were considering emigrating to the United States because they considered this their only alternative if they hoped to establish a family with a black man. In a context in which black men routinely establish domestic partnerships and marriages with white women, relationships between black women and white men remain very stigmatized in Leicester among the black women I interviewed. This is not unique to the black community in Leicester. This same pattern has been found by U.S. scholars working in port cities in England (Brown 1998).

17.   She also interpreted the multiple and varied racial labels that white mothers employed to acknowledge that their children are of European/British ancestry as well as African as evidence that they are racist and don't understand racism. For example, some white mothers, like some black Caribbean parents, employed terms such as "mixed-race," "half-caste," or "African-English" to distinguish between children with one black parent and children with two black parents.

18.   Although he was born in Leicester, England, he self-identifies as Bajan. His parents immigrated from Barbados in the 1960s. His parents refer to the grandchildren who have one white parent as "half-caste."

19.   In his analysis of whites living in Detroit, John Hartigan, Jr. (1997) provides a much-needed analysis of the ways that working-class and poor whites who are located in residential, friendship, and familial networks that include U.S. blacks must manage their own racialization.

20.   My work is indebted to and inspired by that of Ruth Frankenberg (1993), who has argued that racism "rebounds" onto white women.

21.   I thank Jacqueline Nassy Brown for pushing my thinking analytically and for sharing her insights with me from her research in Liverpool.

II

Narratives
of Personhood

4

Baby Things as Fetishes?

Memorial Goods, Simulacra, and the "Realness" Problem of Pregnancy Loss

Linda L. Layne

Contemporary U.S. women who experience a pregnancy loss face a number of culturally and historically conditioned problems. Elsewhere (Layne 1999b, forthcoming) I have described how members of pregnancy loss support groups use the spiritually infused discourse of the gift to deal with some of the moral problems that pregnancy loss in late-twentieth-century North America poses. In this essay I focus on what I call the realness problem of pregnancy loss and show how bereaved parents use the "realness" of material things to deal with this problem.

The realness problem stems from the juxtaposition of two contradictory forces: the growing importance of the fetal subject and an enduring taboo surrounding dead fetuses and neonates.

In the last quarter of this century, a number of factors including earlier pregnancy testing, fetal imaging (medical and public), assistive conceptive technologies, and a smaller family size for many middle-class couples have led to the growing importance of the fetal subject in American culture (Morgan 1996a, 1996b; Michaels and Morgan 1999). Women now may begin to actively construct the personhood of their wished-for child from the moment they do a home pregnancy test. Each cup of coffee or glass of wine they abstain from and each person they inform of the impending birth adds to the "realness" of the baby they are growing within. They may follow the weekly physiological development of their "baby" with a home pregnancy manual, and each prenatal visit contributes to and confirms the growing sense of the baby's realness and to their growing sense of themselves as "mothers." This may be especially true of those visits where one hears the heartbeat, sees the baby moving on the sonogram screen, or is informed of the baby's sex. They may start making or acquiring baby things and preparing a place for the child in their homes, in their lives. They may have quit their job, taken maternity leave, or bought a new house. They may have given it a name or nickname and started talking to it or trying to influence its personality by playing music for it. Their friends, neighbors, or colleagues may have given them a baby shower.

Then, when the pregnancy ends without a baby to bring home, the very people who have encouraged the mother-in-the-making to take on this role and who may have participated with her in the social construction of her "baby" often withdraw their support for these interrelated projects, and act as if nothing of any significance took place. The cultural denial of pregnancy loss challenges the validity of the cultural and biological work already undertaken in constructing that child and belittles the importance of the loss. This cultural denial stems in part from the liminality of dead embryos, fetuses, and neonates. These beings are liminal in two and sometimes three ways. In nearly all cultures, embryos, fetuses, and newborns are considered liminal entities and as such are especially strong sources of "power and danger" that must be ritually controlled (Douglas 1966; Leach 1976). The same is true for corpses. In addition, many pregnancy losses occur because of congenital malformations.[1] As Landsman (this volume) shows, physical differences such as these are often used to challenge individuals' personhood. Thus, the personhood, or what is referred to in native terms as the "realness," of these "babies" may be challenged simultaneously in at least two, and often three, ways.

It is not just the dead fetuses that are liminal when pregnancy loss occurs but the would-be mothers as well. Van Gennep observed that the three phases of rites of passage—separation, transition, and incorporation—are not developed to the same extent in every set of ceremonies, and noted that pregnancy is often dominated by rites of transition (1960: 11). Several studies have documented the transitional character of pregnancy in the West, noting the many pollution beliefs and practices that set pregnant women off from the routines of everyday life (Newman 1969; Comaroff 1977; Paige and Paige 1981). Comaroff describes the pregnant woman as "interstitial in respect both of her social classification and of her behavior" (1977: 116).

Normally, the liminality of pregnancy ends following birth, as the mother is gradually reintegrated into society in her new role through rites of re-incorporation. However, when a pregnancy ends without a live birth, there are no rites to reincorporate the woman. My research with members of pregnancy loss support groups indicates that many participants feel trapped in a liminal social position. One woman reports that after two stillbirths she was told by someone not to worry about "Limbo." Later she says she realized "that there is a Limbo, but it's not for the stillborn babies. It's for their parents," and it was a state that she and her husband felt powerless to escape. "We gave birth—sort of. We had a child—sort of. Our child died—sort of. . . . Soon we learn to speak of things somewhere between birth and death, as we live in our someplace between heaven and hell" (Gana 1986). Another expressed similar feelings in a poem: "A mother without a child. What am I? I had a baby, but she's gone. Am I a mother? What am I?" (Chaidez 1985).

These feelings may be particularly acute for members of the middle class because of the moral valuation placed on finishing what one starts. As one woman who had a miscarriage put it, "No matter how you look at it, you've failed, because if you set out to do something, I believe you've got to finish it" (Down 1986).

While the liminality of dead and/or malformed fetuses and pregnant women who do not give birth to living children may be issues everywhere, there are a number of cultural particularities that contribute to the way pregnancy losses are handled in the United States. Dead babies present an uncontrovertible challenge to our cherished narratives of linear progress. This preferred narrative structure informs the stories we tell about the proper and expected trajectories of individuals' lives and technoscientific enterprises, including biomedicine (Layne 1996a, 1998). In addition, the feelings of bereavement that members of pregnancy loss support groups feel run counter to what Ariès has identified as the modern, and particularly North American, "need for happiness—the moral duty and the social obligation to contribute to the collective happiness by avoiding any cause for sadness or boredom, by appearing to be always happy, even if in the depths of despair" (1974: 93–94).

As a result, a culture of silence continues to shroud pregnancy loss in the United States (Layne 1998, 1990). Since the 1980s pregnancy loss support organizations, hospital bereavement teams, and the popular press have made the subject of pregnancy loss more visible (e.g., Fein 1998), but members of pregnancy loss support groups attest that the suppression and avoidance of these unhappy events remains the norm.

All of these factors contribute to the realness problem of pregnancy loss. A number of members of pregnancy loss support groups describe their confrontations with this problem in their narratives of loss published in support group newsletters. In a piece addressed to a baby she miscarried at eleven weeks, Lisa Jeffries explains the realness problem for her: how to mourn and remember this loss and to get others to participate in this process. "I will remember you in so few ways it hurts. Because I never knew you. And yet you were real and alive in me. I wish I could hold on to something about you. I wish I could show everyone how real you were to me. So then you would be real to them. And then they would know, as I do, that we've all lost someone special in you" (Jeffries 1998). Another example is found in a piece by Anne Ciany (1999) of Anne Arundel, Maryland, entitled "I'm a Mother Too," published in the Mother's/Father's Day issue of *SHARING*. Anne describes how after her first child was born prematurely and died after eighteen hours she sometimes finds herself asking, "Am I a mother?"

and says that family members tell her "that I am not really a mother because I have never experienced raising a child and all the work that is involved."[2] But despite her occasional doubts, Anne maintains that she does feel like a parent because "we have/had a son, we didn't give birth to an 'it.' Collin was real; he existed. If we have/had a son, then we must be parents. If not, what are we? Give us a title if we aren't parents. . . . We've lost so much. Don't deprive us of our motherhood too."

In this essay I show how members of pregnancy loss support groups use things to assert their claim that a "real baby" existed and is worthy of memory and to construct themselves as "real parents," deserving the social recognition this role entails. Through the buying, giving, and arrangement of things, women and their social networks actively construct their "babies" as "real," that is, as individuals who count. This process, which begins during pregnancy (Layne 1999a, forthcoming), is often continued after a pregnancy loss in order to validate the value of the work already done and to claim for themselves the social credit to which they feel entitled as real mothers.

Elsewhere I describe the "uses and trajectories" (Appadurai 1986) of several types of gifts documented in narratives of pregnancy loss—goods purchased or made for the baby-to-be during the pregnancy, goods given in the name of the baby-to-be while in utero, goods given to the baby after its death, and goods given in memory of the baby (Layne 1999a, forthcoming). Here I focus on memorial goods acquired and kept by bereaved parents. Using the semiotic distinction between indices, icons, and symbols, I describe how these goods include those whose relationship with that which they signify is based on physical connection or contiguity (indices), those based on a relation of resemblance or similarity (icons), and those based on a more abstract, arbitrary relationship (symbols).

Babies and their things share a number of physical characteristics—for example, being small in size, soft in both color and texture, precious (in both the sense of being cute and the sense of having great value), capable of dramatic transformation, animal-like in some regards, and possessing a gender but being asexual. In addition to the material qualities of particular baby things, the predominant quality being communicated by bereaved parents through their baby's things is "realness." The irrefutable realness of physical things (even of simulacra, or "fake things") is sentiently apprehended. Things are sentiently apprehended in the same ways that living children are, but that dead children (once they have been buried or disposed of) no longer can be. They can be touched, held, caressed, hugged, and gazed upon. Sometimes they can also be smelled, as in the case of flowers or clothing and blankets, or heard, as in the case of a musical toy or wind chimes. Like children, they can also be cleaned, protected, and displayed for the admiration of others.

In the face of the denial of pregnancy loss, the use of things to make the claim that a real child existed and is worthy of memory is an example of a de Certeauian tactic by which members of subordinated groups use dominant resources for their own interests and desires. As Gorenstein notes, "although most cultural themes embedded in objects are normative and convey and reinforce the generally held cultural themes of a society, the objectification of sentiently-held cultural themes make objects the perfect vehicles for conveying themes that are not commonly accepted in a community" (1996: 8).[3]

Pregnancy Loss Support Groups

This work is based on research with three pregnancy loss support groups in New York and New Jersey: Unite (not an acronym), a regional group with (as of 1995) ten support groups serving Pennsylvania and New Jersey; SHARE (Source of Help in Airing and Resolving Experiences), the nation's largest pregnancy loss support organization with (as of 1995) ninety-seven groups throughout the United States; and the New York section of the National Council of Jewish Women (NCJW) support group in New York City. Over nine hundred such groups were established throughout the country during the 1980s.

My research has involved attending support group meetings—participating first as a parent who suffered multiple miscarriages, and later as a professional at Unite's annual conference—and other special seminars and events sponsored by these groups. I also participated in the New York section of the National Council of Jewish Women's telephone counseling program, completed Unite's training program for support counselors, and interviewed some of the founding members of these and other groups. More recently, I have been engaged in a textual analysis of Unite's quarterly newsletters (starting with their first issue in 1981 and continuing to the present) and the bimonthly issues of the SHARE newsletter (from 1984 to the present), which include contributions from members throughout the country.

Most support group meetings are attended by couples (this was strongly encouraged by the NYJW group), but sometimes a woman and more occasionally a man attends on her/his own. Women, mostly bereaved mothers but also sometimes other female relatives, friends, and nurses, write the vast majority of the newsletter items. Some women, including the editors of both newsletters, contribute multiple items, and these often span a period of years, allowing the reader to piece together a fuller account of the loss and to see how the experience of loss changes over time. Men (again, mostly bereaved fathers but also occasionally bereaved grandfathers or brothers) contribute more regularly to the SHARE newsletter (about 12 percent of the personal items) than they do to the Unite newsletter (about 4 percent).[4]

The membership of these three organizations is predominately middle-class. There is evidence that socioeconomic status influences the rate of pregnancy loss. Like other pregnancy outcomes, the frequency of pregnancy loss varies dramatically from country to country and appears to be linked to socioeconomic factors (MacFarlane and Mugford 1984: 103). Members are also predominantly white, and although white women have a larger total number of pregnancy losses nationwide, the estimated rate of pregnancy loss is nearly double for women of color than for non-Hispanic white women (Ventura et al. 1995: 18). So far as I know, there are no studies available that compare the experience of pregnancy loss for women from different class or ethnic backgrounds in the United States, but it is reasonable to assume that there may be class and/or ethnic differences in the ways that individuals use consumer goods to construct personhood during a pregnancy and after a loss.

All three groups are ecumenical and include Jewish, Catholic, and Protestant members. Testimony of participants at pregnancy loss support group meetings and the personal narratives published in the newsletters indicate that many members of pregnancy loss support groups turn to religion in their search for answers. Judging from these sources, participants vary in the strength of their religious commitment. Religion influences the construction of fetal personhood in a number of ways. For example, according to Jewish religious tradition, one should not buy things for an expected child until after its birth. Similarly, beliefs about life after death undoubtedly have an important influence on the ways goods are used following a loss.

Some founders of pregnancy loss groups are supporters of women's right to choose, while others clearly feel their work in this area complements their antiabortion stand. This divisive issue has remained relatively submerged in the pregnancy loss support movement, as leaders have striven to champion their shared goals and gain strength through unity. It is not safe to assume that individuals who participate in groups share or even know the position of their group's leaders on abortion.

Miscarriages are by far the most frequent type of pregnancy loss. Most pregnancy losses occur during the first trimester, and it is estimated that only 3.1 percent of all intrauterine deaths take place after sixteen weeks' gestation (Bongaarts and Potter 1983: 39). In the medical and social scientific literature the term *stillbirth* is used to designate a loss that occurs after a point in the pregnancy at which the fetus had a chance of surviving ex utero, currently around twenty-four weeks in the United States—not coincidentally, the same gestational age after which abortion is illegal. Later losses (third-trimester and early infant deaths) are proportionately much more frequently represented in the Unite and SHARE newsletters and at support group meetings (Layne, forthcoming). Given the fact that the later the loss, the more "baby things" (and personhood) an embryo/fetus/child is likely to have, it is not surprising that the narratives of loss with the most elaborated accounts of material culture (those on which I focus in this essay) are those describing losses that occurred either later in a pregnancy or after birth. As a result, in this essay I use primarily the "native" terms. It is important to keep in mind, however, that personhood is actively constructed during the course of a pregnancy, and the moment at which this process begins, the pace or paces at which it proceeds once it has begun, and the number of people engaged in this process may vary from person to person and from one pregnancy to the next.

Memories and Things

Many members of pregnancy loss support groups report keeping and/or collecting things that belonged to or symbolize their dead baby. Sometime these items are put away, perhaps in a shoe box (Davenport 1993; Chiffens 1994) or a "memory box" especially designed for this purpose (Memories Unlimited 1994); other times they are displayed in a public area of the home. Whether kept hidden away from view or displayed publicly, these goods help bereaved parents assert, as Hannah Campbell (1992) does of her stillborn son, "He was a real baby with baby things."

In our culture, pregnant women and members of their social networks often make or purchase items for a baby-to-be during the pregnancy. Some women begin to buy or make things from the moment their pregnancy is determined; others wait until the last months of their pregnancy. In addition to purchases made individually by expectant parents, gifts are often given collectively to babies-to-be at baby showers.

After a loss, the goods that had been acquired for the baby are handled in one of two different ways, and these differences do not appear to be directly related to the duration of the pregnancy. For instance, in a poem entitled "Baby Things," about the death of her baby girl two days after birth due to meconium aspiration and hyaline membrane disease, Cindy Foster names, one by one, the things which she accumulated and arranged for her baby during the pregnancy: "Your room was gaily decorated, a rainbow on the wall. / I made bumper pads and a mobile. In gingham they were all. / The playpen is blue. The crib is white. The quilt: blue, yellow and pink." She then tells of how these things were disposed of following the death. "Grandpa took the crib down. / Grandma helped me pack, / All the clothes and toys and things / Into a large sack" (1985). There is a parallel being drawn here between the accumulation of baby things which both accompanied and enstantiated the accumulation of personhood during the pregnancy. With the death, the parallel projects of both the new person and its things are brought to an abrupt end—put into sack and casket. With the baby go the things and all they stood for.

Others use the analogy between baby and baby things to different ends; they use these things to symbolize the baby's ongoing presence in the family. Whereas Cindy Foster put away the baby things "until the time is right for me to have another to share in such delight" (that is, the ownership of these things is revoked with the death and reserved for the next baby), others grant an ongoing ownership to the dead. In these cases, baby things are often used as a stand-in or surrogate for the baby. For example, one woman, in a piece describing the death of her grandson seven weeks after his birth due to a heart anomaly that was diagnosed via ultrasound during the seventh month of her daughter-in-law's pregnancy, writes, "Grief is ... taking a family picture with Alexander's teddy bear instead of with Alexander" (Schneider 1996: 7).

In addition to baby things acquired during the pregnancy, hospitals are an important source of memorabilia for later losses. Many hospitals now have a bereavement team and special protocols for pregnancy losses, which include providing parents with mementos (Baker 1992; Connors 1992; Doherty 1991; Twin to Twin Transfusion Syndrome Foundation 1994). Goods are also often especially purchased for this purpose. Pregnancy loss support newsletters contain numerous advertisements for products designed to assist bereaved parents to commemorate their babies. Some are new products that have been developed by pregnancy loss support organizations or bereaved parents; others are existing products now being marketed to a new consumer niche, such as "portrait plates" on which a photo of a child can be laminated, advertised in the SHARE newsletter "as a means of preserving the memory of your child."

The things that are used to memorialize the child within the family fall into several different categories. Mementos consisting of parts of the body, such as a lock of hair, function indexically, that is, they are "signs whose relation to their objects [is of] a direct nature ... by virtue of [having] been really connected with it" (Singer 1978: 216). Of all the readily separable body parts or fluids, hair has a special place in Euro-American symbol systems. As Miller (1981) notes, "it could be 'safely' admired, since it was not any part of the embarrassing body," and it was particularly appropriate for the commemoration of love and death because of its ability to endure, even after death. According to Rook (1985: 258), hair care (cleansing, cutting, shaping, and anointing) is "the core of most grooming rituals." Sheumaker attributes the popularity of hair as a sentimental object during the eighteenth and nineteenth centuries in the United States to the fact that "hair could embody the supposed essence of individuals and their relationships, symbolize ... ties ... in its tenuous strands" and, because of its durability, " could transcend time, reaching past absence to presence" (Sheumaker 1997: 422).[5]

Handprints and footprints are one step removed from hair semiotically, somewhere between an index and icon in that the print was formed by a direct, physical connection with the baby but then represents the baby from a distance. Like hair, handprints and, even more frequently, footprints have been common mementos of babyhood in Europe and America throughout the twentieth century. *Journal de Bébé*, by Franc-Nohain, published in Paris in 1914, from which the Metropolitan Museum of Art's *Baby's Journal* (1978) was adapted, included a page for the "empreinte du pied et de la main de bébé" and a page for "boucles de chevaux" (personal communication, 1999, Valerie von Volz). The importance of such prints as symbols of early childhood is also evidenced in the frequency with which they are used as motifs in preschool art projects and consumer goods.

Footprints and handprints are important symbols of humanness, bipedalism and an opposable thumb being distinctive characteristics of the species. Since the Victorian era and the discovery of the uniqueness of fingerprints, these prints have come to represent not only generic humanness but the idea of the unique individuality of each person. Infant footprints were also apparently used in this manner. AC Controls Ltd., a British firm that advertises itself as "integrated security specialists," markets a "baby footprinting identicator" kit. According to their promotional material, "obtaining fingerprints and footprints of young children has been undertaken since the early eighties." Up until recently New York state law required that the footprints of all newborns be recorded. This was discontinued recently, as they proved to be nearly useless for forensic purposes, able to identify less than 1 percent of babies (Joaquim Pinheiro, personal communication, 1999).[6]

Footprints and handprints, if the actual prints of a particular person, function on the basis of contiguity, that is, they function iconically. If they are used without direct reference to a particular person, as for instance in the discourse of the antiabortion movement, they function symbolically. In both cases they function as a synecdoche: Part A (fetal feet) equals A (a fetus), which in turn equals B (a human) (Condit 1990). Condit explains how this partiality is key to understanding the importance of fetal footprints in prolife imagery. A "full picture of a young fetus includes features not associated with adult human beings, the placenta, and the umbilical cord," and, if the fetus is young enough, a tail; but fetal feet are "very close to baby feet in shape. . . . Our visual logic 'recognizes' such feet as 'small human feet' and we synecdochically expand the unseen picture to see a full 'small human'" (1990: 68–69).

In the case of pregnancy loss, footprints seem to have an additional meaning (one that privileges them over handprints). Like the trace of someone walking in the sand, the footprints can evoke the sense that someone passed this way, was here, and now is gone.[7] Unlike footprints in the sand, however, those imprinted on specially treated paper are durable reminders of the baby's physical reality. Another way of preserving this physical trace is through plaster casts. In its section of "ideas for remembrance," the SHARE newsletter mentions "a kit for casting baby's hand or foot . . . [which] duplicates in lifelike detail" (Smith 1988).

Sonogram photos and snapshots taken after the birth (whether or not the baby is still alive) also play an important role in authenticating the existence of a "real baby" (Layne 1992). They function iconically as memorial goods. Shapiro (1988: 124) has observed that "of all modes of representation ... [photography] is one of the most easily assimilated into the discourses of knowledge and truth, for it is thought to be an unmediated simulacrum, a copy of what we consider the 'real'" (cf. Sontag 1973).

Sonogram images, while requiring more interpretive effort (that is, not being as "unproblematically 'real'" [Shapiro 1988: 124] as conventional photographs), carry the imprint of medical authority. Oaks (1998) and others have noted how these images play an important role in helping to establish the "reality" of a "baby" for many women during the early stages of their pregnancy. She cites anthropologist Abu-Lughod describing her pregnancy: "I was so unsure of my babies that I worried about their having disappeared if I didn't see them every two weeks or so" (Abu-Lughod, quoted in Oaks 1998: 240). Oaks uses another woman as an illustration of the fact that sonogram images do not necessarily establish reality. One woman reports that even though she had two sonograms she kept the pictures, "because I didn't see it *all* the time, you know, it wasn't *really* real" (1998: 240). If the "reality" of embryos, especially in the early stages of a pregnancy, is problematic for some women because they cannot be seen or felt, the "reality problem" is greatly heightened for women after a pregnancy loss. Sonogram images may be one of the only things available to testify to the fact that a "real baby" ever existed.[8]

In addition to sonogram images, women whose losses take place in the latter half of their pregnancies are often presented with snapshots by the hospital staff. This practice is a modern variation of a nineteenth-century Euro-American practice. According to Ariès, by the second half of the nineteenth century photographs of the dead, especially of children, had become very popular: "Few family albums were without their photographs of dead children" (Aries 1985: 247). Today, photographs of the dead are no longer considered appropriate; it is photographic remembrances of the person in life, not in death, that are valued.[9] But in the case of pregnancy loss, snapshots of the baby after its birth/death may be the only ones possible. Like sonogram images, these photos play a critical role in establishing the reality of the baby. In 1987 SHARE conducted a survey of bereaved parents regarding the importance of photographs after a loss. Of the 438 respondents (who reported losses that occurred between 1966 and 1987), 95 percent "felt that it is important to have pictures of the baby," 63 percent had one or more photographs, 50 percent were offered pictures by the hospital, and 26 percent took pictures themselves (Laux 1988a). The respondents testify to the reality-making function of such photos: "We need to remember her as a real person we were holding. This is our proof"; "Although I get no great comfort from her pictures, I do have them put away for when I do feel the need to see she existed"; "On those days when you feel like it really never happened and people are treating you like you never had a child, you do have a picture to remind yourself you did have a child"; another describes having a picture of her twenty-weeks'-gestation baby "hanging on the wall with the rest of the children. . . . It is proof she existed" (quoted in Laux 1988b). In addition to affirming the reality of a baby, such photographs are used by bereaved parents to stress the uniqueness and individuality of their baby. At the same time they provide important resources for establishing family ties through the rhetoric of inheritance and resemblance. For example, in the film *Some Babies Die,* one woman explains that photos are "so essential" because "you can actually say, 'Well, she has got his nose and my lips.'"

Artistic renderings—sketches and paintings—are another form of visual representation sometimes used to memorialize dead babies. According to Ariès (1962), this practice can be traced to the sixteenth century, when elite European families began to include their dead children in group portraits on, or at, the family tomb. Not until the beginning of the seventeenth century were portraits of individual children common. By then "it had become customary to preserve by means of the painter's art the ephemeral appearance of childhood. . . . Henceforth every family wanted portraits of its children, and portraits painted while they were still children" (1962: 43). Ariès argues that "photography took over from painting" in the nineteenth century (1962: 43), and while there is no denying the importance of photography in contemporary family life, photography has not completely replaced painting. Many middle-class North American families still have portraits done of their children which they hang in public spaces of their homes. The greater cost of such representations and what Bourdieu (1984: 39) has described as the "legitimacy-imposing effects of paintings" make these prestige items. Portraits are, like children, "one of a kind," and although painting is thought to be less "realistic" than photography, good art is thought to capture the essence of its subject (Sheumaker 1997: 423).

Artifacts of civil society are another important type of memorial good. This includes birth and death certificates, hospital identification bracelets, crib cards, baptismal certificates, and in at least one case a measuring tape. Like visual representations, these items bestow authenticity, but they do so via different means. Their authenticating power comes from the civil (or religious) authority that grants them. This in turn rests on the power of positivism, which forms the basis of these bureaucratic institutions. Such goods traffic in weights and measures, dates and times, for these are the prerequisites of civil personhood—what it takes to be counted. According to Hacking, "positivism . . . took for granted that positive facts were measured by numbers." He traces the "avalanche of numbers" to the period between 1820 and 1840 and maintains that by the end of the nineteenth century no one would disagree with the statement of physicist Lord Kelvin "that when you can measure what you are speaking about, you know something about it: when you cannot measure it . . . your knowledge is of a meager and unsatisfactory kind" (Hacking 1991: 186).

Other memorial goods involve more symbolic representations of the baby. In other words, rather than having a metonymic relationship with the child, they represent the child via metaphor. Such goods include sentimental knickknacks for the home purchased specifically for the purpose of memorialization, such as Christmas ornaments and figurines. For example, Hannah Campbell explains that family members gave her a Waterford baby block, a Hummel boy called "I'll Protect Him," and a Hand of God statue cradling a child in memory of her stillborn son, which she keeps in her curio cabinet where she and others can see them and be reminded of him on a daily basis (Campbell 1991b, 1992).[10]

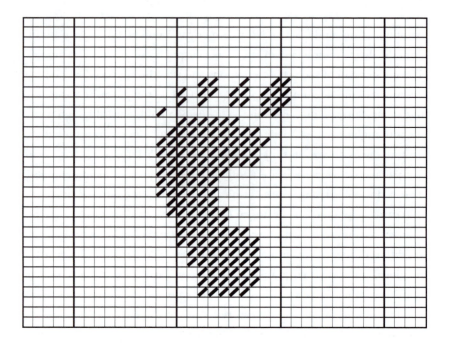

Angels are without a doubt the most popular motif for mementos. The analogization of dead babies with angels accomplished through these goods attributes to babies the qualities of goodness, innocence, and sacredness (Layne 1992) as well as a Victorian valuation of domestic life (Douglas 1977). Baby footprints reappear in a more abstract way in this category of memorial good—not the actual print of a particular baby, but the representation of a generic fetus's or baby's footprint. The SHARE newsletter periodically includes the pattern for making cross-stitch footprints. For example, in 1991 a pattern is presented along with an article on "keepsakes following a miscarriage." The author suggests that the footprint "could include baby's name and date and be framed as a tree ornament."[11] Replicas of tiny feet also are apparently sometimes purchased as memorial objects. According to a piece in the SHARE newsletter, "pewter feet the size of a 10 week gestation baby are available from religious stores" (Lewis 1991).

Another important set of memorial items are objects to be placed in one's yard. Some commonly used items include trees, rosebushes, fountains, benches, birdbaths, and garden statues of children or angels. Like angels, memorial items for the garden convey the qualities of goodness, innocence, and sacredness as well as a romantically construed naturalness (Layne 1994). Whereas most memorial goods are the kinds of mementos that one might possess had the child lived (for example, hospital records, scrapbooks, portraits, toys) and which therefore work to normalize the baby's life, garden memorabilia normalize the child's death. The fact that plants are alive and capable of growth is particularly important in this regard. Cathi Lambert, director of SHARE, tells of "a very special gift" of "a little blue spruce" given to them by family members one December, on the first anniversary of their son's birth/death. The bush becomes a stand-in for a child who is thought of not as dead, but rather as an ongoing, living, miraculous, "angelic presence" manifested through this object of nature. "Our little bush ... immediately named the little 'Christopher' bush ... nurtured and grew" even after having been transplanted to their new home. Each year they decorate "our little bush" with "bright white lights ... the symbol of brightness and purity." Cathi remarks upon the lovingness with which her husband arranges the bush/child in "his radiant white garment of lights," thereby transforming Christopher's bush into Christopher, who "stood glistening alone." At other times the bush is construed not as the child himself but as a vehicle through which Christopher "do[es] his miracles" (Lambert 1992).[12]

Memorial jewelry is also a popular memorial good.[13] The most frequent type of memorial jewelry mentioned is a "mother's ring," which has the birthstone of each of the woman's children (whether living and dead). Sometimes jewelry is more representational—for example, "precious feet" pins and guardian angel pins. Sue Friedeck, a SHARE newsletter editor who had two miscarriages and then had a son who died thirteen days after birth, wears two pieces of jewelry representing her son: "an angel on a chain" and a ring with her son's birthstone, which was given to her as a Mother's Day gift. She writes that she would also like to get a butterfly and heart to wear on her necklace so as to represent "each child lost" (1995a). For Sue, the angel, butterfly, and heart "each represent special qualities of my babies."

Sometimes more than one of the categories of memorial goods are combined in memorial jewelry. For example, the "keepsake pendant" advertised in an issue of SHARE is "a small decorative vessel that holds a portion of a cremated baby's remains or a lock of hair." The pendant can be worn as a necklace or displayed under a blown glass dome (Madelyn Company 1996).

Simulacra and the "Realness Problem" of Pregnancy Loss

In addition to the many consumer goods and memorabilia discussed in the preceding pages, familiar accoutrements of birth and death for middle-class Americans, pregnancy loss support newsletters reveal another category of goods unique to pregnancy loss. These are simulacra of the trappings of fetushood and infanthood. These goods act as substitutes for items that are desired but unattainable. In fact, since the goods that are desired but unattainable are often themselves used as stand-ins for the baby the parents so desperately desire but cannot have, these simulacra represent a particularly clear example of the way bereaved parents use the tangibility of goods to combat the realness problem that pregnancy loss poses for them.[14]

A number of these goods concern visual representations of the baby. As discussed earlier, because embryos and fetuses cannot be readily seen, their "realness" is an issue for many pregnant women and their networks regardless of the eventual outcome. The importance of visual representations in establishing the realness of an embryo or fetus is even greater in the case of pregnancy loss.[15]

If a desired representation is unavailable, pregnancy loss support newsletters provide suggestions on how to attain substitutes. For example, in an article on early losses a contributor to the SHARE newsletter counsels, "If you didn't have an ultrasound, get a copy of Niles Newton's *A Child Is Born* from the library. Photocopy the picture closest to your baby's gestational age" (Lewis 1991). In this case, a photocopy of a reproduction of a sonogram image of some other embryo or fetus may stand in for the coveted image of one's own child, which is in itself a substitute for the coveted child.

Another example is found in descriptions of artistic renderings. Sometimes, much like the case of surrogate sonogram photos, portraits are suggested as a way to fill a void. For example, Kelly Gonzalez, the coordinator in the SHARE group in Colorado Springs, advises, "Even if you do not have any pictures of your baby or you were not able to see your baby, an artist can sometimes work with baby pictures of the parents and/or other children to create a likeness to what you may have envisioned your baby to look like" (Gonzalez 1995; cf. Doerr 1992).

Other times, portraits are suggested as a way of improving on the visual representation(s) one may have, that is, a way of substituting a more desirable representation, one more like the type of representation one would have had if the birth had been "normal" and the baby had survived. This is typically suggested for babies who survived for some time after birth. In these cases, portraits are specifically recommended because the image of the baby can be improved by the removal of unsightly or unpleasant reminders of the child's traumatic birth, for example, tubes and wires, bruises, and birth defects (Friedeck 1995b).

Like visual representations, when the artifacts of civil authority cannot be attained, simulacra are available. For example, the Association for Recognizing the Life of Stillborns (1992) sells "Recognition of Life Certificates," as does SHARE. These certificates are described as "suitable for framing" and "provide a record of birth and lasting keepsake" (Guenther 1991). In 1987 SHARE had two models, one for stillbirth and one for neonatal death. In 1991 they redesigned their certificates and offer "three styles to best suit your experience." Space is provided for personalizing the certificate with "baby's name, parent's name, date and name of support person or hospital representative" (Voegele 1991).

SHARE also provides copies of do-it-yourself baptismal certificates. The certificate was designed by Malinda Sawyer of Marion, Illinois, an active member of Aiding a Mother Experiencing Neonatal Death (AMEND), and shared at a 1983 SHARE conference and then printed in the newsletter (Sawyer 1983). According to Dorothy Van Sant in a piece in a subsequent

Hosanna Amen Hallelujah Shalom Praise Hosanna

Certificate of Baptism
for

_____

_____ *of* _____

LOVINGLY BAPTIZED
In the Name of The Father, Son, and Holy Spirit

Date _____ Place _____
Baptized by _____

"This is my beloved child,
in whom I am well pleased."
Matthew 3:17

Hosanna Amen Hallelujah Shalom Praise Hosanna

© 1982 Aiding a Mother Experiencing Neonatal Death

Hosanna Amen Hallelujah Shalom Praise *(left and right margins)*

Recognition of Life

This is to acknowledge the life of

_____

Who was born into the hearts of

_____

On _____

In an instant you and your
Little one touched hearts. . .
Love is for a lifetime . . .

SHARE newsletter, "anyone can administer the rite of baptism, it is often carried out by a parent or by hospital personnel. For instance, a mother who miscarries at home may baptize her baby" (Van Sant 1986).

This class of goods raises authenticity and legitimacy questions that replicate similar questions regarding the status of the child itself. For example, does a photocopy of a sonogram image from a book count as much as a sonogram image attained at the obstetrician's office? Does a miscarried or stillborn child count as much as one who lives? The equivalent materiality of both types of goods ("real" and "fake") provides a tacit answer to these questions. That is, while a do-it-yourself baptism certificate may not be considered by many to be authentic or legitimate, from the point of view of materiality a homemade certificate is as tangible as any other. The same is true for sonogram images whether they come from an obstetrician's office or out of a book.

Baudrillard defines simulation as "feign[ing] to have what one hasn't" (Baudrillard 1983: 5). "Feigning" has two valences. Its primary meaning has the derogatory sense of fabrication, making something up, or pretending, and it is with this more common sense that I first interpreted the use of these substitutes as "fake goods." Its original meaning was "to form" or "to shape," coming from the Latin *fingere*, meaning "to touch," or "to handle." On reflection, it seems to me that this earlier meaning points to a deeper truth with regard to these goods, namely, that pregnancy (and, later, mothering) are works of fabrication in the sense of being inventive, creative acts that rely heavily on physical touch. The bodily and social work of shaping a child, which begins during a pregnancy and is cut brutally short with a pregnancy loss, creates a painful physical void for bereaved parents. Things not only play an important role in the production of a child during pregnancy (Layne 1999a, forthcoming), they also help bereaved parents define and deal with the painful absence of their wished-for child once it is gone. One of the reasons that things are so effective in both instances is because they are tangible; they can be kept present and regarded or touched at will.

Baby Things as Fetishes?

Gamman and Makinen begin their book on female fetishism with a quote
from Stoller: "A fetish is a story masquerading as an object" (Gamman and
Makinen 1994: 1). The baby things acquired and preserved after a pregnancy loss certainly fit this description. But it is not just any story that such
things tell. They are stories of thwarted desire and tragic loss.

Like narratives of pregnancy loss, contemporary theories of fetishization
and the Baudrillardian notion of "simulation" are fundamentally about
"lack" and "absence" (Baudrillard 1983: 5). Both Freud and Lacan understood fetishism as an individual male solution to the fear caused by the sight
of a woman's "lack" of a penis (Stratton 1996). Stratton has expanded this
notion from the individual to the collectivity and argues that it is a "lack"
felt by people who live under the power of the state, which "provides the
overdetermining context for . . . the twentieth century expansion of consumption" (Stratton 1996: 14). He cites Ewen, who has described how
"twentieth-century advertising encouraged people—especially historically,
women—to think of themselves as incomplete, as lacking" and in turn
"encouraged a constant consumption of new products in order to . . . erase
the discovered and naturalized lack" (Ewen quoted in Stratton 1996: 14).

Psychoanalytically informed theories of fetishization begin with the fear
of a fantasized potential loss. How can the use of things in response to the
actual loss of a wished-for child be understood in terms of fetishization?
Gamman and Makinen distinguish between three types of fetishism—
anthropological, commodity, and sexual. Of the three, the anthropological
model seems best suited for illuminating the ways goods are used in dealing
with pregnancy loss. Gamman and Makinen base their notion of anthropological fetishism on Tylor's 1871 book *Primitive Culture,* in which he says "to
class an object as a fetish demands explicit statement that a spirit is considered as embodied in it or acting through it or communicating by it, or at
least that the people it belongs to do habitually think this of such objects."
(Tylor quoted in Gamman and Makinen 1994: 17). Clearly the "angelic
presence" of Christopher in the little blue spruce tree is one such example.
Another example can be found in Hannah Campbell's story. She ends her

description of "Marc's things" displayed in her curio cabinet by exclaiming, "His Irish ancestors must be proud *he's* in with their Waterford crystal from Ireland!" (Campbell 1992, emphasis added).

Much like the pop fans studied by Fiske, who use things to "help them summon up the star's presence" by using spaces in their homes or their own bodies to construct "'temples' in honor of the star" (Gamman and Makinen 1994: 19), we have seen how some bereaved parents place things in special places in their homes or on their bodies to similar ends. "What the cherishing of objects associated with those we love has in common with the behavior of fans is the desire to maintain a link to an absent person through a fetish object" (Gamman and Makinen 1994: 27).

Gamman and Makinen note the special association of anthropological fetishism with loss and grief. "People mourning lovers, friends, parents, children or animals have been known to develop fetishistic behavior, in order to cope with the loss" (Gamman and Makinen 1994: 27). A number of feminists have argued that loss is a defining quality of motherhood (that is, not an experience restricted to those whose babies die). For example, Simonds and Rothman argue that loss is a "universal" part of motherhood: "The dead baby, the well and truly gone baby, is a symbol for all the babies we lose: the babies of fantasy and the babies of reality, all of whom inevitably leave us" (1992: 13). According to them, this "explains the appeal of ... consolation literature well beyond the narrow audience of grieving parents" (Simonds and Rothman 1992: 13).

A similar point was made by female "fetish artist" Mary Kelly in her 1976 exhibit "Post-Partum Document," in which "she displayed objects associated with her baby, charting his first move away from the breast, at weaning, to the move away from home to go to school" (Gamman and Makinen 1994: 189). Kelly describes the objects exhibited (dirty diapers, a plaster cast of her son's hand, his drawings and gifts of bugs and plants to her, which she "carefully saved," her transcripts of his baby conversations) as "fetish objects that enabled her to disavow the separation" (Gamman and Makinen 1994: 189).

According to Gamman and Makinen, Kelly "was really the first to put the issue of female fetishism on the feminist agenda by arguing that the mother was the prototype fetishist" (Gamman and Makinen 1994: 187). Kelly's work, informed as it is by psychoanalytic traditions, seeks to address human universals; "For women ... the threat of castration does not focus on genitalia but instead takes the form of fear about losing children" (Gamman and Makinen 1994: 189). But historians such as Gillis illuminate the particular cultural and historical context for "the museological mania of the maternal collector/fetishist" (Kelly and Apter 1993: 352). Gillis tells of how collective forms of memory have declined throughout Euro-America during the later part of this century. "Memory work" has become much more individualized and has dramatically increased in volume: "As global markets work around the clock and the speed of communications shrinks our sense of distance, there is both more memory work to do and less time ... to do it. ... It is wives and mothers who pick up the slack. Every attic is an archive, every living room a museum. Never before has so much been recorded, collected; and never before has remembering been so compulsive, even as rote memorization ceases to be central to the educational process. What we can no longer keep in our heads is now kept in storage" (Gillis 1994: 14). As Gillis points out, it is Euro-American women who have come "to serve in various (and usually unpaid) ways as the keepers and embodiments of memory" (1994: 10).

Given the negative evaluation inherent in the concept of fetishism, the application of this term to the collecting and preserving of baby things by mothers (whether or not their babies live) denigrates "women's work."[16] As Gamman and Makinen (1994: 45) point out, all types of fetishism share "the process of disavowal." Whether it is the "disavowal of human labor" in commodity fetishism, the disavowal of the fear inspired by the discovery that mothers lack a penis in sexual fetishism, or the substitution of an object for the original "suppressed" or "hidden" object of desire of anthropological fetishism, a fetishist is by definition someone who "believe[s] the false" (Gamman and Makinen 1994: 45). Thus, fetish theory risks marginalizing and derogating the cultural work of memory assigned to women throughout contemporary North America. The maternal obligation to remember is particularly challenging for would-be mothers following a pregnancy loss.

Ultimately it is unclear whether the concept of "fetish" really adds anything to our understanding of the importance of things after a pregnancy loss. What is clear is that this concept emphasizes the notion of disavowal in the practices of individual bereaved mothers while ignoring the disavowal of pregnancy loss that our society engages in collectively. This is particularly problematic given that this collective disavowal serves as an important impetus for bereaved parents to use objects to make reality claims about their loss in the first place. In other words, if the "realness" of their "baby" and their loss were not disavowed in the first place, bereaved parents might not have such a need to use things in these ways.

Conclusions

Dead fetuses or dead newborns are liminal and as such have the potential for great power and danger. This is even more the case if there is deformity. In our culture, the dangerous valence of these beings is predominant, and like other entities that do not fit into our cultural scheme, they are hidden and ignored.

Narratives of linear fetal and child development form a mainstay of middle-class American's experience of pregnancy and parenthood (Layne 1996a, 1998). Ideas about normal individual development and how a person's life should progress that are apparent in these pregnancy and early childhood manuals reflect ideas that middle-class Americans share about life more broadly. Becker found in her study of mostly white, middle-class infertile couples that people believed "that their lives should follow predictable, coherent, linear paths" (1994: 390). Newman's (1988) study of unemployed white- and blue-collar workers also illuminates how deeply held and widely shared these beliefs are. Pregnancy loss challenges these cherished beliefs.

Most members of our society deal with this challenge, and the threat that these liminal beings present, by pretending that such an event did not happen and that these betwixt-and-between beings never existed. This tendency contributes to additional and unnecessary suffering for those who have a pregnancy loss. In order to combat this tendency, many members of pregnancy loss support groups often adopt the opposite strategy. They work to transform the dangerous ambiguity of that which they lost into power and, as I have shown, they marshal the efficacy of things for this task.

N o t e s

I owe special thanks to Shirley Gorenstein, who was instrumental in focusing my attention on the material culture dimensions of the gifts and provided invaluable comments on earlier drafts, and to Lynn Morgan and Meredith Michaels, who encouraged me to consider baby things as fetishes. Rensselaer Polytechnic Institute provided sabbatical leave, which enabled me to work on this project and for which I am grateful.

I thank the curators of the Department of Drawings and Prints at the Metropolitan Museum of Art, and at the New York State Museum, as well as Dr. Joaquim Pinheiro of Albany Medical Center for sharing their expertise with me.

1.   See Layne 1995 for a historical discussion of medical understandings of the causes of pregnancy loss.

2.   This is an interesting reversal of the primacy of the biological link, particularly as it features in notions about adoption. There the adoptive mother has the requisite experience of raising a child but lacks the required biological link.

3.   The rhetoric of the gift permeates narratives of pregnancy loss. Elsewhere (Layne 1999b) I examine the spiritual gifts that are often felt to flow between God, the "baby," and bereaved parents as the result of a pregnancy loss.

4.   See Layne, forthcoming, for details.

5.   Hair has been associated with mourning since antiquity (Ochs 1993: 54) and was used in the United States as a memento of loved ones, either absent or dead, since the eighteenth century. Victorian mourning lockets often held a lock of hair (Ariès 1985). From the 1780s to the 1820s hair was often woven as the backing for miniature portraits and mourning scenes that were either worn or displayed in the home (Sheumaker 1997: 423). Between the 1830s and 1880s the hair of beloved relatives, and sometimes even pets, was woven, braided, and twisted by middle-class American women, or the professionals they hired, into jewelry, wreaths, or pictures for display behind glass in the parlor (personal communication, archivist at the New York State Museum; Sheumaker 1997; Morley 1971).

6.   According to Dr. Joaquim Pinheiro, a neonatologist at Albany Medical Center, they still do them "because parents like them—they're cute." A nurse educator and social worker at St. Joseph's Hospital in Tampa explains the practice of giving parents footprints as "a token or remembrance of how small the baby was" (personal communication, 1999, Deborah Blizzard).

7.   See Layne 1997 on SHARE's practice of giving "precious feet" pins to "parents who have experienced a miscarriage or ectopic pregnancy," and Layne, forthcoming, for a discussion of footprint iconography in the SHARE newsletter.

8.   SHARE's 1987 Baby Pictures Questionnaire found that of 438 respondents who reported on losses that occurred between 1966 and 1987, 39 percent had ultrasound pictures; "93% of these said they were important keepsakes" (Laux 1998a). It is probably safe to say that the numbers of people with such photos would be greater today given the increased use of routine ultrasound during the past ten years. See Sherman and Newman 1977: 186 on the importance of photographs as "cherished possessions" in our culture. This is particularly true for women, especially for photographs of their children.

9.   See Ariès (1985: 245–47) on the popularity of photographs of dead children in the second half of the nineteenth century; Wozniak 1997 on the importance of photographs in rituals of remembrance among foster mothers in the U.S.; Benjamin suggests that "the cult of remembrance of loved ones, absent or dead, offers a last refuge for the cult value of the picture" (Benjamin 1989: 577).

10.   Wozniak (1997) describes strikingly similar practices among foster mothers in the United States as they tend the memory of foster children they "lost" through death, departure to an adoptive family, or return to their biological families.

11.   Embroidered mourning goods such as memorial pictures, samplers, and mourning handkerchiefs were popular during both the Federal and Victorian eras (Schorsch 1976; Morley 1971; Ariès 1985: 240).

12.   See Schorsch (1976) on the importance of garden iconography in American Federal mourning art and the symbolic association of gardens with the Resurrection.

13.   Most of the jewelry described in pregnancy loss newsletters is memorial jewelry, symbolizing the dead child(ren), worn by bereaved mothers and occasionally by other family members. Several women also tell of burying their children with jewelry that symbolizes the parents (Ashbaker 1993, 1994; Campbell 1990). See Sherman and Newman (1977) on the importance of symbolic jewelry as cherished personal possessions of elderly women, and Ariès (1985: 195, 243) and Morley (1971) on mourning pendants from the Elizabethan and Victorian eras.

14.   As discussed earlier, gender is an important quality of both babies and baby things. In a piece called "Remembering Your Baby," Hely suggests that "even if you miscarried too early for the sex to be determined," one might want to "assign . . . a sex to your

baby," noting that "many times a parent feels s/he knows what the baby's sex is going to be right from conception. Even when parents don't feel they know the sex, they can choose the sex they would have liked for their baby. This makes the baby more real, a person in his/her own right" (Hely 1991).

15.   Benjamin (1989: 575) describes "the desire of contemporary masses ... to get hold of an object at very close range by way of its likeness." Bereaved parents try to get close to their baby by way of its likeness, and sometimes, as in the case of "fake goods," they do so by way of a likeness of a likeness of the child or by a representation of something that would have been a representation of a child, for example, a baptismal certificate that is a substitute for the authentic birth certificate that would have represented an authentic child.

16.   Browne (1981: 1) defines fetishes as "misshapen, bastard icons" and asserts that "the fetish carries the taint of the off-color, an abnormal attachment, a 'closet' devotion, something that the person attached to [it] should be ... ashamed of." Even Gamman and Makinen, who choose not to use Freud's label of "pathological" when discussing sexual fetishism (1994: 38), use the pejorative phrase "obsessive hoarding" (1994: 27) to describe the activities of widows or widowers in preserving some of a partner's effects or of a mother in collecting her child's memorabilia.

5

Missing
Motherhood

Infertility,
Technology,
and Poverty
in Egyptian
Women's Lives

Marcia Claire Inhorn

In Egypt, infertility, or the inability to conceive, is a devastating problem for women. They face a triple burden: blame for the failure to conceive; negative evaluation and social ostracism as dangerous, un(re)productive members of society; and responsibility for overcoming the infertility through a reproductive quest that is often traumatic and unfruitful (Inhorn 1994a, 1996). This quest for conception—or the "search for children," as Egyptian women themselves call it—involves remedies of quite disparate origins and natures and is a near-universal phenomenon for infertile Egyptian women of all social backgrounds. So powerful is their desire to have children and so mighty is the force of social pressure that comes to bear upon them that many infertile women may risk all that they have, including their lives, in their quest for conception (Inhorn 1994a).

Underlying this sometimes desperate, often relentless quest is a patriarchal fertility mandate requiring all Egyptian women to be mothers (Inhorn 1996). Women who are unable to achieve entrance into the "cult of motherhood" (Bouhdiba 1985) are seen as being less than other women, as depriving their husbands and husbands' families of offspring, and as endangering other people's children through their uncontrollable envy.

As members of a predominantly Muslim society, infertile women's greatest social threat comes from husbands, who have the right under Islamic law to replace an infertile wife through outright divorce or polygynous remarriage. Although husbands of infertile women are often reluctant or totally unwilling to claim such rights, replacement of this sort is usually urged by husbands' extended family members, who view a wife who thwarts her husband's virile procreativity as, at best, "useless" and, at worst, a threat to the social reproduction of the patrilineage at large (Inhorn 1996). Thus, in Egypt, infertile women of all backgrounds tend to face tremendous social pressures, ranging from duress within the marriage to stigmatization within the extended family network and outright ostracism within the larger community of fertile women. Indeed, of all the types of persons that one could be, there are very few less desirable social identities than that of the infertile woman, or *umm il-ghayyib*, "mother of the missing one," as Egyptians sometimes call her, giving this particular identity all of the classic features of a stigma. Goffman (1963: 3) defined a stigma as "an attribute that makes [her] different from others in the category of persons available for [her] to be, and of a less desirable kind—in the extreme, a person who is quite thoroughly bad, or dangerous, or weak. [She] is thus reduced in our minds from a whole and usual person to a tainted, discounted one. Such an attribute is a stigma, especially when its discrediting effect is very extensive."

Given the grave social onus of infertility, it is not surprising that infertile Egyptian women—who are seen as "missing motherhood"—are quite willing to subject their bodies to a variety of treatment modalities. These range from five-thousand-year-old pharaonic prescriptions to the latest in new reproductive technologies. In this essay, I will explore both ends of the therapeutic spectrum, from the most "traditional" to the most "modern" treatments being offered to infertile women in Egypt today. I will begin by exploring what might best be described as "old" medicine in Egypt—not only traditional ethnomedical practices grounded in centuries-old medical traditions, but also outdated biomedical practices that are still commonly used in infertility treatment in contemporary Egypt. Then I will fast-forward to more recent developments in Egypt—in terms of both my own ethnographic research and the advent of high-tech reproductive technologies that have taken the country by storm and revolutionized the practice of infertility medicine.

Problematizing Infertility

In this essay, my goal as a medical anthropologist and feminist scholar concerned with women's health and well-being is to highlight the various considerations and constraints infertile Egyptian women face when assessing treatment options, including those associated with the relatively recent introduction in Egypt of in vitro fertilization, known as *atfāl l-anābīb*, or literally "babies of the tubes." As part of this discussion, I will put forward three major arguments. First, the experience of infertility treatment in Egypt is extremely gender-biased: women tend to be blamed for infertility problems in their marriages, are therefore expected to seek treatment services with sometimes minimal support from their husbands, and are subjected to highly invasive, often agonizing therapies, even in the face of documented male infertility problems. Second, the experience of infertility treatment in Egypt has become inextricably linked to one's class position in this markedly class-based society: the poor continue to receive "older" infertility therapies, be they ethnomedical or biomedical, for most cannot begin to afford the newer, more efficacious treatment modalities available primarily to the educated elite of this society. And, finally, the experience of infertility treatment in Egypt cannot be understood without reference to religion, specifically Islam, and its particular patriarchal ideologies and dogmas about the nature of gender, kinship, family life, motherhood, and the role of God in the control of science and medicine.

As a prelude to this discussion, I intend to explore the "local moral world" (Kleinman and Kleinman 1991) of one poor urban Egyptian woman, Fadia, who found herself caught in a struggle to achieve motherhood with the current reproductive technologies and treatments available to her.[1] Fadia's story clearly illustrates the plight of poor infertile Egyptian women who, in their culturally mandatory attempts to become mothers, must also avoid financial ruin, moral opprobrium, bodily harm, marital collapse, and psychic despair. I would argue that understanding the desperate quest for motherhood that women such as Fadia face is important for three major reasons.

First, from the widest global perspective, infertility is a significant although seriously underrecognized public health problem. Because international population efforts have been directed almost entirely to fertility reduction through family planning, few population programs consider infertility to be a population issue, and thus the mission of most family planning programs rarely involves helping infertile couples to build families. Yet such neglect of infertility as a global population problem seems misguided. In many societies, high infertility rates can be shown to coexist with high fertility rates, especially in the wake of epidemics of sexually transmitted diseases (STDs) that produce sterility. Perhaps nowhere is this more evident than in the AIDS-stricken "infertility belt" of Central Africa, where as many as 30 to 50 percent of all couples in some populations are unable to conceive, leading to further depopulation (Collet et al. 1988; World Health Organization 1987).

Given its location slightly to the north of this African infertility belt, Egypt has a much less prevalent infertility problem. Yet infertility still occurs in a significant proportion of Egyptian couples, making Egypt more similar, demographically speaking, to many Western nations. A recent World Health Organization–sponsored study conducted in seven diverse locations around Egypt placed the total infertility prevalence rate among married couples at 12 percent (Egyptian Fertility Care Society 1995). This included the 4.3 percent of couples experiencing so-called primary infertility, or the inability to conceive after one year of trying with no history of previous pregnancy in the woman, as well as the 7.7 percent of couples with so-called secondary infertility, or the inability to conceive after one year of trying in light of at least one previous pregnancy in the woman. Unfortunately, Egypt, like the vast majority of the world's societies, has made no provision in its long-standing population efforts to address the issue of infertility as either a population problem, a more general public health concern, or an issue of human suffering for its citizens, especially women. In other words, little effort is made in Egypt to address the concerns of the infertile subpopulation, given the historically exclusive focus on hyperfertility and overpopulation as matters of national importance.

A second general problem impeding our current understanding of infertility involves the scholarly lacuna associated with women's cross-cultural experiences of, and desires for, motherhood. Relatively little is known beyond the most superficial, survey-based level about why women worldwide want and/or need to have children. (Equally important and even less clearly understood is why men need to prove their fertility and may desire both children and the experiences of fatherhood.) This is perhaps especially important in high-fertility societies such as Egypt, where women unable to achieve culturally valorized motherhood roles suffer significantly over their infertility. Because feminist analyses of motherhood and, more recently, analyses of the new reproductive technologies tend to decry the patriarchal motherhood mandate, they often (although not always) fail to acknowledge the issues of women's agency and desire—namely, that women in places such as Egypt are genuinely enthusiastic about having children, will go to great lengths to bear and nurture their offspring, and consider themselves fulfilled rather than oppressed by their motherhood roles. Thus, infertility is a particularly cruel misfortune in such pronatalist, matrifocal settings.

A third, related issue is the Western bias in reproductive technology discussions. The vast majority of the social scientific, feminist, and ethical discussions surrounding motherhood, infertility, and the new reproductive technologies focus on Western women, particularly those in the United States, Western Europe (especially Britain), and Australia, which is largely (although not exclusively) where these technologies have been developed. In general, these discussions tend to be highly polemical in nature and textually based, rather than ethnographically enriched by the experiences of real women. In such discussions, furthermore, the issues surrounding the transfer of new reproductive technology to the so-called developing world are rarely acknowledged, perhaps because of unexamined, Eurocentric, even neo-Malthusian prejudices surrounding the "hyperfertility" of non-Western women and their inherent unworthiness as candidates for these technologies.

Nonetheless, given that significant infertility problems exist in the developing world, it should come as no surprise that the transfer of high-tech reproductive technology to the developing countries is occurring on a massive scale. Perhaps nowhere is this technological globalization process more evident than in the nearly twenty nations of the Muslim Middle East, where IVF centers are present in countries as minuscule as Bahrain and Qatar to those as large as Saudi Arabia and Egypt, which alone boasts thirty-six IVF centers. Most important, when new reproductive technologies reach places like Egypt, they do not enter cultural voids. Rather, local considerations, be they cultural, social, economic, or political, shape the way these Western-generated technologies are both offered to and received by non-Western subjects. In other words, the assumption on the part of global producer nations that technologies are "immune to culture" and can thus be "appropriately" transferred and implemented anywhere and everywhere is subject to challenge once local formulations, perceptions, and consumption of these technologies are taken into consideration. In the case of the regionally underprivileged nation of Egypt, infertile women and men willing to consider the use of new reproductive technologies face a series of culturally specific constraints. As will be highlighted in this paper, these range from the particular culturally infused dynamics of gender relations to class-based barriers to access, and local versions of Islam, that legislate upon the "appropriate" use of these technologies and thus restrict who can benefit from them.

Such culturally specific considerations speak to the need for greater historical and local grounding of ethical, feminist, and technoscience debates surrounding the various impacts of reproductive technologies. Currently, moral, scientific, and gendered discussions of these technologies tend to be situated in Western histories, discourses, and understandings. But, as we shall see in this essay, the use of reproductive technology in Egypt involves not only a unique history but different understandings of the body, medicine, and morality, all of which profoundly influence women's decisions about whether or not to utilize these technologies.

Research Setting and Methodology

The research upon which this paper is based encompasses two distinct time frames. The first period is the late 1980s, or what may be called the early IVF period in Egypt. In 1988–89, when I conducted fifteen months of anthropological fieldwork on the problem of infertility in Alexandria, Egypt, IVF was neither widely available nor widely understood in the country. During this initial period of research, I based my inquiry in the University of Alexandria's large public ob/gyn hospital catering to the infertile. At this hospital, popularly known as Shatby, I conducted in-depth, semistructured interviews with one hundred infertile women and a comparison group of ninety fertile ones. With few exceptions, these women were poor, uneducated, and illiterate or only semiliterate, and most had never been employed in wage labor outside their homes.[2] Furthermore, many of these women came from first- or second-generation rural migrant families who had moved to Alexandria, Egypt's second largest city, in search of an improved quality of life. It is important to note here that my research among these women began in the hospital but eventually took me to the homes and home communities of these women, where I conducted additional unstructured interviews and participant observation. Furthermore, it was through my research in women's homes and communities that I met a variety of traditional healers, who also participated as willing informants in my study. It is also extremely critical to note here, given the later focus of this essay on IVF in Egypt, that many of the infertile women participating in my study were seeking treatment at Shatby Hospital specifically because of the hospital's widely publicized claims of a free, government-sponsored IVF program. Yet by the end of my fifteen-month tenure in Egypt, it had become apparent to all my poor IVF-desiring informants that an IVF program at this public hospital had yet to arrive. Furthermore, it appeared that

IVF was not going to be the promised government freebie for poor infertile women with infection-blocked fallopian tubes.

Moving ahead, the second period of research is the late 1990s, or what may be called the IVF boom period in Egypt. Egypt is now in the midst of massive reproductive technology transfer, with new urban IVF centers cropping up on a regular basis. In the midst of this IVF explosion, I spent the summer of 1996 in Cairo conducting participant observation and in-depth, semistructured interviews with sixty-six middle- to upper-class women and their husbands undergoing IVF (or a small variety of closely related new reproductive technologies) at two of the major IVF centers in this city of nearly twenty million inhabitants. Both of these IVF centers were situated in private hospitals in Heliopolis and Maadi, elite neighborhoods on the outskirts of Cairo. The patients presenting to these IVF clinics were generally well-educated, professional, comparatively affluent women, who were often accompanied by their husbands. Indeed, in 40 percent of the interviews conducted in these clinics, husbands were present and participated, often enthusiastically, in discussions. Moreover, whereas interviews in the first study were conducted entirely in colloquial Egyptian Arabic, many of the women and men who participated in the second study spoke fluent, even flawless English, and chose to conduct the interview in their second language.

Thus, this essay offers both a diachronic and class-based comparison of infertile women seeking treatment in the two largest cities of Egypt. The essay reveals how the treatment experiences of poor and elite women differ by virtue of economic resources, and how a time span of less than ten years has dramatically altered the infertility treatment landscape in Egypt. However, the essay places primary emphasis on the plight of poor Egyptian women, who continue to be excluded from the high-tech revolution in infertility treatment in Egypt today. The case of Fadia, to whose story we now turn, illustrates the special problems that infertile women who are members of the Egyptian underclass face, and how their treatment decisions are affected by their gender, class, and religious identities as poor Muslim women.

The Story of Fadia

"All my life was despair and torture and sorrow and sadness. Sometimes I would sit like this and cry, and I say, 'Even God, when I got married, he doesn't want to be generous with me, I mean [to] bring a child to stay. I mean, even if anything happened between me and Osman [her husband], disagreements or anything, this child of mine would make me stay [with Osman], would not make me go. Go where? If I went away, the same thing that happened to my mother would happen to me.' So, you find me crying and scared all the time. When I sit alone, I'm upset. I cry. I'm afraid. I'm thinking. And I say, 'Who knows what will happen tomorrow? Who knows what the years are hiding?'"

These are the words of Fadia, a poor urban Egyptian woman whose life has been marred by infertility and by the husbands and male family members who, in claiming their patriarchal authority, have oppressed and abused her. Like so many of the lower-class migrants to Egypt's northern cities, Fadia was born and raised in the south of Egypt, a land called Sa⁢ʿid by Egyptians, home of the major monuments of Egypt's pharaonic past and a place of renowned cultural conservatism and respect for tradition. Fadia's father, a local ne'er-do-well, fled Saʿid for Alexandria, leaving behind a wife and four young daughters. As a child, Fadia was raised alternately by her impoverished and disempowered mother and by her paternal grandparents and uncles, who withdrew Fadia from school at the age of twelve, treating her as their servant.

Because of her mother's inability to control the events surrounding Fadia's life and her father's complete abnegation of his parental responsibilities, Fadia's marriage prospects, per Saʿidi custom, were under the control of her paternal uncles. Like her mother, the adolescent Fadia had become a real beauty, with flowing black hair, smooth olive skin, dark almond-shaped eyes, and a perfect smile and figure, neither too plump nor too thin. Although the local Arabic teacher was in love with Fadia and asked for her hand in marriage, Fadia's paternal uncles decided that she should marry her maternal first cousin Iid, a man who was physically and emotionally repugnant to her. Although her relatives told her, "Maʿlish [never mind], you'll love him tomorrow," "tomorrow" never came for the eighteen-year-old Fadia. In her brief marriage to Iid, Fadia endured life-threatening physical violence (her husband beat her and once stabbed her in the back), marital rape, and continuous emotional abuse. Only through a desperate suicide attempt involving the ingestion of mercurochrome and iodine was Fadia able to convince her husband (and the various paternal and maternal relatives pitted against her) to give her a divorce.

However, as a divorcee in a small Saʿidi town with no real family or home to call her own, Fadia decided to flee to Alexandria to live with the degenerate father who had never treated her as his child. Before Fadia left, her mother pleaded with her not to go: "Your father is difficult. Your father will beat you. And your father will disgrace you in front of people. He's bad, not good. If he was good, we would have lived with him. We could have stayed. And nobody would have forced you into anything. You could have been educated. Your father is not good." But, believing that temporary escape from the suffocating environment of her Saʿidi relatives was her only alternative, Fadia decided to migrate to the north.

Everything Fadia's mother told her daughter turned out to be true. When Fadia arrived in Alexandria, she found her drug-addicted father living in a small room with neither furniture nor a wardrobe nor food to eat. Although he agreed to take Fadia in, he proceeded to abuse her viciously, just as Fadia's mother had predicted. This included chaining Fadia to the door, heating a knife over a gas flame, and then putting the knife on Fadia's body so as to burn and scar her for life.

Obviously Fadia needed a way out of yet another intolerable situation, and Osman, a divorced neighbor of Fadia's father, provided the vehicle of escape. One day, when Fadia was walking down the street to buy some milk, Osman spotted her and, admiring her beauty, came to inquire about her from some neighbors. Discovering that she was a divorcee, Osman proposed immediately. Although Fadia found the balding, chain-smoking Osman unattractive and too old (he was ten years her senior), she sensed that he might be kind to her, especially in comparison to her sadistic father. Furthermore, as a divorcee who had already lost her virginity—thus depriving a future husband of the "delight and deliciousness" of penetrating a woman who is still "blocked"—Fadia, feeling devalued and stigmatized, believed her chances of attracting a more desirable husband were slim. Thus, reluctantly and without ceremonial fanfare, Fadia married Osman, moving into the poor carpenter's ground-floor, one-room apartment in a lower-class Alexandria neighborhood.

As with Fadia, Osman's conjugal track record was not good. He had already wed four women, including one who turned out to be a true hermaphrodite, and he had executed the writing of a formal marriage contract with a fifth woman, whom he had divorced even before undertaking an official wedding ceremony. However, all of these serial marriages had ended quickly and inauspiciously, without children resulting from any of the unions. With the young, lovely Fadia, Osman hoped that his marital and procreative luck would improve.

Indeed, within the first two years of her marriage to Osman, Fadia became pregnant three times. But she miscarried each time in the first trimester. The third miscarriage was particularly traumatic, for Fadia bled profusely, was hospitalized for twenty-two days, and underwent two painful episodes of *tausīᶜ wi kaḥt,* or dilatation and curettage (D&C) of her uterus. According to Fadia, the experience reminded her of the time, a decade earlier, when, following her circumcision by a traditional midwife, she had bled profusely and spent a month in a government hospital in order to convalesce from the hemorrhage.

Unfortunately for Fadia, her reproductive luck with Osman did not improve. Following the third miscarriage and a trip home to Saᶜid to visit her poor mother, Fadia did not become pregnant again. Osman, vexed over Fadia's failure to bear his children, became increasingly short-tempered—smoking as many as four packs of cigarettes a day, suffering severe impotence problems, and insulting, threatening, and beating his wife from time to time out of sheer frustration over yet another ill-fated marriage.

Yet Fadia convinced Osman to let her seek treatment for her infertility, which Fadia helped to finance by joining neighborhood savings clubs and selling off all her bridal gold. Fadia tried many *waṣfāt baladī,* or traditional remedies, including, among other things, stepping over the gravedigger's tools in a local cemetery, sitting on a freshly delivered placenta, wearing black glycerin-imbued vaginal suppositories, undergoing cupping to draw "a glass of air from her back," wearing a band of rubber with a padlock around her waist, placing Qur'anic amulets under her pillow, licking a rock at a shrine of conception until her tongue bled, and visiting spiritist healers who prescribed elaborate and expensive animal sacrifices to appease the angered spirit-sister under the ground.

However, when none of these remedies worked to make her pregnant, Fadia stopped the folk remedies altogether and started going again to the doctors who had cared for her during her previous miscarriages. Several of them requested a semen analysis from Osman, which he grudgingly underwent three times. The semen analyses revealed a chronic prostate infection and poor sperm motility, for which Osman was prescribed expensive drug therapy. Fadia, meanwhile, underwent both drug therapy and invasive procedures, including the painful *kayy*, or cervical electrocautery, in which her cervix was thermocauterized by a heated instrument, as well as hydrotubation, or injections of antibiotic and anti-inflammatory drug "cocktails" into her uterus. Eventually laparoscopy, a diagnostic surgical procedure to examine the inner recesses of Fadia's pelvis, was performed at the University of Alexandria's public ob/gyn teaching hospital. There Fadia was diagnosed as having a large ovarian cyst, a severe pelvic infection, and blockage of both fallopian tubes. Following an operation to remove the cyst and to "clean out" the fallopian tubes, a young physician told Fadia that her chances of conceiving normally without the help of Egypt's newest treatment modality, in vitro fertilization (IVF), were nearly impossible. Fadia refused to believe the doctor and was incensed that he should predict such a hopeless future for her fertility.

Meanwhile, the religiously devout Osman was sometimes generous and compassionate toward Fadia, telling her that he would support her in her treatment efforts, while at other times he was tyrannical, blaming her for their continuing childlessness and yelling at her, "Get out! I don't want you." When Fadia broached the subject of IVF with Osman, he was adamantly opposed—not only because of the extraordinary expense, which was well beyond their means, but also because a popular televised cleric had deemed IVF to be *ḥarām*, or forbidden by Islam. According to Osman, the sinfulness of this procedure certainly derived from the fact that "another man's sperm" might be introduced during the IVF procedure. Thus, "a man would be raising someone other than his own child; a man should *never* allow his wife to do that [IVF]."

Unfortunately for Fadia, however, the young doctor was right about Fadia's need for IVF. Although Fadia herself was willing to try IVF, which she believed had been discovered in and imported from America, she realized her chances of undergoing this treatment were remote, given her ongoing poverty and her husband's moral opposition to the procedure. Thus, with few treatment options left open to her, Fadia hoped that Osman's own "weak worms" (sperm of suboptimal quality) and lack of children from his previous marriages would keep him "silent" on the subject of divorce. For if Osman divorced her, as was his right under Islamic personal status law, she would truly have nowhere else to go.

Persistently worried and depressed over this increasingly likely eventuality, the infertile Fadia lamented her fate. "My circumstances are bad. I don't find help. I don't find defense. I don't find somebody to stand by me. So I'd better take it from the start and live and it's finished. It's a life anyway. It has no love. It has no happiness, but it's not important. What's important is that I'm living, and that's it. If I was working, I would have been a free individual. No one would be able to stand in my way. But I don't work. I have no profession in my hand or a job or anything to have a *piaster* [i.e., a penny] out of it or to do something with it. No, I need someone to feed me, to provide me drink, and to support me. What can I do? I live. Yes, it's possible if I'm working, if I'm an employee, no one would be able to stand in my way. But I'm weak. Why? I'm helpless. I have no profession or a weapon in my hand or anything. It's my fate. Naturally, [if I had] children, to me, a child calms his mother. If she doesn't bear children, he [the husband] gets married [to a second wife], and he has children, and he leaves her, he forgets her—even if they have constant love between them. He forgets her and goes back to his children.... Of course, to me, I want [children]. I want because if anything happened to him [Osman], no one can take the apartment away from me. No one can take the furnishings. No one can take anything from me. But if I don't have children—and send evil away!—if anything happened to him, they will take everything, his brothers. By God! And I go out like this—just like a servant.

"It's torment. I am in torture. [But] thank God. There is nothing in my hand that I can do [to have children]. If there were anything in my hand, I would have done it. But I have *nothing* in my hand.... This is my life story. I said it, and I talked. It's finished."

Little did the despairing Fadia realize that her story, told to me in its entirety in December 1989, had yet to "finish" and, in fact, was soon to take a turn for the better. In the fall of 1992, I received the following letter from Fadia:

"In the name of God, my friend and sister, Doctor Marcia, I send my greetings and eagerness to you and your husband and to the family, young and old. A thousand thousand salutations to your father and one thousand to your mother and brothers. I send my best wishes from the beautiful, generous Egypt. Congratulations on your recent marriage and may you have babies. I am very eager to see you, and I cannot forget you for a moment, and I am always speaking about you.

"I am fine, thanks be to God, and I have new information to tell you—that a misunderstanding happened between me and Osman and we separated from each other [divorced], and I left the apartment and everything [behind]. Then God gave me a prize: I married a young god, a beautiful and decent man, who works as a general bus driver. He loved me, and I loved him affectionately, and I gave him everything. We got married on November 11, 1991, after the divorce from Osman on August 28, 1991. My new husband's name is Mohammed. I wish you can visit Egypt and know him. He is very good and he loves me.... Thank you very, very much for you are still remembering me."

Procreative Ideologies and Women's Bodies

For most infertile Egyptian women such as Fadia, their stigmatization and their desperate attempts to be cured of their infertility are exacerbated by their inability to achieve motherhood through other institutionalized means, including adoption. Islamic law disallows adoption, although it specifies in great detail how orphans are to be treated (Esposito 1982, 1991). The permanent, legal fostering of abandoned infants—which, for all intents and purposes, is tantamount to adoption as it is known in the West— is available in Egypt, but it is unacceptable among Egyptians of all social classes for a host of cultural reasons (Inhorn 1996).[3] Thus, biological parenthood—actually giving birth to a child—is the only tenable option for most Egyptian women.

However, among Egypt's large urban underclass, the "biology" of parenthood can be seen to vary considerably from that which most Westerners assume to be universal. Instead of a child "belonging" equally to both parents—who, in the duogenetic theory of procreation found in the West, are seen as contributing equally to the hereditary substance of their offspring— children in Egypt are seen by most less-educated, lower-class men and women as being "created" primarily by their fathers. In other words, in the popular, monogenetic theory of procreation found throughout Egypt, as well as in other parts of the Middle East (Delaney 1991; Good 1980; Greenwood 1981), men are seen as creating preformed fetuses through spermatogenesis; these fetuses are then carried in men's sperm (or "worms," as sperm are referred to among the urban poor) to women's wombs through the act of sexual intercourse. In other words, if men's "worms carry the kids," as Egyptians are apt to put it, then women's wombs are seen as mere vessels, or receptacles, for men's most essential, substantive input.

Two alternative theories do grant women some procreative role, although the substances they contribute to fetal formation are deemed less important than those of men. In one version, women supply menstrual blood as an actual product of conception, which "mixes with the man's worms." However, because menstrual blood is deemed insalubrious and polluting, many Egyptian women who hold this view are also troubled by what they perceive to be the contribution of a dangerous, defiling substance to the development of a healthy fetus. A much less commonly held view, but one that is beginning to gain credence with the spread of Western-style education to the poor, regards women as egg producers—eggs that must necessarily unite with sperm in order to produce a fetus. However, this seemingly duogenetic theory of procreation remains androcentric; women's eggs are deemed less important, contributing "less than half" or "little at all" to conception when compared to the major role afforded to men's sperm.

Moreover, women are blamed for endangering masculine procreativity by virtue of wombs that fail to facilitate conception and thus men's dominant role in this process. Given that men are widely believed to engender their own offspring, it is a truly ironic, patriarchal paradox that women, rather than men, are generally blamed for failures in the reproductive realm. As long as a man retains his ability to ejaculate his worm-borne fetuses into a woman's waiting womb, he is deemed both virile and fertile. The notion of male infertility has reached the masses in Egypt due to the widespread dissemination of semen analysis technology over the past two decades. Thus, men such as Fadia's husband Osman are known to suffer from "weak worms," as sperm pathologies are generally referred to by lower-class Egyptians. However, male infertility is rarely entertained as the absolute cause of any case of childlessness. This is because worms are thought capable of being invigorated, even enlivened, by a variety of "strengthening" medications. In other words, the actual clinical severity of many male infertility problems, which rarely respond well to drug treatment alone, remains unrecognized by the vast majority of Egyptians.

Rather, women are typically blamed for being infertile, because their reproductive bodies are seen as more complicated than those of men and, hence, more prone to mechanistic failures of the "reproductive equipment." Such "equipment" includes the uterus, fallopian tubes, and ovaries, which are viewed as unstable (even "wandering"), mechanically fragile, and thus subject to both injury and internal failure. Women are viewed as having "many things that can go wrong" with their reproductive bodies, a view that is supported when women seek infertility treatment and are subjected to numerous painful and time-consuming diagnostic and therapeutic procedures. The degree to which Egyptian women view their own reproductive bodies as fragile, potentially malfunctioning, and difficult to treat is remarkable, as is their willingness to accept and then internalize patriarchal ideologies of reproductive blame. Indeed, women who are told by physicians that their husbands are suffering from serious male-factor infertility typically continue to seek treatment for themselves, under the assumption that something *must* be wrong with them, too. This well-internalized view of women's reproductive bodies as the site of numerous potential problems makes sense when considered in light of the five-thousand-year history of Egyptian gynecology.

Egyptian Ethnogynecologies

In Egypt, rather than there being only one hegemonic form of gynecology, it is more accurate to speak of multiple gynecologies, or multiple, historically based philosophies regarding the appropriate diagnosis and treatment of women's reproductive bodies. For heuristic purposes, it is easiest to divide these gynecologies into two major categories: biogynecology, or "modern," Western-derived, biologically based gynecology, and ethnogynecology, or nonbiomedical, "traditional" forms of gynecological care. However, such a dualistic and seemingly dialectically opposed representation of the Egyptian gynecological realm is nothing if not simplistic. Instead, numerous healing philosophies are still present in Egypt, leading to a multifaceted array of etiological, diagnostic, and therapeutic beliefs and practices regarding the nature and treatment of infertility.

These multiple healing philosophies are the result of the dynamic syncretism of four major literate medical traditions in Egypt, the most recent of which is colonially produced Egyptian biomedicine. Prior to the introduction of biomedicine in the mid-1800s, Egypt was home to (1) pharaonic medicine, a five-thousand-year-old medical system known to us through a variety of medical papyri (Leake 1952) and involving the extensive use of an herbal pharmacopoeia by pharaonic medical practitioners (Manniche

1989); (2) *yūnānī* medicine, the most historically influential, colonially produced system of Greek medicine, which was the basis of Arab medicine
throughout the Middle East for many centuries. Hippocrates and Galen,
the fathers of *yūnānī* medicine, were major proponents of "humoral pathology," in which the physiological functions of the body were seen to be regulated by four basic humors, blood, phlegm, yellow bile, and black bile,
which required equilibration through various hot and cold, wet and dry
therapies to ensure bodily well-being; and (3) prophetic medicine, which
emerged following the rise of Islam in the seventh century A.D. Prophetic
medicine was based on the Prophet Muhammad's teachings about health
and hygiene in the Islamic scriptures and was particularly popular with the
masses, for it incorporated traditional concepts and practices from Arab
folk medicine (Millar and Lane 1988). These included methods to ward
off the evil eye, the writing of religious sayings in curative amulets, and
the practice of cupping, or the placement of a glass jar over a lit object
on the skin, all of which are widely practiced in Egyptian infertility treatment today.

In fact, although none of these ancient medical traditions continues
today as recognizable systems of medical practice, their influence is defi-
nitely felt in the realm of contemporary Egyptian ethnogynecology, where
healers of various types treat the infertile with the materia medica and the
power of beliefs derived from these earlier traditions. The primary ethnogynecologists in Egypt today are *dāyāt,* or traditional midwives, who
treat the ailments of the infertile as well as deliver the majority of Egypt's
babies. However, *dāyāt* are not the only ethnogynecologists. In urban Egypt
today, poor infertile women may seek the help of one or more *sittāt kabīra,*
or elderly lay women healers known for treating the most common bodily
complaints of women; *ʿaṭṭārīn,* or herbalists, who deal in the herbs and
minerals necessary for various healing appurtenances; *munaggimīn,* or spiritist healers, who tend to specialize in sorcery nullification, and spirit invo-
cation and appeasement; and, finally, *shuyūkh bil-baraka,* or blessed shaikhs,
living and dead, who provide divine intercession for infertile women on

their healing pilgrimages to saints' tombs and other "shrines of conception" (Betteridge 1992).

Some poor infertile women eschew the services of such healers, placing their entire faith in "God and doctors." However, as seen in the case of Fadia and her pursuit of a variety of traditional remedies, the vast majority of lower-class women continue to rely on these popular, indigenous practitioners at least as a first line of resort; for it is these healers, and not doctors, who recognize, diagnose, and treat the many ethnogynecological causes of infertility.

Kabsa, also known as *mushāhara,* is considered by most poor, uneducated women to be the primary cause of infertility. *Kabsa* involves the entrance of a polluted individual or substance into the room of a new bride or newly delivered mother, rendering their reproductive bodies "bound" by the pollutant. Although *kabsa* is extremely complex and is described in great detail elsewhere (Inhorn 1994a, 1994b), suffice it to say that a woman who has been affected by *kabsa* must undergo one or more depolluting rituals of consubstantiality, in which she is "unbound" through reexposure to the putative pollutant (blood, urine, sexual excreta, the discharges of death, or gold, which is thought to pollute the poor).

Second, many women experience *ruṭūba,* or utero-ovarian humidity contracted through exposure of the genitals to cold drafts or cold water. *Ruṭūba* is thought to be remedied through either cupping or vaginal suppositories called *ṣūwaf,* which are thought to drain the moisture from an affected woman's reproductive organs, but which, in fact, may be ethno-iatrogenic, causing ascending, sterilizing infections in some women (Inhorn 1994a).

Third, *dahr maftūḥ,* or an open back, is another common cause of infertility, believed to be caused by overexertion. This condition requires cupping, traditional cauterization, or an externally worn belt and padlock to "close" the back, which cannot properly "carry" a pregnancy.

Fourth, *khaḍḍa,* or a severe shock or fright, is thought to render both men and women infertile and must be remedied either by countershocking or by placing edible substances in a special pan called the *ṭast it-tarʿba*, or "pan of shock."

Similarly, *ʿamal*, or sorcery, is believed to be a cause of both male and female infertility and requires divination and nullification by mostly male spiritist healers, who are often viewed with skepticism as being unscrupulous and immoral.

Finally, there is the *ukht taht il-ard*, or spirit-sister under the ground, a mostly benevolent subterranean spirit counterpart who, when angered by her earthly sister, can render the latter infertile until she is properly appeased through small animal sacrifices or the provision of gifts, usually food.

Although poor women vary in the degree and extent to which they accept these ethnoetiologies and act upon them in their treatment quests, suffice it to say that ethnogynecological beliefs, treatments, and practitioners are alive and well in Egypt among the urban underclass, providing an alternative therapeutic realm for poor infertile women that is rich and varied in its content.

On one hand, these ethnogynecological therapies tend to be much more accessible, affordable, and, on some levels, culturally acceptable than foreign-based biogynecological treatment modalities. Furthermore, although their efficacy is both unknown and questionable, these ethnogynecological therapies tend to be much less invasive and potentially less iatrogenic than biogynecological "cures."[4] On the other hand, ethnogynecological therapies are not entirely unproblematic for poor infertile Egyptian women. Some procedures, such as cupping, are extremely painful, while others, especially the practices revolving around *kabsa* (which involve, among other things, exposure to miscarried fetuses, the bloody by-products of birth, cemeteries, morgues, and skeletons) are reported by many women to be repulsive and traumatizing. Furthermore, in the era of AIDS and other blood-borne infections, the exchange of blood and bodily fluids required in many of these ethnogynecological practices can only be seen as ultimately health-demoting. Finally, for many poor Egyptian women who are sensitive to the ever-increasing Islamist discourse in the country, these ethnogynecological practices may produce great moral ambiguity and anxiety, because at least some of these practices, especially those associated with sorcery, have been directly condemned as pre-Islamic superstitions that go "against the religion."

Indeed, although most poor infertile women consider and attempt to counter one or more of these possible ethnogynecological causes of their infertility, they acknowledge and agree with the Islamist discourse stating that infertility and its solution are ultimately up to Allah, God the Almighty, who decides who will be infertile and who will not, as well as who will overcome her infertility with his help. Because God created medicine so that believers might seek the solution to their own suffering, poor infertile Egyptian women take very seriously their quests for conception, attempting to demonstrate to God their belief in his healing power. Thus, today, most infertile Egyptian women are peripatetic pilgrims, embarking on relentless healing quests. For many women, these quests take them from healers to holy sites and, not inconsequentially, to numerous physicians.

Egyptian Biogynecology

For many poor women, ethnogynecology remains an especially appealing avenue for therapy, because of the considerable constraints to proper infertility care posed by Egyptian biomedicine. In the biomedical management of infertility in Egypt, it is women's bodies—not men's—that tend to be subjected to expensive, invasive, agonizing, and often iatrogenic methods of surveillance and control. In fact, Foucault's (1977) notion of "biopower"— in which human bodies become the site of ideological control and are disciplined, punished, and in other ways manipulated through "technologies of the body" designed to create, ultimately, politically docile subjects— seems quite germane to this discussion. Egyptian biomedicine, a historically recent British colonial import that remains the institutionalized source of biopower in this setting, has created through subtle hegemonic coercion and consent (Gramsci 1971) a class of docile, subordinated infertile women; these women are too readily subjected to, and accommodating of, various forms of biogynecological bodily invasion, touted by many physicians as being high-tech biomedical "fixes" for infertility. That mostly male biogynecologists with little if any training in infertility management willingly invade infertile women's bodies—both vaginally and abdominally—in the pursuit of blatantly patriarchal and capitalist ends is the source of what might best be called the "untherapeutic therapeutics" rampant in the Egyptian biogynecological setting (Inhorn 1994a).

In Egypt today, those women who cannot afford IVF and the other new reproductive technologies are typically subjected to an array of outdated, inefficacious, and even iatrogenic therapies that are widely practiced by Egyptian biogynecologists. In many cases, the subjects of these iatrogenic practices are poor, minimally educated women, who, having been convinced of the superiority of biomedicine or simply desperate to be cured, may sell virtually everything they own in order to finance their biomedical quests to doctors who can only be described as second-rate. Typically, these physicians engage in the blatant abuse of fertility drugs—overprescribing them to patients and failing to monitor sometimes serious side effects, which may lead to additional infertility problems. Furthermore, infertile Egyptian women typically undergo multiple invasive procedures.

One of these invasive procedures is tubal insufflation, or *nafq* in Arabic, an antiquated diagnostic procedure in which carbon dioxide is pumped into the uterine cavity to purportedly "blow open" blocked fallopian tubes. This procedure, which was introduced in the United States decades ago as a method of diagnosis, continues to be a routine treatment in Egypt, although it was never intended to be used therapeutically and now is found only in the annals of gynecological history in the West (Speert 1980). Furthermore, tubal insufflation actually produces further infertility problems in some women, by forcing pathogenic bacteria from the lower part of the genital tract into the upper part, where these bacteria lead to sterilizing infection (Inhorn and Buss 1993).

Second, many infertile women are subjected to dilatation and curettage (D&C), or *tausi^c wi kaht* in Arabic, involving the purported "cleaning" of the uterine cavity through scraping off the endometrial lining by a sharp curette. Although D&C is indicated for postmiscarriage bleeding, it has been obsolete for decades in the treatment of infertility in the West, and thus is no longer included in contemporary texts in reproductive medicine (Carr and Blackwell 1993).

Finally, many infertile women undergo the painful procedure called cervical electrocautery, or *kayy* in Arabic, another irrational and obsolete procedure, in which the purportedly "eroded" cervix is thermocauterized by a heated instrument, leading to potential destruction of the glands providing the cervical mucus necessary for the transport of sperm into the upper genital tract.

In addition to this most popular triad of biogynecological infertility treatments, many infertile Egyptian women such as Fadia undergo an array of other nonsensical and potentially deleterious invasive procedures, including the injection of drug "cocktails" into the uterus, surgical removal of "wedges" of the ovaries, and various tubal surgeries, where the delicate fallopian tubes are cut and resutured without the benefit of a surgical microscope, leading to their shortening and permanent scarring.

Although a detailed cultural critique of Egyptian biogynecological practices is beyond the scope of this essay and is presented elsewhere (Inhorn 1994a), suffice it to say here that an indigenous critique is beginning to emerge from within the Egyptian biogynecological community itself. It involves the subversive discourse of primarily younger, often university-based physicians, who rail against the irrational, inefficacious, and harmful practices of many of their community-based colleagues. According to this small physician elite, most Egyptian biogynecologists continue to perform these procedures for two reasons: first, because of their outdated medical knowledge, which derives from an antiquated, colonially produced system of medical education in Egypt (El-Mehairy 1984; Sonbol 1991) and which is accompanied by a blatant lack of physician accountability through any form of systematic continuing medical education or malpractice; and second, because of physicians' frank greed for money in a climate of economic uncertainty and stiff competition for paying clientele. Poor infertile women, who are uneducated and often too easily impressed by male physicians' authority, constitute easy prey for unscrupulous physicians, who may justify their largely inefficacious treatments as a harmless form of hope for their desperate female patients. As physicians practicing in a developing country, they realize all too well that it is such poor patients who will never be able to afford IVF and the other new reproductive technologies introduced to Egypt during the last decade. Thus, older reproductive technologies, which are applied in a cavalier and harmful fashion, are even justified as a form of "mercy" treatment by physicians who are incapable of offering the newer reproductive technologies to their poor patients.

The Advent of IVF

Thus, as it now stands, with few exceptions, poor Egyptian patients such as Fadia are simply unable to obtain IVF and the other new reproductive technologies, even if they are aware and highly desirous of such treatments. Among the poor, and even among most of the middle class, IVF is absolutely unaffordable—and probably will continue to be so indefinitely, given the personal expenditures required for such therapy in privately held IVF clinics.

It has now been more than ten years since the first IVF center in the Muslim Middle East opened in Cairo as a private concern, and the first Egyptian "baby of the tubes"—a little girl named Heba Mohammed—was born in 1987. By the early 1990s, the University of Alexandria's Shatby Hospital, where I conducted my original research, opened its own public IVF center, and the first Alexandrian "baby of the tubes" was born in early 1992. But since those early publicity-driven days of free, government-sponsored IVF, fewer and fewer test-tube babies have been born to poor Egyptian women. As Egypt's one and only public IVF program, the Shatby Hospital IVF clinic continues to operate, but on such a low volume that very few patients receive treatment and success rates are compromised. For the most part, the physicians charged with running this clinic put their energies into their private IVF concerns—which, as is typical for most Egyptian physicians working in the public sector, they run on the side.

With only this one, rather suboptimal exception, the rest of the thirty-six IVF centers in Egypt today are private concerns, charging comparatively high prices for the procedures that patients pay out of pocket (since health insurance in Egypt is new and not widespread). The doctors who run these centers, many of whom are university professors and are Western-trained, comprise a small, elite corps of highly educated and biomedically sophisticated reproductive medicine specialists in Egypt. Not surprisingly, their patients are also drawn from a relatively small group of educated, elite Egyptians, who are sophisticated about their medical options and can afford to pay for high-tech therapies. For the most part, these women are highly educated professionals who often speak English or French and are employed as doctors, lawyers, architects, engineers, accountants, bankers, professors, businesswomen, and even movie stars. Furthermore, many of these women and their husbands are members of the Egyptian "brain drain" generation—they increase their wealth by working in the petro-rich Arab Gulf countries, returning home annually on month-long vacations in order to undertake a trial of IVF.[5]

In other words, over a relatively short time span, the IVF scene in Egypt—once touted as being open to even the poorest public-hospital patients—has become extremely class-based and exclusionary, the arena of a handful of elite doctors and their upper-class patients. This does not mean that elite doctors and patients are without sympathy for the poor and even middle-class women who cannot afford IVF therapy. For example, one IVF doctor in Cairo described his futile, ten-year campaign to introduce IVF at Cairo's largest public university teaching hospital, bemoaning the lack of political will that had frustrated his efforts. Furthermore, affluent women themselves lamented the high cost of IVF therapy and the need to repeat the therapy if it did not succeed, typically at a cost equivalent to nearly $3,000 per trial. They agreed that such therapy is exceedingly expensive, especially in light of what they view as a poor salary structure in Egypt and a generally low standard of living in this developing country. Yet most of these patients also admitted that they and their husbands could afford repeated trials of IVF. And many stated bluntly during interviews that these therapies are "not for everyone"—the "everyone" in this case tacitly referring to poor women such as Fadia, who are often known to wealthy women only in their capacity as domestic servants.

Indeed, echoed in this exclusionary discourse is the same kind of Euro-centric prejudice that, as noted earlier, seems to underlie much Western discourse on infertility and the new reproductive technologies and which is certainly rife in the Western-generated population discourse on Egypt. In this discourse, the new reproductive technologies to combat infertility *should not* be "for everyone," because, the equation goes, those who cannot afford these technologies certainly cannot afford to have children. In this model, poor women do not deserve to be mothers, and any reproductive technology directed at them should inhibit—not facilitate—their fertility.

Religion and New Reproductive Technologies

Even if some affluent Egyptians think this way, rarely do they express this self-serving, neoeugenic argument openly, for it militates against the teach-ings of Islam, which state that every child is born with its own *rizq*, or source of sustenance. Egypt is a decidedly Muslim country, with more than 90 per-cent of its citizens Sunni Muslims and with public expressions of religiosity increasing under a two-decade-long wave of Islamic fervor. Although Egyptian Muslims are certainly heterogeneous in terms of religiosity and degree of religious expression and practice, it is also true that Islam pro-vides a source of guidance for many Egyptian Muslims in a variety of arenas of human activity, be they spiritual, economic, educational, medical, or political. Instruction that informs or regulates the everyday activities of Muslims can be found in a number of theological documents, including the Qu'ran and the *hadīth* (the traditions and sayings of the Prophet Muhammad), which are the primary Islamic scriptures. Together, these sources make up the body of Islamic jurisprudence called the *sharī'a*. Those issues, such as the new reproductive technologies, which are not discussed in the centuries-old *sharī'a*, are regularly legislated upon by the most vener-able Islamic jurists in the form of written religious proclamations called *fatwās* (Lane and Rubinstein 1991).

Even before IVF emerged on the scene in Egypt, the grand shaikh of Egypt's world-renowned Al-Azhar University issued a *fatwā* on the religious permissibility of IVF. He declared that IVF and similar therapies were an acceptable line of treatment—as long as they were carried out by expert scientists with sperm from a husband and ova from a wife with "no mixing with other cells from other couples or other species, and that the conceptus is implanted in the uterus of the same wife from whom the ova were taken" (Aboulghar, Serour, and Mansour 1990). In other words, in Egypt and in the rest of the Middle Eastern Muslim world, Islamic jurists have clearly spelled out which individuals undergoing reproductive therapies have the right to claim the status of "mother" and "father"—namely, only the *biological* mother and father, who thereby maintain "blood ties" to their IVF offspring. Sperm, ova, and embryo donation are prohibited, as is surrogacy.

It is interesting to note that although this *fatwa* on IVF was issued as early as 1980, uncertainty about the Islamic position on IVF reigned throughout the pre-IVF period in Egypt, as evident in Fadia's husband's belief that IVF was religiously prohibited. By the mid-1990s, however, much of this moral uncertainty had given way to a kind of moral clarity abundantly apparent in the discourse of Egyptian women undergoing IVF. Stating that the religious aspect of IVF is its "most important" element, Egyptian IVF patients interviewed in the 1996 study were experts on the religious dimensions of IVF. As they explained, sperm, egg, or embryo donation leads to a "mixture of relations." Such mixing severs blood ties between parents and their offspring; confuses issues of paternity, descent, and inheritance; and leads to potentially incestuous marriages of the children of unknown egg or sperm donors. Thus, for the Egyptian women undergoing IVF in this study, the thought of using donor sperm from a sperm bank was simply reprehensible and was tantamount in their minds to committing *zina*, or adultery. Surrogacy, in addition, tampers with the "natural maternal bond," which is meant to be an exclusive link between one mother and her biological child.

Furthermore, much of this righteous discourse was constructed in relation to discourses about the corrupt Christian West. In Egypt, news stories and television movies imported from America and Europe show women who "rent their wombs," only to struggle over custody of the children they bear or IVF doctors who impregnate hundreds of women with their own sperm, only to be sent to prison; or IVF mothers who bear twins, one black and one white, by two fathers because of careless sperm admixtures in western IVF laboratories. Proclaiming that this would never happen in Egypt—where women assume that their IVF doctors are good, religious Muslims—women in Egyptian IVF centers described in incredulous terms the immoral horror of Western IVF practices. They concluded smugly but apologetically to the American anthropologist researcher that "each society has its own traditions and customs."

But, as an American anthropologist interested in understanding such "traditions and customs," I also perceive what most infertile Egyptian Muslim women are unwilling to contemplate—namely, the paradoxical downside of Islam's patriarchal moral code. On one hand, Islam glorifies motherhood and all it entails, insisting that women are endowed with a "natural maternal instinct" (Schleifer 1986). Yet, because of Islam, infertile women who attempt to realize their maternal instinct by resorting to reproductive technologies are particularly limited in their technological options. Moreover, these constraints are even greater when one considers that Islam prohibits adoption, again for reasons having to do with lack of a natural "maternal bond" between an adoptive mother and her child and, more important, the lack of "blood ties" between adoptive fathers and their offspring, leading to nagging questions of paternity, descent, and inheritance.

Finally, a particularly cruel irony that is occurring with increasing frequency in Egyptian IVF centers today has to do with male infertility. A brand-new reproductive technology called intracytoplasmic sperm injection (ICSI)—pronounced "iksee"—is allowing men with severe male-factor infertility to have "biological" children using their own sperm. Those Egyptian wives who have "stood by" their infertile husbands for many years but who are now too old to produce their own ova for the ICSI procedure are increasingly being "replaced" through divorce or polygynous remarriage. Because egg donation, sperm donation, and surrogacy are all strictly forbidden by Islam, infertile Egyptian husbands see their own reproductive futures as lying with younger "replacement" wives, who are allowed to men under Islam's personal status laws.[6] These laws, coupled with the Islamic position on the need for biological paternity in the practice of IVF, place infertile Muslim women in a true reproductive bind.

Conclusion

It would seem appropriate to quote from Cris Shore's recent essay on anthropology and the new reproductive technologies:

> Attitudes toward conception communicate key structural principles about the nature of society: in this case, a patriarchal society still rooted in an ideology that stresses the importance of blood ties, the primacy of the nuclear family, and the superiority of paternity. . . . The lesson from anthropology is that every society has a vested interest in controlling reproduction, and in each, we tend to find dominant institutions—the church, the state, the medical profession, or whatever—competing to monopolize the discourses through which legitimate reproduction is conceptualized. (1992: 30)

Through my own anthropological inquiries into infertility in Egypt, I hope to have shed some light on the ways in which the reproductive destinies of infertile Egyptian women are being controlled, for better or for worse, by the male-dominated medical profession, the state-sponsored religion, and the overarching political economy of a society divided into a few haves and many have-nots. Unfortunately, for many of these infertile Egyptian women, rich and poor, their efforts to be cured of their infertility are often fruitless and thus their future remains unclear. Both collectively and individually, they face a "medical and emotional road of trials" (Sandelowski, Harris, and Black 1992)—one whose end is rarely in sight. That they journey down this tortuous road with such fortitude, dignity, and conviction is a testament to their spirit as pilgrims, whose "search for children" holds in store the promise of a better life.

Notes

1. The name Fadia is a pseudonym.

2. For additional detail on the study population and research methodology, see Inhorn 1994a.

3. Not only is adoption culturally unacceptable among the urban poor, but it is also unacceptable among the wealthy, as apparent in my more recent research, carried out in 1996. Of the sixty-six couples participating in my study of IVF, only one couple was legally fostering a child. Most other couples had rejected this option out of hand, claiming it was "against the religion."

4. Neither I nor any other contemporary researcher has attempted to assess whether the ethnogynecological treatments for infertility used in Egypt are, in fact, efficacious. Some of the herbal substances used in various ethnopharmacologically based infertility remedies (e.g., suppositories) have been shown to have medicinal properties (Bedevian 1936). From a strictly biomedical standpoint, however, it is unlikely that any of the traditional remedies are substantially efficacious, and some are potentially iatrogenic in terms of exposing women to further genital tract infection.

5. Although a few women in this study had also traveled to Europe or the United States in order to try IVF, traveling outside the Middle Eastern Muslim world was generally not condoned by study participants as a wise or feasible option. In addition to the logistical difficulties of securing access to medical personnel, facilities, and housing, many women were concerned about the moral standards of non-Muslim Western IVF practitioners. They felt that the possibility of sperm and ova "mixups" was much higher in the West, either through careless laboratory practices or through intentional efforts on the part of physicians to increase their success rates. Most women were convinced that such "involuntary donation" of sperm and ova would never take place in Egypt or another Muslim country. Thus, most women chose to remain as patients within the Middle Eastern region.

6. Although I do not intend to suggest that Islam is more or less patriarchal than any other world religion, many feminist scholars (e.g., Badran 1993; Coulson and Hinchcliffe 1978; Hatem 1986; Smock and Youssef 1977; White 1978) have argued that Islam's personal status laws governing divorce and polygyny provide a glaring example of the nexus between patriarchal ideology and practice in the Middle East.

6

"Real Motherhood," Class, and Children with Disabilities

Gail Landsman

New reproductive technologies and high-profile custody battles have brought to the fore the contested nature of the term *mother* in United States culture. Should the defining criteria for "real motherhood" be a woman's contribution of genetic material to a child, her provision of the body that carries and gives birth to the baby, or her nurturance of (and perhaps prior contract for) a child after it is born? New technologies have opened the possibility that each of these component roles may be fulfilled by a different person; similarly, open adoptions and calls for a "reformed custody approach" to surrogacy (Narayan 1995) leave open the possibility of maintaining a broad array of parental claims.

Yet each of the criteria assumes the existence of a culturally recognized and valued "real child." How is motherhood defined and experienced by those raising children who do not meet society's standards of quality? Whyte and Ingstad argue that "if personhood is seen as being not simply human, but human in a way that is valued and meaningful, then individuals can be persons to a greater or lesser extent" (1995: 11). In these terms, we know that in American society disability diminishes personhood (Longmore 1997; Mitchell and Snyder 1997; Wendell 1996; Zola 1993). Thus we can ask whether for mothers of infants with disabilities motherhood is diminished as well, and if it is, how motherhood is reconstructed by those who nurture children with disabilities.

Methods

This chapter is based on data collected as part of a larger study, the goals of which are to map the different U.S. cultural meanings of the terms *normal* and *disabled* that different mothers initially bring to their birth experience, and to identify and explain the factors affecting any redefinitions of disability and motherhood that take place through the actual experience of mothering a child with disabilities. Data collection began in August of 1995 with the cooperation of the Newborn Followup Program of the Department of Developmental Pediatrics at the Children's Hospital of Albany Medical Center in Albany, New York, and continued for more than two years. The Newborn Followup Program has a twenty-five-county catchment area. It serves children who have been hospitalized in the neonatal intensive care unit (NICU), as well as children who have been referred through other sources such as pediatricians, family practice physicians, child care providers, or parents' own concerns.

The program serves as an evaluation site for determining eligibility for early intervention services. Depending on the child's needs, such services might include physical therapy, speech therapy, special education, nursing services, occupational therapy, teachers for the visually impaired, psychological services, and/or assistive devices. In accordance with Part H (now Part C) of PL 94-142 (Individuals with Disabilities Education Act), all children from birth to age three years who are determined to have disabilities or significant developmental delays are eligible for early intervention services free of charge. Thus collecting data through the Newborn Followup Proram offered the possibility of recruiting a broad range of participants across class lines.

The protocol was as follows. I met mothers in the waiting room, prior to their appointment with a developmental pediatrician at the Newborn Followup Program. There I explained the project and stated that I am myself the mother of a child who had a traumatic birth, spent time in the neonatal intensive care unit, and has since had some difficulties (at a later time I also tell parents that my child has cerebral palsy). Consent was received to observe and record on audiotape the child's session with the doctor, including the discussion between physician and mother when a diagnosis is made and explained. Ages of children included in the study range from newborn to four years old. Over 120 developmental pediatric evaluations of children at risk for disability have been recorded. Physicians' examinations of a child for potential disability generally involved far more than diagnosis alone, however, lending themselves to discussion of pre- diction as well: What will the future be like for this child? Will the child ever attain specific developmental milestones, such as walking independently or attending regular school? What can or should be done in the best interests of the child?

If she so chose, each mother could continue participation in the study by agreeing to an in-depth, audiotaped interview in her own home or place of work, generally within a month of the physician's evaluation. For about one-third of the women, a second interview took place one year following the original interview. Comparative analysis of the doctor's actual wording (as taped during the evaluation sessions) with the mother's own interpreta- tion of her child and of her role as mother (as collected in two interviews one year apart) was therefore made possible and will enable me to deter- mine how various factors in mothers' lives may be associated with different approaches toward medical predictions. Future analysis will address the question of how mothers integrate their own experiences and beliefs with the interpretations presented by the medical system regarding their chil- dren, and with what impact on their mothering, that is, how mothers incor- porate, reject, or reconstruct elements of the physicians' narratives in their own interpretations of their children and in the decisions they make on their behalf.

To date, fifty-eight in-depth, first-round interviews with mothers of chil- dren identified as disabled have been carried out and recorded on tape. These interviews lasted from one to three hours: specific data were col- lected on the mother's age, education, work history, marital status, religious background, current religious affiliations, prenatal testing, number of pregnancies and children, and prior experience with disability, as well as on the type of disability with which the child has been labeled. However, the bulk of each interview was devoted to the collection of the mother's story, in her own words, of finding out about and living with her child's disability, and to descriptions of the ways in which she represents her child to herself and others.

Mothers interviewed reside in urban, rural, small-town, and suburban settings of upstate New York, and include both married and single women. They range in age from teenagers to women in their early forties, and with educational levels from high school dropout to Ph.D. While some of the children seen for evaluations at the Newborn Followup Program had disabilities associated with fetal exposure to alcohol and drugs or as a result of child abuse, none of the children of mothers I interviewed had disabilities that doctors attributed to maternal behaviors. To my knowledge, none of the mothers interviewed had seriously explored the option of placing their disabled children in an institution or putting the child up for adoption; at the time of the interviews all were raising their child at home.

The current and former occupations represented by women in the study cover a broad range and include homemaker, waitress, schoolteacher, accountant, college professor, housecleaner, cashier, college student, nurse, secretary, seamstress, factory worker, medical claims examiner, transcriber, university administrator, and occupational therapist, among others; in addition, some unemployed and underemployed women in the study were on public assistance. Although Jews and African-Americans have not been well represented in the study (neither have Muslims, Buddhists, and various other religious and ethnic groups), the study did capture a broad cross-section of socioeconomic classes in the region. I had expected that class would be a major factor in how mothers interpret both their disabled children and their own motherhood. Analysis of the data, however, does not support this view, and it is the goal of this essay to attempt an evaluation as to why that is the case.

The Challenge to "Real Motherhood"

"Real motherhood" exists as an issue for mothers of infants with disabilities in part because such mothers hold themselves or feel they are held accountable by others for the failure to produce a normal child despite their access to expert medical knowledge. Mothers of all classes represented in this study indicated that they were aware of experts' advice about how best to ensure the birth of a healthy baby. The vast majority of mothers' narratives include some statement of how the mother thought she had done everything right and therefore believed she should not have had a child with disabilities. For mothers, "doing everything right" involved getting regular prenatal care from medical professionals, including various diagnostic tests, and refraining from smoking, drinking, and using any illegal or over-the-counter drugs during pregnancy; some mothers also included in "doing everything right" either waiting to have a child until they were married or financially secure, or having their child early when they were still young and healthy. Exercising regularly, giving up caffeine, and gaining the "right" amount of weight were also often pointed to, although just what was considered the right amount of weight varied widely. In general the image that had been accepted by these mothers is one in which positive pregnancy outcomes are in the control of women in compliance with medical advice.

Thus, upon receiving a diagnosis, most mothers report at least initially assuming that they personally must have done something wrong to account for the disability; for example, one mother of a child with a missing hand tried to find out the point during a pregnancy when the fetus's hands develop, in order to determine whether that time coincided with the evening she had had a drink at a relative's wedding (before she even knew she was pregnant). Another woman questioned whether the effect of cooking Christmas dinner had brought on a premature delivery. Yet another felt "haunted" by the one Tylenol she had taken during her pregnancy. With the exception of five women—two adoptive mothers, one woman who drank heavily during her pregnancy (knowing it was dangerous but just "not caring" at the time), one who was on birth control during the early phase of her pregnancy (of which she was unaware), and one who had received amniocentesis results indicating Down syndrome—no mother in the study expected during her pregnancy that she could have a child with a disability. In this sense, mothers of all socioeconomic backgrounds originally felt "misplaced" in the category of mother of a child with a disability.

"Real motherhood" is also problematic for these mothers because, particularly when the disability is known from birth, the cultural markers publicly acknowledging motherhood are sorely lacking. "When she was born and people heard there was something wrong, like, the congratulations disappear. You don't get any of that. It's like you don't have a baby," commented the mother of a child with Down syndrome and a heart defect. Responding to a question about what she had planned for the day of her newborn's discharge from the hospital, a nurse who is the mother of a ten-week-old boy with spina bifida commented, "I thought my mom would be here, and we would have family here, and it would be a big show-off thing. I had announcements actually in my drawer that I was going to do, but I never did. I don't know. I just didn't." A mother of a premature baby who suffered serious bleeding in her brain spoke of the pain of lost opportunities for the kind of motherhood she had planned.

> I remember people stopping by, and I wanted so badly for somebody to say congratulations. Instead, I'm in this room by myself. People sent some flowers, but nobody knew what to say or to do, and it was the most horrible feeling, because it's ... like it is a tragedy and it is horrible, but especially the first-time mom, you want some real experiences. I don't know. Probably if they said congratulations, I would have chopped their head off and said, "What do you mean, congratulations? This is not a good thing. This is a terrible thing to go through." It's like nobody wanted to see pictures of her. You know what I mean? Nobody, like, oohed and aahed. When Melissa was in the hospital, a friend of mine—I had five friends who were having babies in May when Melissa was due. We were all due at the same time, and I went to visit one of them

that I was really close with. The other ones, I couldn't hack it, but one of them I was really close with, and I went to visit her when she had her baby. And . . . I realized how much I missed out on having my first baby. Having the family come in to see her, to see the child. They all want to hold the baby, and no strings attached, no cords. The baby is already sucking, and all those things. All the rituals. I missed out on showers. I missed out on everything. There was nothing that was pleasure about her birth, and even after her birth. You know, you don't send out announcements, because what's there to announce? That you had a one-pound-five-ounce baby, you know? It's all those rituals. They shouldn't mean anything, but they do.

This sense of the loss of the experience of first-time motherhood is reported by participating women of all classes whose children are born with an identified disability or risk of disability or death, as is the case for very premature infants. For mothers receiving a diagnosis of their child's disability at a later time, in the course of a developmental exam, it is often the doctor who is seen as diminishing the personhood of the child. A medical technologist turned homemaker talks about her child's examination:

The evaluation, I think, was a totally foreign process to me, and an eye-opener, because here they were objectively categorizing my child in a way that I never saw him that way. And it hurt. I mean, I cried. I cried when they told me that my two-and-a-half-year-old had the cognitive ability of a nine-month-old.

The mother of a young child with a chromosomal abnormality reports the impact of the developmental pediatrician's evaluation of her child, and her struggle to recapture, for herself, her own definition of her child and her role of mother.

And of course, it was tough for us, Gail, because even though Dr. Jones—another thing I didn't care about Dr. Jones in the beginning was he pointed out every one, I mean, I think my son was so hand-some and then he just ripped apart his face. "He has all these dys-morphic features. His eyes are widespread. He has no bridge on his nose. His ears are too low.... He's got what they call a shawl scrotum, and he's dwarfed in size," and all of that.... I felt like I wanted to wring my own neck because I would look at my son and find myself picking—"Oh, my God, he does look like that." It was awful. Then I would look at his portraits on the wall and I would say, "Oh my." So every Christmas picture I took after, I would say, "He's got that look." I would look at him in a certain way when he was sleeping at night, and I said, "Becky, you've got to stop this because you can't let doctors do this to him." ... There were days I would just—being part-time too, and being home a lot, I would just sit and cry. I would look at Billy and just cry.... Like even with this latest thing with Dr. Jones about the attention deficit, I was so devastated when I came out of there, I said, "That's it. We're going to Disney World next year." It's a stupid thing to say, but that's the only way I can, as a mother, feel that I want to do something for him because I figured that I don't know what his future's going to be so I'm going to make sure, if I can't do anything else, he's going to enjoy his life. We've been trying to save. It's going to be real tough for us, but I said, "We're going," because I want to bring him a little bit of joy.

Physicians at the Newborn Followup Program feel called upon to give an unambiguous diagnosis, and they are aware of research suggesting that par-ents are dissatisfied if they feel they are not given enough information. Doctors may assume that in seeking information, mothers are also asking doctors to predict outcomes for their children, and indeed this is often overtly the case. Yet such predictions and labels often lead to bad feelings. In the first round of interviews mothers in this study commonly rejected the application of a label to their child, particularly if that label was one about which there are entrenched societal stereotypes. Thus a mother was more likely to agree with a diagnosis of periventricular leukomalasia or pervasive developmental disorder, which conjures up no particular images in U.S. culture, than with one of cerebral palsy, mental retardation, or autism, about which a mother is likely to already have some preconceived culturally based stereotypes that in turn do not fit her understanding of the child she is raising.

Mothers of children diagnosed with autism, for example, often mention the movie *Rain Man* and contrast their child to the film's autistic savant main character, played by actor Dustin Hoffman. Similarly, upon first hearing a diagnosis of cerebral palsy, mothers often (mistakenly) assume both that they are being told their child will necessarily be unable ever to walk and that the term implies mental retardation. In U.S. culture mental retardation may indeed hold the lowest possible rank in the "pecking order of disabilities" (Ferguson 1996: 20). Mothers from all classes question or resist such diagnoses, claiming that the doctor only "played" with the child during the evaluation; that the parents were given different information from doctors elsewhere, such as in Boston or Buffalo; that with time and therapy (such as massage for spasticity) the child will outgrow his or her symptoms; or that the child was perfectly able but simply chose not to perform tasks for the doctor within the short period and particular setting of the evaluation.

The labeling of a child with a particular disability challenges the mother's capacity to define for herself her child's disabilities and abilities. Doctors may explain diagnoses in clear medical and/or lay terms, but in the short period of time they have with parents they are unable to disassociate certain terms from the cultural devaluation of a person so labeled. A mother, in asserting her child's full personhood, therefore often first attempts to disassociate her child from the diagnosis that culturally diminishes him or her. This is what physicians and psychologists refer to as the stage of "denial." I suggest that rejection or reinterpretation of the physician's label and prognosis cuts across all classes, probably because discrimination against persons with disabilities does so as well.

Mothers reasserting the personhood of their child therefore do so in large part against the definition provided by the medical system. Mothers'

narratives are full of the-doctors-were-wrong stories, stories in which mothers present neonatologists' and developmental physicians' dire predictions,
ranging from a child's not living through the night to being mentally
retarded to never walking, as having all been proven wrong by a child. For
instance, in disagreeing with a doctor's diagnosis of her child as mentally
retarded, a mother of a child who had experienced a stroke pointed to the
fact that despite that same doctor's earlier prediction of permanent blindness, the child's sight had indeed returned.

Researchers have found that most American women "regard information derived from technology as inherently authoritative knowledge"
(Browner and Press 1997: 113; Davis-Floyd 1992; Rapp 1987), and indeed
mothers in the study generally did not question diagnoses based on clinical test results such as MRIs, CT scans, chromosome analyses, and blood
tests. However, in cases where diagnoses are based primarily or exclusively
on physician observation of the child's behavior, mothers often assert that
the child behaves differently at home, performing tasks or exhibiting
knowledge there that was not demonstrated to the physician in the office,
or which was interpreted incorrectly by the physician, who can never know
the child as well as the mother does. Countering the authoritative knowledge of the physician with the mother's nurturance-based knowledge
reasserts not only the full personhood of the child, but the status of "real
motherhood" as well.[1]

The Child as Lesson

While struggling to overcome the sense of inadequacy as a mother—that is,
wondering what one must have done wrong during a pregnancy—many
mothers of infants and children with disabilities of all classes are adamant
that they are stronger, different, and better mothers as a consequence of
having a child with special needs. In an age where "at-home" motherhood is
no longer the norm, professional women who had already decided to stay
home to raise their children find that having a child diagnosed with disabilities justifies their decision, and may give them a new purpose and focus. A
mother of a child newly diagnosed with autism describes its impact:

Being with kids all the time, after having an active professional life, was a huge adjustment, very difficult adjustment for me. . . . It's a very odd thing to say, and I had to say all that to put it in context, but the fact of Brendan's disability has almost saved me in a way. It gave me something to focus on. It gave me something to learn about again. It's so weird to think that that could be the cause of, that could be the catalyst for regaining something in myself that I had lost when I decided to stay home, which I have never regretted. I would much rather stay at home than put stockings on every day or makeup, or do laundry at eleven o'clock, or whatever. It hasn't been an altogether bad thing, really. It's given me a new purpose, something to work for.

Similarly, a college-educated mother of a child multiply handicapped as the result of a stroke states:

Before this happened, I didn't feel like I could accomplish anything in my life. I was going through a period where I have a child, and I saw all my friends getting their master's and stuff, and I was feeling like I wasn't making anything of my life. I was just a mother, a housewife. I just hated that word, *housewife*. . . . I said to my husband one night, "I just want to make a difference in someone's life." And this is what I was chosen to do. . . . People would give me praise when she first got sick and stuff, and I hated that. I hated people saying to me, "Oh, you're doing so well. We're so proud of you." I would say, "Please, wouldn't you do that for your kid?" I used to say "I'm not looking for that," not that I'm looking for it now, but I can look back and honestly say I accomplished a really hard task as best I can. If I never really do go on to school, or whatever, just me having Lisa survive what she has. The reason why she says "mama," "baba," and "dad" is because of me.

This woman later built her child's experience into her analysis of the role of motherhood across generations.

I don't know if you've heard that song "Because You Loved Me," that new song that's out . . . from that movie *Up Close and Personal*. It says, "You were my voice when I couldn't speak. You were my eyes, when I couldn't see," and it goes on, and my mother called me crying, and she goes, "Did you hear that song? It reminds me of you and Lisa." I said "Yeah, I did, Mom, but it reminds me of you and me." And it goes on and on. It's just the circle of life, really. My mother almost died, and my grandmother was at her bedside almost every day, and my mother was with me, and I was with my daughter. You must fight for your kid until the end. No matter what. . . . You're never going to regret fighting for your child. You're never going to look back and regret it.

In having to fight even harder for their children with disabilities, these mothers have revalued motherhood as a worthy endeavor. Mothers across all classes in the study justify their not being on the "fast track" by their commitment to their disabled children. A mother of a child with Down syndrome likes her job as a part-time waitress because her hours ensure that either she or her husband will always be home with their daughter. Similarly, a clerical worker for the state explains, "I was able to go part time to be with Billy and to do all the services and all the things I've had to do, where maybe if I went to college and was working someplace else I wouldn't have had that option. To me, right now more so than getting a tremendously high-paying job or having an education, I want to just make sure Billy gets the best hopes that he can."

Like those women who currently or had previously held professional positions, working-class mothers describe changes in their personalities, relationships, and values. A stay-at-home mother whose husband works at a convenience store talks about changes as a result of the birth of her child, Faith, who is deaf and visually impaired and has motor impairments.

Before it was—This is going to sound stupid. Before it was I was a good mother, and I had my kids, but my husband was always more important. I was just obsessed with this man that I had been with since I was seventeen, and Phil was just absolutely everything. . . . I would do absolutely anything for him. If it meant taking my kids out at three o'clock in the morning, I would do it, but now I don't care. I don't care what he does. I don't care how he affects my life. Faith is more important than anything because she needs me, and it's made me wake up and grow up real quick because it's a pretty important thing, and it's just something drastic that changes your life.

Mothers who work outside the home commonly describe a shift in their concerns such that everyday issues at the workplace now seem petty and trivial. One mother who places print ads for a local manufacturer of heavy gardening equipment described workers' concerns about a much-publicized potential factory relocation in such terms.

I think you look at life differently. You go to work and you hear people getting stressed out over the stupidest things. If you put things in perspective, who cares? Who really cares? . . . Yeah, the company may close down, who cares? I've always said, "Live for today," but I think more—I really believe it more now, and actually grew up more now.

For many the child becomes a vehicle for reassessing one's life. This statement is from a woman who had worked in her parents' flower farm business and now is at home with her toddler, a boy diagnosed with mental retardation.

It just opens up the realm of all the people that are going to touch your life in a very different way, and it changes the shift of your thinking to becoming much more compassionate and I think that is to me, the whole crux of the Bible is that we become more compassionate of people, and to love God, and to love others. I mean, they're the two greatest commandments, and how do you learn to do that without ever having it put to the test, you know, and I really like this situation just—it must, I have to believe for all other parents, I know I am just speaking for me, but to create much more of a compassion in your heart, not only for disabled people, but for their loved ones, for everything. I mean, it just changes your whole heart. I mean, it really kind of scrapes off some of the hard surface and just softens us to people.

These statements are not at all unusual. Mothers of all ages, educational levels, and occupations attributed meaning to their child's disability. Mothers varied greatly as to whether they believed that "God gives special kids to special parents."[2] But most mothers in all socioeconomic classes in the study told stories in which the child's disability became a lesson about true priorities. A teenage single mother of a child with a seizure disorder and multiple disabilities as the result of a stroke described her child's purpose as being a lesson to teach doctors more about this type of problem so as to make life better for other children. A middle-class suburban housewife sees her child teaching compassion to others. A single mother working as a waitress and raising two children in a trailer park sees her child, diagnosed with Asperger's syndrome, as her teacher. She described a conversation she had at her local church. The pastor, trying to bring her into the church, told her that were she to live her life in Jesus Christ she would realize that "'you have Mac for a reason and he's here to teach you a lesson and blah blah blah blah.' Jeez, I know that!" she stated emphatically, and told a story of a "personal moment" once when she had prayed and wished that she could know what unconditional love was:

I have these relationships and I love them *if* they're good, and *if* they give me cards, you know. . . . I don't know what unconditional love is. Well, it's like, hello, be careful what you ask for because you just might get it, you know. And like, patience! I mean, look at the things he's taught me, patience, unconditional love—all that stuff.

In asserting their child's full personhood within a cultural context that diminishes it, mothers' stories occasionally become even broader critiques of inequities in U.S. society. Extending full personhood to their own child leads to the extension of personhood to other groups whose humanity has been diminished, albeit for different reasons. A white high-school-dropout who is the mother of a child diagnosed with both Down syndrome and autism offered this commentary in which lessons learned about her child in turn became an analysis of racism in the United States.

> I said to my mom the other day—it might sound cold, but I'm not meaning to be cold—if everyone in the world had one person in their family that had a problem, that had Down's syndrome or you know, cerebral palsy, or whatever, people wouldn't be so quick, the world wouldn't be such a mean place. . . . And I guess even, I was never a really prejudiced person, but I never really looked at how black people felt or whatever. You really think about it today and it's all along the same lines. People judge how a black person is and that's not fair. I guess it's really opened up another world for a lot of people. My father is a prejudiced person. . . . I used to hear him say things when I was younger and now I think about it and think that was really bad for him to say around us.

A mother who works as a medical transcriber and whose child has mental retardation as a result of hydrocephaly similarly extends her newly trans-formed view of personhood from her daughter to others: "You look at things differently. And you thank God for every day you have. No matter what. No matter how people look at her, she's still beautiful to you. And *every* kid, it doesn't matter. Your kid is a beautiful kid."

Conclusion: On the Relevance and Irrevelance of Class

Recognizing the full humanity and personhood of their own child in a soci-ety in which disability diminishes personhood, many mothers of children with disabilities see themselves as being in a class by themselves. Mothers describe themselves as people who have gained access the hard way to knowledge about priorities and values that is denied those who have not suffered through their trauma. Mother after mother told me that nobody could possibly know what it was like without having gone through the experience themselves; some claimed that it was only the fact that I myself have a child with a disability that made it possible for them to believe I would understand. The relevant divide for them was not socioeconomic class or education, but nurturance of a child with disabilities.

This is not to say that socioeconomic class does not affect access to resources for a child with disabilities or that mothers in the study were unaware of class-based inequities regarding the treatment they and their children received. Women whose children's health care was funded by Medicaid sometimes complained that medical staff looked down on them, and they worried that doctors made choices based on financial concerns rather than on the best interests of the child.[3] Some middle-class women similarly commented upon what they saw as the greater attention and respect they could command from doctors and nurses compared to less educated and/or less financially secure parents they had come to know in the hospital.

Certainly many mothers are embittered and resentful; they speak of being envious of mothers of "normal" children, and they experience anxiety about the financial costs of what for many will be lifelong care. These concerns may vary with the economic circumstances and social supports available to the family.[4] Yet women across all classes construct stories in which their motherhood is reestablished not just as equal to the form of motherhood and nurturance available to mothers of typical children, but in many cases as better and more important.

This transition of identity is exemplified in the story of a mother, working as a part-time accountant, who chose to adopt twin premature babies at high risk for serious disabilities including cerebral palsy, visual impairment, and mental retardation. As told, the story began eleven years ago, when the woman had a placental abruption and gave birth to an extremely tiny premature baby. She went through years of being told her son was mentally retarded and of advocating for him against enormous odds. She told me how she used to imagine that when she died she would go to heaven and ask God what she had done wrong to have such a child.

> I spent eleven years wondering what I did wrong. It was my body. Who else could you say? ... I used to feel for years that when my time was up and I hopefully went up there, my first question was going to be, "So what did I do wrong?"

Then one cold winter day it came to her that she *hadn't* done anything wrong; she had simply been "in training" for her girls. She told me how her father had come to see the newly adopted twins, who, combined, weighed a total of three pounds.

> "It took eleven years," he said, "but you have your answer now." He says, "Because of two little girls coming along the line that needed you." We always tell people that at our house good things come in *real* small packages!

Further analysis of the data in this study may indeed show subtle class differences in how mothers of children with disabilities interpret their children and their own motherhood. These differences may well be accentuated as children reach school age, when disabilities become more obvious and resources an even more significant factor in advocating for one's child.

Nevertheless, mothers of all classes represented in this study originally felt miscast in the role of parents of a disabled child. I suggest that this is because medical technologies, the availability of selective abortion of defective fetuses, and the widespread dissemination of expert knowledge about ensuring healthy pregnancies produce an illusion of control and of the potential for "perfect" babies for mothers of all socioeconomic classes who have access to and utilize the medical system; and because discrimination against persons with disabilities extends broadly across class lines in U.S. culture.

Nancy Press and colleagues (1998) found that in their study among European-American and Mexican-American women in southern California, socioeconomic status played no detectable role in pregnant women's attitudes toward disability.[5] They found that conflicting discourses prevailed: while pregnant women might verbalize some of the positive, romanticized images of children with disabilities, when asked about the implications of a possible disability in a child of their own, women of all socioeconomic classes in their study generally responded with negative and fearful imagery. Indeed it is this same imagery that most North American women who do give birth to children with disabilities bring to their experience of birth and of their child's diagnosis.

Challenging their own prior prejudice against persons with disabilities, on one hand, with love of their own disabled child, on the other, many mothers tell stories in which they attach meaning and purpose to the disability and reflect on their own personal growth. In the process of reinstating the personhood of one's disabled child, both to oneself and to others, mothers often come to extend the status of full personhood to other people with disabilities and to other groups in society whose personhood has been diminished for other reasons, and to reconstruct for themselves an image of normal motherhood of a different but perhaps richer kind.

Notes

The research on which this paper is based was funded through the National Endowment for the Humanities, Program in Humanities, Science and Technology. It also draws on work carried out during a pilot study funded in part through a Faculty Research Award of the State University of New York at Albany, and through the Small Grants Program of the Institute for Research on Women, State University of New York at Albany. I am deeply indebted to the physicians, nurses, and secretarial staff of the Newborn Followup Program of the Children's Hospital at the Albany Medical Center for creating such a supportive atmosphere for this work, and to the many mothers who have generously shared their stories with me. Another version of this paper was presented at a session of the annual meeting of the American Anthropological Association in 1996 in San Francisco. Many thanks are due to Heléna Ragoné and France Winddance Twine for co-organizing such an exciting session and to the discussants, Rayna Rapp and Emily Martin, for their useful insights.

1.   Brigitte Jordan (1993) introduced the notion of authoritative knowledge in her book *Birth in Four Cultures,* first published in 1978. Since that time the concept has been elaborated and celebrated, most notably in a recent collection addressing the cross-cultural study of birthing (Davis-Floyd and Sargent 1997). The "central observation" of the concept of authoritative knowledge "is that for any particular domain several knowledge systems exist, some of which, by consensus, come to carry more weight than others, either because they explain the state of the world better for the purpose at hand (efficacy) or because they are associated with a stronger power base (structural superiority), and usually both" (Jordan 1997: 56).

2.   See Landsman 1999 for an analysis of the cultural meaning of this adage and its interpretation by mothers of children with disabilities at different points in their lives.

3.   A recent study of women who entered obstetrical care at low risk found that "similar care and resources were expended on Medicaid-insured and on privately insured women" (Dobie et al. 1998), but the study did not address comparative expenditures on the children born to the two groups of women.

4.   *Social support* is a term that refers to "the subjective sense of receiving something from network members," with network members being those persons one has contact with who could provide support, such as family members, persons in the community, and paid professionals (Patterson et al. 1997: 384). Social support can be in the form of information, tangible help, and/or emotional support, and is widely recognized in the literature as a major factor mitigating the negative impact on individuals of stressful life circumstances (Patterson et al 1997: 383).

5.   Press and colleagues (1998) suggest that this may be due to the reasonably homogeneous nature of their study population, that is, there was a high level of acculturation among the Mexican Americans and little variation in educational level. It is significant to note, however, that in my sample there is great variation in educational level, yet no differences in interpretation of disability and motherhood were found to correlate with socioeconomic status.

III

Blurred Boundaries

Legal, Political, and Economic Parameters of Motherhood

7

Nonbiological Mothers and the Legal Boundaries of Motherhood

An Analysis of California Law

Susan Dalton

In 1997, two mothers, each of whom entered a co-parenting relationship with her female partner by assisting her in achieving pregnancy and then, with the partner's encouragement, forming a mothering relationship with the resulting children, were denied the legal right to contact their children following the breakdown of the adult relationships. As in previous lesbian co-mother cases, the judges in these cases declared the nonbiological mothers legally unrecognizable as mothers per se.[1] What is interesting about these cases is that in each the trial court judge attempted to maneuver around the legal, biologically based definition of a mother for the purpose of preserving the relationships between the nonbiological mothers and their children.

The difficulty California judges have in recognizing social mothering performed by women who are neither birth parents nor genetic parents is neither new nor limited to lesbian co-parent cases. Indeed, the tendency of judges not to recognize social mothering that is performed by nonbiological mothers is tied to the historical development of American law, which has traditionally enabled judges to consider both social and biological

reproduction in determinations of father status but only biological reproduction in determinations of mother status. In this analysis I examine four
lesbian co-mother custody cases and three surrogacy cases involving hetero-
sexuals to explore how recent changes in the two-parent family, brought
about by changes in both the organizational structure of lesbian and gay
communities and reproductive technology, have "alter[ed] the means and
meaning of human reproduction [as well as] the meaning and scope of
family" (Dolgin 1997: 1–2). By focusing on the court's understanding and
use of sex, gender, and sexuality in legal cases involving both lesbian and
heterosexual nonbiological mothers, this analysis demonstrates how the
treatment of these variables as interchangeable within institutions such as
the law works to naturalize institutional heterosexuality to the apparent
detriment of all social mothers.

What Is Motherhood?

Feminists often ask what makes a person a mother on a purely social level—
that is, what the relationship is between the day-to-day physical and emotional care individuals perform with regard to children and the status the
U.S. courts assign them. Should men, for instance, who do primary child
care labor on a daily basis be assigned the status of mother? Or should
the practices of "othermothering," common in African-American communities,[2] or *ohana,* common in native Hawaiian cultures,[3] lead to the legal
recognition of social mothers as legitimate mothers?

More recently the question of what makes a person a legitimate mother
has emerged within the legal arena as well.[4] Recent advances in medically
based infertility treatments have worked to "defamiliarize what was once
understood to be the 'natural' basis of human procreation and relatedness"
(Ragoné 1998: 118). Medical procedures such as in vitro fertilization (IVF)
have created situations in which the very act of physically reproducing a
child, traditionally considered the incontestable determinant of mother
status, may now be divided between two women simultaneously, one who
contributes the genetic material (the egg) and another "who gestates the
embryos but who bears no genetic relationship to the child" (Ragoné 1998:

119). Procedures such as these act to seriously complicate even the most traditional constructions of the category "mother."

Likewise, changes in lesbian and gay communities over the past thirty years, coupled with the use of usually low-tech intervention strategies such as alternative insemination, have led to the emergence of yet another family formation, families consisting of lesbian or gay couples who choose to bear and raise children within their intimate relationships (McCandish 1987; Patterson 1992, 1994, 1995; Kurdek 1993).[5] Like families created through most surrogacy arrangements, lesbian two-parent families contain at least one parent who physically and emotionally nurtures children with whom she shares no genetic or biological link.

One way nonbiological parents, both heterosexual and homosexual, have for creating a legally recognizable relationship between themselves and the children they parent is through adoption. For married heterosexual couples who become parents through surrogacy arrangements, two types of adoption are available. The first, the stepparent adoption, would be indicated anytime one member of the marital couple is biologically related to the child while the other is not. This is often the case in traditional surrogacy arrangements, where the husband's sperm is used to impregnate the surrogate. In these cases, the nonbiological parent, usually the wife, is considered a stepparent because she is married to the child's biological and custodial father. The independent adoption is available to couples when neither is biologically related to children they help produce through a surrogacy arrangement. In instances where a heterosexual couple acquires a donation of both sperm and egg and then pays to have that genetic material implanted into a surrogate for gestation, neither is biologically related to the resulting child, and thus both must adopt the child to acquire legal parental status.

For lesbian couples who become parents by using donated sperm to impregnate one member of the couple, the only type of adoption available is the limited consent adoption, a modified version of the independent adoption that legally resembles the stepparent adoption.[6] The major drawbacks of the limited consent adoption include its unavailability in many parts of the country (including numerous counties in California), its prohibitive cost, and the unfamiliarity of many lesbian and gay parents as well as family law practitioners with the procedure.[7]

For whatever reason, many adults who become parents either through surrogacy arrangements or private co-parenting agreements fail to legally establish themselves as legitimate parents via a formal adoption procedure. In the seven cases discussed in this essay, the courts were asked to make parenting determinations when the agreements between adults, designed to make clear their intended parenting arrangements, broke down. In some cases the parenting agreements began to fail before the children were even born, while in others the agreements did not begin to unravel until years after the parent-child relationships had been firmly established. In each of these cases, the courts attempt to answer the question: What makes a person a mother under California law? What this analysis makes apparent is that legal determinations of parental status are heavily influenced by gendered notions of biological reproduction, sexuality, and parenthood, leaving men differently situated than women, and married couples differently situated than legally single lesbian couples in the eyes of the courts.[8]

This analysis builds on Rubin's observation that while feminist theorists understand sex and gender to be different systems, related yet distinct, most "fail to separate gender and sexuality analytically," leading them to understand "the oppression of lesbians in terms of the oppression of woman" (1989: 308). Feminist scholars theorizing the effects of gender on social and legal constructions of the family have, for example, either lumped lesbians and heterosexual women together or disregarded lesbianism completely, leading them to ignore the interaction between sex, gender, and sexual orientation (see Brown 1981; Hartmann 1981; Rhode 1989; Weitzman 1985; Smart and Sevenhuijsen 1989; Smart 1991). While some authors do differentiate between heterosexual and lesbian mothers to specify that lesbians are often denied custody of children because of their sexual orientation (see Chesler 1991), they still fail to fully conceptualize sex, gender, and sexual orientation as distinct analytical categories. At the same time, gay and lesbian legal scholars, theorizing the effects of homosexuality on child custody decisions, have traditionally lumped lesbians and gay men together, forgoing a more nuanced analysis into the ways sex, gender, and sexual orientation, both separately and in combination, affect child custody decisions (see Susoeff 1985; Richards 1979, 1993; Sherrill 1993; Wilson and Shannon 1979; Arriola 1992; Byrne 1993; Stivison 1982; Robson 1992; Rivera 1982; Rubenstein 1993).

As Ingraham argues, a failure to fully develop sex, gender, and sexual orientation as independent variables leads to the construction of a theoretical framework that "closes off any critical analysis of heterosexuality as an organizing institution" (1996: 169). By defining gender simply as "the cultural side of the sex-gender binary," feminists continually naturalize a male-female binary that relies upon unquestioned assumptions of heterosexuality (Ingraham 1996: 186). A critical analysis of sexuality, according to Namaste (1996: 204), must "examine the rhetorical, institutional, and discursive mechanisms needed to ensure that heterosexuality maintains its taken-for-granted status."

In this essay I analyze seven custody cases from the 1990s to explore how legal conceptualizations of reproduction, sex, gender, and sexual orientation affect legal determinations of both mother and father status. I focus on the legal construction of motherhood to explore how judicial conceptualizations of biological reproduction, sex, and gender affect social mothers' ability to be recognized as mothers in a court of law. Here I determine that the courts, through the development of legal fictions concerning reproduction, untie parenthood from biological reproduction, first for married men and later for a few married women. Because the use of these legal fictions relies on the blurring of the boundaries between marital status and reproductive status, however, individuals who do not fit within the organizational logic of the fictive reproductive scenario remain excluded. Finally, because the legal fiction requires that judges at least imagine the nonreproductive parent as the child's biological parent, and because men and women play significantly different roles in the reproductive scenario—men produce sperm, while women gestate and give birth—women have a much more difficult time than men convincing judges to imagine them as having fulfilled their gender-appropriate role in the reproductive scenario and thus granting them legitimate parental status. Following a brief review of California's presumed father statute, which is used to explain that development of the legal fiction, the analysis shifts first to the four lesbian co-mother cases, followed by the three surrogacy cases.

The Legal Development of the Presumed Father

In an insightful 1965 anthropological study of California's family law, Herma Hill Kay argues that if we examine the law as it pertains to the legitimation of children, we can observe an "evolving ... legal concept of the family" (1965: 57). This evolution of the legal conceptualization of the family is founded on a broadening of the legal definition of fatherhood that occurs in two primary ways. First, the California legislature adopted Civil Code 230, which encouraged judges to consider men's social fathering when making fatherhood determinations. This act encouraged judges to emphasize the social aspects of parenting for men but not women. Second, California legislators, through the adoption of the presumed father statute, developed a legal fiction that was grounded in the reproductive scenario and used to blur the boundaries between biological and social reproduction for a particular set of married men.

An examination of English laws throughout the seventeenth and eighteenth centuries—from which California family law was adopted—shows that children's legitimacy status was originally inseparable from the marriage of their biological parents (Kay 1965). In 1872 California legislators, wishing to soften the effects of illegitimacy on children, broke with English law and established the legal means by which biological fathers who were not married to their children's biological mothers could legitimate their children retroactively (Kay 1965). This retroactive legitimation, called "conduct legitimation," was achieved when

> the father of an illegitimate child, by publicly acknowledging it as
> his own, receiving it as such, with the consent of his wife, if he is
> married, into his family, and otherwise treating it as if it were a legit-

imate child, thereby adopts it as such; and such a child is thereupon deemed for all purposes legitimate from the time of its birth. (Kay 1965: 61)[9]

In addition to Civil Code 230, which allowed courts to declare unmarried men fathers, California adapted from English law a presumed father statute. This statute, Civil Code 193, established that whenever a child is "conceived during a time when the mother [is] living in the same house with her husband ... and the husband is not impotent, ... the child is conclusively presumed to be legitimate" (Kay 1965: 61).[10] This statute, while purportedly based on an inference about biological fact, actually "grows out of a normative aspiration" that quickly becomes "a prescriptive command about marriage and family" (Shultz 1990: 317). The important issue, Shultz argues, becomes "not who is, but who *should* be having sex with the mother: her husband" (emphasis in original).

The enactment of Civil Codes 230 and 193 was undoubtedly driven, at least in part, by the economic empowerment of men but not women that occurred during the eighteenth and nineteenth centuries. As Ariès (1970), Brown (1981), Hartmann (1981), Basch (1992), Rhode (1989), and Chused (1992) all argue, women living in early American society experienced both legal and economic subordination that largely prevented them from accessing or acquiring wealth independent of their relationships with men. This legislation, which encouraged judges to consider men's biological and social connections to children separately, allowed judges considerable maneuverability in granting father status to men willing to economically care for children.

Today, the presumed father statute is subsumed under the Uniform Parentage Act, first enacted in 1973. Once married, adults in California fall under the jurisdiction of this act, which, among other things, facilitates the creation of legal relationships between married adults and children either born or adopted into their families. Under the Uniform Parentage Act, for example, children born to a married woman are legally presumed to be the children of her husband even in cases where the husband is not the biological father (Bancroft and Whitney 1996).[11] According to the Uniform Parentage Act:

> A man is presumed to be the father of a child if ... (a) [h]e and the child's natural mother are or have been married to each other and the child is born during the marriage, or within 300 days after the marriage is terminated; (b) [b]efore the child's birth, he and the child's natural mother have attempted to marry each other by a marriage solemnized in apparent compliance with law; (c) [a]fter the child's birth, he and the child's natural mother have married, or attempted to marry, each other by a marriage solemnized in apparent compliance with law ... and either of the following are true: (1) [w]ith his consent, he is named as the child's father on the child's birth certificate, [or] (2) [h]e is obligated to support the child under a written voluntary promise or by court order; [or] (d) [h]e receives the child into his home and openly holds out the child as his natural child. (Bancroft and Whitney 1996: 478)

In stark contrast, the Uniform Parentage Act provides only one means of determining mother status: proof that a woman claiming to be a child's "natural" mother did in fact give birth to the child herself.

Creating a Legal Fiction: The Division of Fatherhood into Biological and Social Components

Both the presumed father statute and Civil Code 230 encouraged judges to divide fatherhood into separate components, biological and social. While Civil Code 230 allowed the consideration of social reproduction only in the presence of biological reproduction, the presumed father statute allowed judges to replace biological reproduction with social reproduction entirely. This was accomplished with the creation of a legal fiction that allowed judges to replace biological fact with a very loosely construed presumption of that fact.

The ability of the judges to rationalize the legitimation of presumed fathers rested on their ability to invoke a legal fiction that they used to blur the boundaries between social and biological father status for married men. At the core of the construction of this legal fiction is human reproduction requiring a male and female engaged in heterosexual activity. In creating the presumed father statute, legislators relied upon the normative ascription regarding the marital relationship—that is, that wives engage in an exclusive sexual relationship with their husbands—to mask their substitution of biological reproduction with social reproduction for married men. This was remarkably easy to accomplish because, after all, the biological father's role in the reproductive scenario is both extremely limited and usually performed in private. For judges to imagine that a fertile husband had engaged in an act of sexual intercourse with his wife, thus rendering her pregnant, required very little imagination at all.

While the presumed father statute allowed judges to separate biological reproduction from legitimate fatherhood for some married men, the structure of the statute worked to obscure the presence of the legal fiction by making the presumption itself unrebuttable (see *Estate of Mills,* 1902).[12] In presumed father cases, the substitution of social reproduction for biological reproduction for married men is continually glossed over: judges use marital status and an indication that sexual activity between a husband and wife is occurring while simultaneously refusing to hear any evidence to the contrary (see *Dawn D. v. Jerry K.,* 1997).[13]

Finally, while social reproduction became interchangeable with biological reproduction for most married men, heteronormativity worked as the unspoken logic that allowed this legal maneuver to be employed without disrupting the belief that biological reproduction is central to the legal conceptualization of the family. By restricting the use of the legal fiction to the institution of marriage, the state maintained the all-important ideological link between biological reproduction, gender, sexuality, and parental status.

As I will demonstrate using the seven cases below, however, the courts' insistence on maintaining this ideological link works to exclude virtually all social mothers who, although situated very closely to the presumed father with regard to their relationship to biological mothers and their children, lack the ability to fit easily into the reproductive scenario upon which the legal fiction supporting presumed father status is based. This means that while the legal definition of fatherhood has become, relatively speaking, broadly constructed, the legal construction of motherhood remains remarkably narrow. The *only* determinant for "natural" motherhood that exists under California law is the act of reproduction. Simply put, the courts continue to reserve the legal definition of "natural" mother for those women who biologically reproduce children.[14]

All of the material for the cases below, with two exceptions, comes from the published decisions of the state appellate and supreme courts. These decisions, with one exception, contain virtually no information regarding the racial composition of the families involved. While several authors have discussed the influence of both race and class on surrogacy arrangements as well as court decisions regarding those arrangements (see Grayson 1998; Ragoné 1994; Hartouni 1994), very little information exists pertaining to the racial composition of lesbian two-parent families or the link between the race of the adults in these families and the children they produce.[15] Considering the lack of judicial notice regarding the race of the litigants in all but one of the cases, however, it is probably safe to assume that all the litigants, except those in the case where race was noticed, were white. Likewise, considering the high cost of bringing this type of case before the court, it is reasonably safe to assume that all of the litigants, at least those initiating the cases, were middle- to upper-class. Regrettably, the absence of concrete information regarding the race, ethnicity, or social class of the litigants in these cases, coupled with a judicial silence regarding these variables, prevents me from developing an analysis that speaks to racial, ethnic, or class differences.[16]

When Is a Mother Not a Mother?
The Legal Invisibility of the Nonbiological Mother
in the Lesbian Two-Parent Family

The first two cases in which judges were asked to recognize the parental status of lesbian nonbiological co-mothers occurred in 1990 and 1991. In both cases, the nonbiological mother sued her former partner, that is, their children's biological mother, following the breakdown of their intimate relationship when the biological mother refused the nonbiological mother visitation with children they had co-parented from birth. In both cases the courts attempted to resolve the question of whether a woman who is not a genetic, birth, or adoptive mother can be granted legitimate mother status.

Curiale v. Reagan

In the first case, *Curiale v. Reagan* (court of appeals, 1990), Angela Curiale and Robin Reagan began living together in an intimate and exclusive relationship in April 1982.[17] Two years into the relationship the couple made a decision to jointly parent a child. Together they acquired sperm with which Robin was impregnated by means of artificial insemination. In June 1985 Robin delivered a child and for the next three years Angela acted as the family's sole financial provider. In December 1987 Robin and Angela ended their relationship and Angela left the family home.

Following the breakdown of their relationship, the women voluntarily entered into a written agreement that included joint physical custody of the child. Six months after their breakup, however, Robin informed Angela that she intended to sever the co-parenting agreement and from that point forward refused to allow Angela any contact with the child. Angela responded by filing a complaint with the court seeking recognition as the child's de facto parent and requesting court-ordered visitation rights.

In court Angela argued that she should be legally recognized as the child's de facto parent because both she and Robin clearly expressed their intention to co-parent the child. Angela argued further that the child had come to recognize her as a parent. Both the trial and appellate courts responded to Angela's claim by ruling that there existed "no statutory basis for a claim of parental status." Because they could not legitimate her status as mother, the justices argued, they were "without jurisdiction to award [her] custody or visitation."

Nancy S. v. Michele G.

In *Nancy S. v. Michele G.* (court of appeals, 1991), a case remarkably similar to *Curiale*, the court again faced the question of whether a woman who is not a genetic, birth, or adoptive mother can be granted legitimate mother status by the courts.[18] According to the transcripts in this case, Nancy and Michele began living together in August 1969. In November of that year they celebrated their commitment to each other with a private "marriage ceremony." Eleven years later they decided to become parents and secured donated sperm, with Michele impregnating Nancy via artificial insemination. In June 1980 Nancy gave birth to the couple's first child. Several years later Michele and Nancy decided to add a second child to their family and Michele again used artificial insemination to impregnate Nancy. Their son was born in June 1984. Michele was listed on both children's birth certificates as their father and both children were given her family name. Pursuant to their co-parenting arrangement, both children developed strong and loving attachments to both women and referred to each as "Mom."

In January 1985 the couple separated and began sharing custody of the children. Following a jointly agreed upon visitation schedule, the older daughter began living with Michele five days a week, while the younger son lived with Nancy five days a week. Additionally, both children spent considerable time in each home, overlapping at one or the other house four days a week. After approximately three years, Nancy sought to change the visitation schedule so that each woman would have custody of each child 50 percent of the time. Michele, unhappy with Nancy's proposed changes and unable to broker a compromise that was acceptable to both women, turned to the courts for assistance. In order to be heard by the courts, however, Michele had to first establish herself as a legally recognizable parent.

The key legal issue for Michele, like Angela before her, was convincing the courts to recognize her as a legitimate mother. In her attempts to establish herself as a mother in the eyes of the court Michele argued that (1) she was a de facto parent, (2) she stood in loco parentis with regard to the children, (3) because both she and Nancy taught the children to recognize her as their mother, Nancy should be legally estopped from denying both her and the children that relationship, and (4) she fit a "functional definition of parenthood."

De Facto Parent

In support of her claim of de facto parent status, Michele argued that a de facto parent is "that person who, on a day-to-day basis, assumes the role of parent, seeking to fulfill both the child's physical needs and his psychological need for affection and care."[19] Given that she "helped facilitate the conception and birth of both children and immediately after their birth assumed all the responsibilities of a parent," she clearly met the definition of a de facto parent. To this argument the court responded, "These facts may well entitle appellant to the status of a 'de facto' parent. It does not now, however, follow that as a 'de facto' parent appellant has the same rights as a parent to seek custody and visitation over the objection of the children's natural mother."

In Loco Parentis

In making a claim of in loco parentis, Michele cited the decision in a 1964 appellate case, *Loomis v. State of California,* in which the justices had ruled that "a person who has put himself in the situation of a lawful parent by assuming the obligations incident to the parental relationship, without going through the formalities necessary to legal adoption, does stand *in locus parentis,* and *the rights, duties and liabilities of such person are the same as those of a lawful parent*" (appellant's reply brief to the trial court in *Nancy S.:* 8, emphasis in original).[20]

In response to Michelle's claim of in loco parentis, the appellate court noted that in the context of torts,

> the doctrine of "in loco parentis" has been used to impose upon persons standing "in loco parentis" the same rights and obligations imposed by statutory and common law upon parents. It has also been applied to confer certain benefits upon a child, such as more favorable inheritance tax treatment ... or workers' compensation benefits.... The concept of "in loco parentis," however, has never been applied in a custody dispute to give a nonparent the same rights as a parent.

Clearly the court has used the concept of in loco parentis at various times to extend a variety of rights and benefits to children who would normally be disadvantaged simply because the people acting as their parents held no legal status as parents. When the courts have decided it is in children's best interests to have their relationships with putative parents legally recognized, they have generally recognized those relationships. It is hard to imagine anything more important to a child than maintaining an ongoing relationship with an adult who has acted as a primary parent for five and nine years, respectively. Given the fact that Michele was, by all accounts, an outstanding parent, it is difficult to understand the court's decision not to protect her children by recognizing and protecting their relationship with her.

Interestingly, as the court noted, a similar decision was reached in *Perry v. Superior Court* (1980), in which a husband of six years was denied visitation with his wife's children from a previous marriage. Following that decision, however, the California legislature, reacting to intense lobbying by the courts, amended the law by enacting Civil Code section 4351.5, allowing judges to grant visitation to stepparents within the context of divorce settlements. This law was specifically created to allow courts to recognize the development of social parent-child relationships that commonly occur within families, for the purpose of preserving those relationships. While Civil Code section 4351.5 appeared to directly address the principal issue in *Nancy S.,* there was one caveat. Because Michele and Nancy were both women, the state of California did not recognize their marriage ceremony as valid. Thus, the court argued that Nancy and Michele, as an unmarried couple, remained outside the scope of this particular law. Although theoretically the courts could have set aside the marriage requirement in Civil Code section 4351.5, arguing that its unavailability made it unenforceable with regard to lesbian and gay couples, they chose instead to argue that the law simply did not apply to lesbian and gay couples.

Equitable Estoppel

The third argument made by Michele employed the legal concept of equitable estoppel. The term *estoppel*, which originated in contract law, means to prevent someone from alleging something they had previously denied, or denying something they had previously alleged. In 1975 the appellate court in *Valle v. Valle* reasoned that the elements of estoppel could be used to determine that a father-child relationship was legitimate even though the social father in that case was not the biological father of the child in question, had not legally adopted the child, and was not married to the child's legal mother.[21] In *Valle* the court determined that the elements of estoppel come into play with regard to parental status decisions if (1) a putative father "represented to the child that he was his father, (2) the child relied on the representation by accepting and treating [him] as his father, (3) the child was ignorant of the true facts, and (4) the representation was of such duration that it frustrated the realistic opportunity to discover the natural father and to reestablish the child-parent relationship between the child and the natural father." Finally, the court declared that equitable estoppel is specifically a condition that "runs in favor of the child."

Valle was an interesting and important decision because it represented the first time the courts used the legal fiction first developed for presumed fathers to legitimate a social father who was not married to a child's birth mother at the time of the child's birth.[22] In order to accomplish this feat, the court modified the legal fiction to focus specifically on the child. Here the court argued that as long as the child believed that his social father was in fact his biological father, the courts could and should prevent that man from later abandoning the fathering role at cost to the child.

Michele attempted to invoke the elements of equitable estoppel by claiming in part that "the children developed the deep psychological bonds of a parent-child relationship" with her based on Nancy's insistence that they were "equal parents both legally and functionally" (appellant's reply brief to the trial court: 10–11). The court, however, rejected Michele's claims on two grounds. First, they argued that although equitable estoppel has been used "for the purpose of imposing support obligations on a husband," it "has never been invoked in California against a natural parent for the purpose of awarding custody and visitation to a nonparent." Second, the court noted that while "other states . . . have begun to use the doctrine

... to prevent a wife from denying the paternity of her husband ... even where tests had excluded the husband as the natural father," the use of the doctrine stems from "one of the strongest presumptions in law [, i.e.,] that a child born to a married woman is the legitimate child of her husband." As the court aptly noted, "No similar presumption applies in this case."

These arguments, however, strip the equitable estoppel claim of its intent as originally spelled out in *Valle* and later reiterated in *Johnson*.[23] In those cases the justices asserted that equitable estoppel could be used to assist the courts in maintaining parent-child relationships provided it was determined that a child had developed a parent-child relationship with a person the child believed to be its natural parent. Neither of the arguments forwarded by the court in *Nancy S.* addresses this issue directly. Although there is ample evidence within the case file indicating that the children had developed a parent-child relationship with Michele based on their belief that she was their parent, the court appears to ignore this evidence entirely.

One explanation for the court's refusal to support Michele's equitable estoppel claim lies in the fact that Michele, as the co-mother of slightly older children, disrupted the legal fiction normally used to support the equitable estoppel claim. In other words, by the ages of five and nine, Michele's children theoretically would have known enough about reproduction to understand that only one of their mothers could be a "natural" parent. If the legal fiction used to support the equitable estoppel argument rests upon what the children believe regarding their biological parentage at the time of the trial, it would cease to function, in lesbian co-mother cases, as soon as the children are old enough to understand the biological particulars of human reproduction.

This argument, of course, assumes that once children are disabused of the belief that their social parent is also their biological parent, they will alter their relationship with the social parent such that it ceases to be important. There is no psychological evidence, however, showing that children whose social parents are not also their biological parents (adopted children, for instance) seriously alter their relationship with those parents once this fiction is debunked, especially if the information has generally been available to the child all along. This raises the question of why the courts were willing to deny Michele's children an important parental figure if theoretically they could have used the equitable estoppel reasoning to prevent that loss from occurring.

One answer, which gains some support in the court's rejoinder to Michele's "functional parent" claim, is that the courts always imagine the ideal two-parent family as heterosexual. Within this heterosexual configuration mothers and fathers play distinct yet complementary roles. Because these roles are gendered, however, the only role available to women is that of mother. Within this normative family context the child-rearing labor performed by Nancy, the children's biological mother, would be seen as crucial, while the labor performed by Michele, a second mother, would be seen as redundant.

Functional Definition of Parenthood

Finally, Michele urged the court to adopt a "functional" definition of parenthood in order to "protect on-going relationships between children and those who function as their parents." Michele argued that a "functional" parent would include "anyone who maintains a functional parental relationship with a child when a legally recognized parent created that relationship with the intent that the relationship be parental in nature." The court rejected this argument as well. This time, the court argued that "expanding the definition of a 'parent' in the manner advocated by appellant could expose other natural parents to litigation brought by child-care providers of long standing, relatives, successive sets of stepparents or other close friends of the family."

The courts' refusal to expand the definition of parent to include co-parents such as Michele because a recognition of Michele's mothering would expose other natural parents to litigation brought by "child-care providers" or "close friends of the family" assumes that marriage is the only means available to the courts for reliably establishing the existence of legitimate families in which valid parent-child relationships develop. At the same time, excluding women from accessing the legal fiction that allows social parents to be recognized as legal parents serves to keep motherhood tightly tied to genetics. This in turn has prevented judges from developing a social category of motherhood. Judges, unused to visualizing the social aspects of mothering with any depth or variety, appear unable to see co-mothers as capable of providing their children with nurturing that is fundamentally based on and enriched by their unique personalities. Instead of seeing co-mothers as unique individuals and thus mutually important to the children's development—something that routinely occurs with heterosexual couples—the courts appear to view the nonbiological mother's contribution as simply redundant, something that won't be especially missed.

As long as the legal fiction that is used to rationalize the replacing of biological parents with social parents remains housed within the institution of marriage and marriage remains limited to male/female couples, the courts will remain unable to recognize social mothers who co-parent with other women or social fathers who co-parent with other men as legitimate. This effectively limits their ability to conceptualize the two-parent family as anything other than heterosexual. Taken together, the courts' use of a legal fiction that assumes a heterosexual model, coupled with their repeated rejection of any other family models, creates a system of circular reasoning in which heterosexuality as the basis of the two-parent family is continually assumed, required, and reproduced within family law.

With all routes to mother status effectively blocked in the *Nancy S.* decision, lesbian nonbiological mothers began searching for new ways to have their mothering status recognized by the courts. In the two cases that follow, the nonbiological mothers appear to first abandon their mother status, in an effort to gain the right to sue for visitation, and then reinvoke that status in an attempt to convince the courts to recognize their visitation requests as valid.

The More Things Change, the More They Remain the Same

In 1997, two additional lesbian mother cases were brought before the California superior courts.[24] Both involved children who had been conceived within the context of long-term lesbian relationships with the understanding that the two women would share parental rights and responsibilities. In neither case had the nonbiological mother adopted the children, and at some time following the dissolution of their intimate relationship, the biological mother refused visitation to the nonbiological mother. These cases are different from all previous lesbian co-mother cases because in both the superior court judges attempted to find a way to recognize the parental status of the nonbiological mothers for the purpose of granting them visitation rights.

K.C. v. L.W.

In *K.C. v. L.W.* (1997) the nonbiological mother attempted to gain legal recognition for her social mothering based on the fact that she was a de facto parent and that as such, she had grounds for requesting visitation.[25] Unlike the two previous cases, however, the nonbiological mother in this case structured her suit as a guardianship action, claiming to be a guardian rather than a parent in an attempt to avoid the biologically based definition of mother contained within the Uniform Parentage Act.

This guardianship action raised several issues for the court. First, guardianship requests traditionally seek a change of custody, that is, that the children be removed from the parent's (or parents') home and placed with the guardian. This is known as a full guardianship action. To support a full guardianship claim the courts generally require the guardian to demonstrate that a failure to remove the child(ren) from the home of the custodial parent(s) will be physically, emotionally, or mentally detrimental to the children. In this case, however, the nonbiological mother was using a guardianship claim to seek visitation with the children, and at no time did she argue either for a change of custody or that living with the biological mother was, in and of itself, detrimental to the children. Simply put, she was claiming to be a guardian because the court would not recognize her as a parent. Although she was not seeking a typical guardianship action, she hoped that the court would support her attempt to modify that action.

The court responded to this somewhat unusual request by noting that while "guardianship is an unusual vehicle for what the nonbiological mother is seeking . . . it is all that is available under California law for a lesbian . . . seeking court-ordered contact with children with whom she has no biological or adoptive connection." Because the nonbiological mother was using the guardianship action in an attempt to gain limited visitation and not full custody, the court allowed the claim to proceed.

Having agreed to hear the case as a "nontraditional" guardianship action, the court turned its attention to the issue of detriment. Building on its categorization of the case as nontraditional, the court further determined that "a limited 'visitation guardianship' should be granted if it is proven that a natural parent harms her children unnecessarily by denying them visitation with a meritorious de facto parent who is out of favor." Because the petitioner was not seeking the long-term removal of the children from the biological parent, the court concluded that it was reasonable to modify the application of the detriment standard by focusing on the effects of a denial of visitation rather than on the quality of the biological mother's relationship with the children per se. This modification led the court to ask whether a denial of limited visitation with a meritorious de facto parent would be unnecessarily detrimental to the children.

In the end, the court determined that while it might be willing to grant some form of limited visitation to a meritorious de facto parent in a similar case, the nonbiological mother in this case did not live up to the court's measure of a meritorious parent. Indeed, the court determined that while the "petitioner was clearly a de facto and psychological parent of the [children] during the time she lived with respondent and the children and for a period of time thereafter . . . for a number of reasons she lost that status in the period that followed [, leaving] the court [un]prepared to say that [her status] remains at the level of 'psychological parent.'"[26]

While the nonbiological mother in this case failed to gain court-ordered visitation, she did succeed in convincing the court that there existed legal grounds upon which such a claim could be heard. By situating herself as a legal guardian instead of a legal parent, she successfully maneuvered around the restrictive definition of parent contained within the Uniform Parentage Act and gained the right to be recognized as a party able to bring such a suit.

Ironically, after being forced to abandon her claim to mother status as a condition of having her case considered, this same mother was then required to convince the court that she was not just a parent but a meritorious parent in order to win the right to continue her mothering relationship with the children. In the end it may have been the very grounds upon which she gained the hearing—the fact that she was a guardian and not a parent—that opened the door to the intense scrutiny under which she eventually lost the right to continue parenting. Had she been a legitimate parent in the eyes of the court, her legal right as a parent to maintain a relationship with her children would have far outweighed her less-than-meritorious behavior that occurred following her former partner's refusal to allow her access to the children. Indeed, the very same behavior that hurt her, such as her attempts to see the children despite her former partner's insistence that she and the children end their relationship, would probably have been excused as the desperate acts of a mother unfairly denied access to her children.

West v. Superior Court

In the final lesbian mother case, *West v. Superior Court* (court of appeals, 1997), a nonbiological mother sued her former partner, the child's biological mother, in civil court, alleging breach of contract.[27] Here the nonbiological mother claimed that she and the child's biological mother had entered into an oral agreement to have and raise a family together. Pursuant to this agreement, she argued, the parties sought out and obtained sperm with which to impregnate the biological mother (chosen due to her superior health care coverage). Additionally, the nonbiological mother agreed to support the family while the biological mother was at home caring for the child during its infancy. Finally, she argued, the couple specifically communicated to each other their mutual intent to jointly raise that child, and that while she had "performed all of the conditions, covenants and promises required by her ... in accordance with the terms and conditions of the agreement," her ex-partner had "breached the agreement by preventing her from continuing in her role as parent." Thus, she was seeking the court's assistance in having the contract upheld.[28]

The purpose of filing this case as a breach of contract case in civil court as opposed to a child custody case in family court was again to sidestep the restrictive legal definition of a mother contained within the Uniform Parentage Act. In explaining the rationale behind this filing, one attorney close to the case reported that "there is no case law that says that you can't create a contract to transfer parental interest or to create visitation and custody rights in a child. [In] fact, the only cases on that point are cases between parents that say that the court can enforce those agreements as long as they're not contrary to the best interests of the child." Furthermore, this attorney explained, the courts should uphold all contracts that are not deemed to be against public policy, and it is not against public policy for "a child to have two parents, both of whom are being responsible for providing love, comfort, [medical] benefits, and everything else." [For approximately one year in 1977 I conducted a series of face-to-face and telephone interviews with many of the attorneys involved in the lesbian mother cases discussed in this paper. These quotes are taken from one of those interviews.]

Although the superior court agreed with the nonbiological mother and ordered that visitation be restored, the appellate court sided with the biological mother and agreed to hear the appeal as a more traditional custody dispute. In its reversal of the trial court's decision, the appellate court noted, "As a person unrelated to [the child], [the nonbiological mother] is not an 'interested person' and, therefore, may not drag [the biological mother] into the courts, under the Uniform Parentage Act, on the issue of visitation with [the child]."

While the nonbiological mother attempted to sidestep the restrictive definition of mother contained in the Uniform Parentage Act by emphasizing her contractual relationship with the biological mother rather than her mothering relationship with the child, her attempt failed because the appellate court refused to apply the elements of contract law to the institution of the family. As Dolgin (1997: 43) argues, although "American law has steadfastly concerned itself with relations between, or rights and obligation of, autonomous individuals . . . [f]amily law has been a remarkable exception. Family matters, handled by a separate and distinct body of law . . .

[are] largely regulated with reference to the family, not the autonomous individual, as the smallest unit of social relevance and value." By redefining the case as a rather run-of-the-mill visitation dispute rather than a breach of contract case, the appellate court once again invoked the Uniform Parentage Act as the relevant body of law. Using the Uniform Parentage Act, the court then determined that the nonbiological mother was not a legal parent. As a legal outsider to the family unit, the court concluded, the nonbiological mother had absolutely no right to seek visitation with the child.

Together these four lesbian nonbiological mothers presented a total of six legal arguments, four of which attempted to convince the courts that they were legally recognizable mothers and two of which attempted to sidestep a determination of their mother status altogether. In response to all but one of these claims, the appellate courts immediately chose to categorize the nonbiological mothers as simply single women seeking custody of children they had neither birthed nor adopted. Using this particular conceptualization, the courts then identified the nonbiological mother as a non–family member, a legal stranger to the child and its family. As an outsider, the nonbiological mother became a threat to the integrity of the family unit. To grant her visitation request was seen as tantamount to allowing a baby-sitter to demand ongoing visitation with children removed from her care.

This legal conceptualization of the family relies upon unspoken assumptions regarding both reproduction and parenting. To begin with, it assumes a family model based on the idea of biological reproduction—in other words, a family consisting of one father and one mother. Within this paradigm, although legal fictions may be used to replace a biological father with a social father, there exist no legal fictions that allow a biological father to be replaced with a social mother. Thus while men may be readily substituted into a vacant father role, women are never seen as viable substitutes for a missing father.

This means that claims to parental status made by women who co-mother children must always be heard as a set of competing rather than complementary claims. Because the paradigmatic family consists of only one mother, the courts immediately defined its role in the above cases as determining who that mother should be. This is importantly different from the courts' role in typical custody cases, where claims to father status do not directly compete with claims to mother status—in other words, where the courts can recognize the social parent (usually the father) without having to displace the child's custodial birth parent (usually the mother).

In all of these cases, what the lesbian nonbiological mothers were really asking the courts to do was to expand the legal definition of the family to include the possibility of two parents of the same sex. In order to accomplish this, the court must begin to unhinge the legal definition of "natural" mother from the act of biological reproduction, that is, they must figure out a way to apply the legal fiction to women. As the three surrogacy cases below demonstrate, however, judges, for the most part, remain wedded to the idea that parenting is first and foremost a biological activity: people become parents by biologically reproducing children. And the courts appear to have a much more difficult time imagining women as interchangeable figures within the reproductive scenario than they do men. These cases raise some interesting questions regarding the application of the legal fiction to women in general as well as the courts' continued conflation of biological reproduction and motherhood in an age where technology is increasingly leading to the medical separation of the two.

Surrogacy Cases and Their Effect on the Legal Definition of a Mother

There have been few cases in California in which women, having gained motherhood status through surrogacy arrangements, have turned to the courts seeking legitimation of that status. As Dolgin (1997: 1–2) notes, however, "Since 1978, with the birth of the first child conceived in vitro, reproductive technology has developed at an astonishing pace, altering the means and meaning of human reproduction, and inevitably, the meaning and scope of family." Here I examine California's three surrogacy cases to explore how innovations in reproductive technology affect judges' legal conceptualizations of motherhood.

Johnson v. Calvert

In *Johnson v. Calvert* (supreme court, 1993), California's first surrogacy case, Mark Calvert and his wife, Crispina, wishing to biologically reproduce a child despite Crispina's earlier hysterectomy, entered a surrogacy agreement with Anna Johnson. [29] Their contract provided that "an embryo created by the sperm of Mark and the egg of Crispina would be implanted in Johnson and the resulting child ... would be taken into Mark and Crispina's home 'as their child.'" In accordance with this contract, Johnson agreed to "relinquish 'all parental rights' to the child in favor of Mark and Crispina."

In January of 1990 a zygote created from Mark's sperm and Crispina's egg was medically implanted into Anna Johnson's womb, successfully impregnating her. Soon thereafter, however, relations between the Calverts and Johnson began to deteriorate. As communications became strained, Johnson sent a letter to the Calverts in which she demanded the balance of payments due her via the surrogacy contract and threatened to withhold relinquishment of the child until her demands were met. The Calverts responded by filing a lawsuit "seeking a declaration that they were the legal parents of the [as yet] unborn child." Johnson responded to this legal maneuver by filing papers of her own seeking a declaration that she, and not Crispina, was in fact the legal mother of the child.

In this case the courts were faced with two women making a claim to legal mother status using the legal terminology contained within the Uniform Parentage Act. Crispina, on one hand, argued that she had produced the egg from which the child grew; thus she was the child's biological mother. Johnson, on the other hand, argued that she physically gave birth to the child; thus she was the child's birth mother.

The California Supreme court, citing the Uniform Parentage Act, agreed with both women. [30] In Anna's favor, the court explained, "Civil Code section 7003 provides, in relevant part, that between a child and the natural mother a parent and child relationship 'may be established by proof of her having given birth to the child.'" In Crispina's favor, the court noted that under the Uniform Parentage Act, paternity may be presumed if blood testing positively identifies a man as the likely biological genitor of a child. Applying a liberal interpretation, the court reasoned that this section of the act should be applied equally to both men and women and that because blood tests showed that Crispina had provided genetic material for the baby, she too had a viable claim to parental status.

The justices then determined that the best way to resolve the issue was to move backward in time to focus on the women's original intent. Here the court found that

> Mark and Crispina are a couple who desired to have a child of their own genetic stock but are physically unable to do so without the help of reproductive technology. They affirmatively intended the birth of the child, and took the steps necessary to effect in vitro fertilization. But for their acted-on intention, the child would not exist. [The court concluded that] although the Act recognized both genetic consanguinity and giving birth as means of establishing a mother and child relationship, when the two means do not coincide in one woman, she who intended to procreate the child— that is, she who intended to bring about the birth of a child that she intended to raise as her own—is the natural mother under California law.

This case is particularly interesting because the courts, for the first time, faced a situation in which two women were recognized as mothers simultaneously. Because of the continuing effect of institutional heterosexuality on the legal definition of family, Anna and Crispina battled each other over the singular category of mother. And because of the continuing effect of institutional racisim on Euro-American kinship ideology, this was a battle that Crispina, who shared her racial makeup with the child, was particularly likely to win.[31] As Grayson (1998: 545) argues, "To say that Johnson [a black woman], could be the mother to baby Christopher [a child of both white and Filipino heritage] would be to indicate a willingness on the part of the courts and the public to relinquish or, at minimum, to blur, racial-familial boundaries."

In contrast, once Mark's biological relationship to the child was determined via blood testing, his father status was deemed unassailable because Johnson, as a woman, could not challenge Mark for the status of father. Thus institutional heterosexuality both prevented Johnson from challenging Mark's parental status, although her claim could be read as complementary to his, and required that her claim be seen as competing with but not complementary to Crispina's similar claim.

If we were to simply switch the sex of the litigants for a moment, imagining that both Crispina and Johnson were men, it becomes evident that the court has faced similar cases many times before, that is, two men claiming simultaneous fatherhood—albeit one biological fatherhood and the other social fatherhood. In these instances, drawing on the presumed father statute, the courts have repeatedly ruled that when the social father is married to and living with the child's biological mother at the time the child is conceived and born and he accepts the child into his home and treats it as his own, he alone is the child's legal father.

In this case, Crispina Calvert's position appears even stronger than that of most presumed fathers. Crispina is, for instance, both a biological mother and a social mother competing against another who is neither a social mother nor genetically related to the child.[32] In addition, Crispina was married to and living with the child's biological father at the time the child was conceived and born. And although she was unable to produce a child herself, she did consent to her spouse's reproductive activity, as required in Family Code section 7613.[33] Yet, even with all this going for her, the supreme court determined that it could not apply the presumed parent/father statute to Crispina and proceeded to decide the case on other grounds.

Why was Crispina not found to be a presumed parent, as the Calverts' lawyer argued? One explanation might be that the court felt uncomfortable splitting women's maternal role into separate biological and social categories. To do so would have meant questioning deeply rooted beliefs that giving birth is what makes a person a mother and biological mothers are generally better for children than nonbiological mothers (Andrews 1996; Bartholet 1993). Although the courts do split the maternal role from biology in cases of adoption, this occurs only with the consent of the biological mother or following a court's determination that the biological mother is unfit to parent (Hollinger 1996). In the absence of these two circumstances, the courts always prefer biological mothers over nonbiological mothers.

Another explanation involves the legal fiction that is typically used by the courts to support presumed father determinations. When judges invoke the legal fiction they do so by imagining a biologically based reproductive scenario and then substituting the biological father with the presumed father in this scenario. This is fairly easy to do with regard to men because the male's participation in the reproductive scenario is relatively short-lived. Although Crispina was genetically related to the child in this case, a fact that aligned her closely with the biological father in the reproductive scenario, she, as a woman, would have to take on the role of birth mother in the court's imagination. To grant Crispina presumed parent status under these conditions would require the court to either imagine Crispina as the birth mother, a feat made all the more difficult by the fact that the actual birth mother was a litigant in the case, or imagine the reproduction of a child sans a birth mother.

By deciding the case based on Crispina's genetic relationship with the child coupled with her original intent to parent, the court sidestepped the issue of the differential impact of its use of the legal fiction on social mothers versus social fathers while simultaneously maintaining the stance that biological reproduction is central to the legal definition of mother. Although it could be argued that a consideration of Crispina's intent to parent cracked the door to a legal consideration of women's social mothering, as the decision in the next case makes clear, the court's consideration of Crispina's intent to parent followed its determination that her mother status was legitimate. Without this prior determination, her intent would have probably been considered irrelevant.

Moschetta v. Moschetta

In *Moschetta v. Moschetta* (court of appeals, 1994), we witness a similar refusal by the courts to allow women access to social motherhood via the presumed father statute.[34] In this case, Cynthia and Robert Moschetta, wishing to raise a child but unable to produce one themselves due to Cynthia's sterility, entered into a surrogacy agreement with a woman by the name of Elvira Jordan. Their contract provided that "Jordan would be artificially inseminated with Robert Moschetta's semen so as to bear his 'biological offspring.'" Additionally, "Jordan promised that Robert Moschetta could obtain sole custody and control of any child born" and that she would "sign all necessary papers to terminate her parental rights and 'aid' Cynthia Moschetta in adopting the child." For this service, the Moschettas agreed to pay Jordan $10,000 and provide for her living expenses.

In November 1989 Jordan became pregnant using Robert's sperm. By January 1990, however, the Moschettas were experiencing marital problems and in April Robert informed Cynthia he wanted a divorce. When Jordan heard of the Moschetta's marital problems, on May 27 while in labor, she began to reconsider the surrogacy agreement and refused Robert's attempt to visit the child for several days immediately following its birth. Three days later, after receiving a promise from the Moschettas that they would stay together and work out their marital problems, Jordan relented and allowed the couple to take the baby home.

By November 1990, however, the Moschettas' marriage had deteriorated further and Robert left the family residence, taking the child with him. Cynthia responded by filing court papers seeking a legal separation from Robert and a determination by the court that she was the child's "de facto mother." In February 1991 Jordan joined the legal action, claiming that she and not Cynthia should be granted legal parental status.

The principal question before that court was who the legal mother of Marissa was. Or, from Cynthia's position, was there any way under California law for a woman who is neither a child's genetic mother nor the birth mother to establish herself as a legal parent sans a formal adoption? In its initial ruling the superior court determined that Robert Moschetta and Elvira Jordan were the child's legal parents and that as such they should share joint legal and physical custody of Marissa.

Robert, in his appeal of this ruling, contended that his wife and not

Jordan should be designated Marissa's legal mother. The crux of Robert's argument was fairly simple. Basically he argued that the Uniform Parentage Act allowed for the legal recognition of presumptive fathers and that if the court simply replaced the term *father* with *mother,* it could easily grant Cynthia presumed parent status as well.

The appellate court refuted this argument on several grounds. First, the judges argued that "in cases directly involving human reproduction, individuals of different sexes may be distinguished on the bases of different reproductive roles." This biological difference, they argued, allows judges to systematically exclude women from consideration under the presumed father statute because, after all, women become mothers differently than men become fathers.

Turning to the presumed father statute, they then argued that in order for the court to grant a married man presumed father status he must be considered fertile and theoretically capable of impregnating his wife. As was made clear in the surrogacy agreement, Cynthia was in fact sterile and thus physically incapable of producing a child. According to the court, Cynthia's presumed parent claim fails "because the court is already aware that she is not the child's "'natural' mother."

It is informative at this point to imagine what might have occurred if the tables had been turned, that is, if Robert had been sterile instead of Cynthia. Under these conditions, instead of approaching a surrogate mother to assist Robert in reproducing a child, the couple might have approached a male friend to assist Cynthia in reproducing a child. Had this occurred with routine medical supervision, Robert's presumed father status would have been protected under Family Code section 7613, which specifically protects the presumed parental status of sterile husbands whose wives, with their consent, conceive a child via physician-assisted artificial insemination. In fact, Family Code section 7613 is specifically designed to protect sterile men who enter into parenting agreements with their wives from challenges made by the children's biological fathers.

Additionally, the court argued that even if it set aside Cynthia's sterility for a moment, Robert's claim that Cynthia should be determined to be a

presumed parent still fails "because the presumption is not absolutely con-
clusive, and may be defeated by blood tests which show that the husband is
not the genetic father of the child." Although it may be the case that biology
has at times been used to trump presumed father status, the courts have traditionally allowed this to occur only when the biological father is actively
involved in the child's life. In this case, the biological mother, Jordan, relinquished Marissa when the child was just three days old and at that point
ceased to be the child's social parent.

The court's conclusion in this case treats biology as the definitive factor
in determining parental status, something the courts have historically applied with respect to women but not men. Indeed, as recently as 1998, the
California supreme court refused to entertain an "alleged" biological father's attempts to prove his parental status via a blood test over the objections
of the child's mother and her husband, even though the mother had been
both living with the "alleged" father and sexually active with him at the time
of her conception, and her husband made no attempt to assert that he was
genetically related to the child (see *Dawn D. v. Jerry K.,* 1998). By simply
refusing to entertain the evidence, the court shielded the husband from the
"alleged" biological father's claim.

The final argument made by the court refuting Robert's claim that
Cynthia should be recognized as Marissa's presumed mother rested on the
question of whether or not Cynthia had the ability to treat Marissa as her
natural daughter. Here Robert argued that

> because he and Cynthia took Marissa home from the hospital and
> Cynthia afterwards held the child out as her own, Cynthia should
> be presumed to be the natural mother because she "received" the
> child into her home. Therefore, just as Robert's "receiving" Marissa
> into his home would establish that he was the presumed father ...
> Cynthia's "receiving" Marissa into her home made Cynthia the
> child's presumed mother.

To this the court responded, "On the simplest level, the argument is
unpersuasive because Cynthia never held Marissa out as her 'natural' child.

There never was any doubt that Marissa has no biological, natural or genetic connection with Cynthia."

To understand the courts' refusal to allow Cynthia access to presumed parent status it is useful once again to reconstruct the reproductive scenario a court uses in these cases. This reproductive equation involves one male and one female who, as the court noted, play different reproductive roles. Put rather simply, with the exception of a brief flurry of activity surrounding ejaculation, males play a passive role in the reproductive scenario while their female partners perform all of the labor necessary to physically reproduce a child.

When Robert argued that Cynthia should be considered a presumed parent because she was married to him, the child's biological father, at the time of the child's conception and birth, he was unwittingly invoking this reproductive scenario. Within this scenario, the only role available to Cynthia, as a woman, was the physically active role. To successfully invoke the legal fiction supporting the presumed father statute the court would have to imagine the alleged presumed parent fulfilling his or her sex-appropriate role in this reproductive scenario. For men this means that judges must be able to imagine that they successfully completed an act of sexual intercourse with their wives. For women, however, this would require that judges imagine the wife physically reproducing the child herself, that is, achieving pregnancy, physically gestating the fetus, and giving birth. This, according to the court, was clearly impossible in this case.

In some ways Cynthia's dilemma resembles that of the lesbian nonbiological mothers. In both instances the courts' reliance upon a heterosexual model of the two-parent family in which the parental roles are highly gendered seriously limits the legal conceptualization of the mothering role. Indeed, mothers remain little more than women who physically reproduce children. And, as with the lesbian mother cases, to rule in favor of the nonreproductive mother would have required the courts to seriously disrupt the reproductive scenario by redefining women as potentially passive partners in reproduction.

Planting the Seeds of Change? *Buzzanca v. Buzzanca*

In a final case, *Buzzanca v. Buzzanca* (court of appeals, 1998), the court was faced with a marital dissolution case in which a wife sought her husband's support of a child they obtained through a gestational surrogacy agreement.[35] In this case, Luanne and John Buzzanca arranged to have an embryo, genetically unrelated to either of them, implanted in a surrogate who agreed to carry the fetus to term and then relinquish it to them.

Following the implantation procedure but before the child's birth, Luanne and John separated. When the baby was born Luanne took custody and began raising it as her own. When John sought formal dissolution of their marriage, Luanne filed a separate petition seeking to establish herself as the child's mother and requesting court-ordered child support from John. John responded by arguing that because neither he nor Luanne was biologically related to the child, and neither had legally adopted the child, they were not the child's legal parents. Because he was not a parent, John argued, he could not be held financially responsible for the child. If anything, he concluded, the child's surrogate mother was its natural mother and her husband its presumed father. The surrogate, in response to John's attempt to invalidate their contract and foist motherhood upon her, argued that she had—per their surrogacy contract—voluntarily relinquished all claims to the child and thus neither she nor her husband was its legal parent.

The superior court reached the conclusion that the child had no legal parents. After accepting a stipulation that neither the surrogate mother nor her husband was the child's legal parent, it went on to conclude that Luanne "could not be the mother because she had neither contributed the egg nor given birth [a]nd John could not be the father, because, not having contributed the sperm, he had no biological relationship with the child."

The appellate court, however, disagreed and ruled that Luanne and John were indeed the child's legal parents and that John, as the child's father, could be held financially responsible. This appellate decision is particularly interesting because the court proceeds to recognize a social

mother who by all accounts has no biological, adoptive, or stepparent relationship to a child. The court accomplishes this by first appointing John
parental status via the presumed father statutes, and then extending that
status to Luanne by arguing that she, as John's spouse, should have the
same access to presumed parental standing as does John. According to the
appellate court,

> The trial judge erred because he assumed that legal motherhood,
> under the relevant California statutes, could only be established in
> one of two ways, either by giving birth or by contributing an egg. He
> failed to consider the substantial and well-settled body of law hold-
> ing that there are times when fatherhood can be established by con-
> duct apart from giving birth or being genetically related to a child.
> The typical example is when an infertile husband consents to allow-
> ing his wife to be artificially inseminated.
>
> The same rule which makes a husband the lawful father of a child
> born because of his consent to artificial insemination should be
> applied here. Just as a husband is deemed to be the lawful father of a
> child unrelated to him when his wife gives birth after artificial insem-
> ination, so should a husband and wife be deemed the lawful parents
> of a child after a surrogate bears a biologically unrelated child on
> their behalf. In each case, a child is procreated because a medical
> procedure was initiated and consented to by intended parents. The
> only difference is that in this case—unlike artificial insemination—
> there is no reason to distinguish between husband and wife.
>
> So it is, of course, true that application of the artificial insemi-
> nation statute to a gestational surrogacy case where the genetic
> donors are unknown to the court may not have been contemplated
> by the legislature. Even so, the two kinds of artificial reproduction
> are exactly analogous in this crucial respect: Both contemplate the
> procreation of the child by the consent to a medical procedure of
> someone who intends to raise the child but who does not have any
> biological tie.

If a husband who consents to artificial insemination under >section 7613 is "treated in law" as the father of the child by virtue of his consent, there is no reason the result should be any different in the case of a married couple who consent to in vitro fertilization by unknown donors and subsequent implantation into a woman who is, as a surrogate, willing to carry the embryo to term for them. The statute, is, after all, the clearest expression of past legislative intent when the legislature did contemplate a situation where a person who caused a child to come into being had no biological relationship to the child. Indeed, the establishment of fatherhood and the consequent duty to support when a husband consents to the artificial insemination of his wife is one of the well-established rules in family law.[36]

Furthermore, the court differentiated its reasoning in this case from all previous decisions rendered in lesbian mother cases by arguing that

we are dealing with a man and woman who were married at the time of conception and signing of the surrogacy agreement, and we are reasoning from a statute, >section 7613, which contemplates parenthood on the part of a married man without biological connection to the child born by his wife.... It is enough to say that because the >Nancy S. and >West cases ... involve[ed] non married couples at the time of the artificial insemination, they are distinguishable.

Following this line of reasoning, the court concluded that John is a legal father because he "caused [this child's] conception every bit as much as if things had been done the old fashioned way." Luanne, the court determined, is a legal mother because she "is situated like a husband in an artificial insemination case."

Here, for the first time, California judges appear to crack the door on the venerable domain of the presumed father. They do so, interestingly enough, through a section of the Uniform Parentage Act (7613) that was specifically designed to extend presumed father status to infertile married men whose wives achieve pregnancy via artificial insemination—in other words, in cases where men other than the husbands are indisputably the biological fathers. The problem the court faces in attempting to employ section 7613 is that neither John nor Luanne really fits the definition of a parent as it is constructed in the statute.

The court resolved this apparent dilemma by focusing first on John and Luanne's marital status and then using that status to argue that John, as a married man, falls under the jurisdiction of section 7613. Here the court conveniently ignored the fact that the legislature clearly intended that married men be responsible for children born to their wives via assisted reproduction and that John, although married, was not married to either of the women biologically involved in reproducing this child. Having set that detail aside, the court then reasoned that married men, under section 7613, are legally responsible for children born via in vitro fertilization if their consent to the procedure can be reasonably interpreted as causing the birth of the child.

This argument was employable with regard to John because John, as a male, fits neatly into both the language of the statute and the gendered notions of biological reproduction that support it. In other words, John gains parental status, at least in part, because as a male, he has a gendered identity (man, husband, father) that coincides with both the language of the statute and the role the statute assigns to men as husbands. According to the statute, John, as both a man and a husband, could legally consent to the impregnation of a woman for the purpose of becoming a father.

It is telling that the court does not simply replace John with Luanne in the above reproductive scenario. In Luanne's case her gendered identity (woman, wife, mother) clashes with both the language of the statute and the role the statute assigns to women as wives. As both a woman and a wife, Luanne receives no statutory support when it comes to consenting to her spouse's reproductive activity. Not only is she, as a woman, considered incapable of consenting to the in vitro fertilization of her spouse, but even if she were seen as a wife consenting to her spouse's reproductive activity, that consent would be meaningless because wives don't automatically become the legal mothers of their husband's biological children.

To get around this hurdle the court engaged in a two-step maneuver. First, the court made John a father. Then, focusing on John and Luanne's marital status, they linked Luanne to John and declared her to be situated just like John in the reproductive scenario. By arguing that Luanne, through her marriage to John, was legally situated just "like a husband," they granted her honorary male status. As an honorary husband, she was ushered into the world of presumed parents based on the fact that her legal spouse had just acquired (reproduced?) a child.

Conclusion

The process of determining legal parental status for men and women in California is heavily influenced by gendered notions of reproduction and parenting. While biological reproduction requires both a male and a female, the act of parenting can be accomplished by any number and configuration of people. Historically, however, both the California legislature and the courts have used a biological model of reproduction as a template for the social family. This practice of tying social reproduction to biological reproduction has led the courts to conflate sex with gender in legal determinations of parental status, which has resulted in widely varying outcomes for men and women.

The most obvious example of the disparate treatment women and men receive as a result of this conflation of sex with gender involves the development of normative pathways to motherhood and fatherhood within the law. While legal determinations of "natural" motherhood remain tightly tied to biological reproduction, legal determinations of "natural" fatherhood encompass both biological and social reproduction. While some courts have concluded that these disparities are the result of the different biological roles men and women play in the reproductive scenario and are thus biologically determined making them both natural and inevitable, in reality these differences are social constructions whose origins remain deeply hidden within legal fictions lawmakers use to link together biological reproduction and social families.

These legal fictions, which are typically used to obscure the substitution of social fathers for biological fathers by allowing judges to pretend that the former is also the latter, simultaneously work to conflate gender (the social act of fathering) with sex (the biological act of fathering), making them appear inseparable within the legal construct of the "natural" father. Because judges are required to at least imagine that the social parent could be the biological parent before employing the legal fiction—thus maintaining the fictitious link between biological reproduction and the legal construction of family—the gender of the social parent in the legal fiction remains tightly tied to the sex of the missing reproducing parent.

This heterosexualization of the social family seriously limits the courts' ability to legally recognize mothers who co-parent with other women. Although a nonbiological mother co-parenting with a child's birth mother may act exactly like a comparably situated nonbiological father, the courts are unable to employ the legal fiction with regard to the nonbiological mother because she, when coupled with the biological mother, cannot be imagined to be a reproducing pair. While this use of a biological model of reproduction has led the courts to believe the issue to be about the sex of the co-parent, in reality the issue is not the nonbiological mother's sex but rather the court's interpretation of what she theoretically could or could not have accomplished because of her sex. As soon as the court moves away from genetic consanguinity, however, the issue ceases to be about the sex of the co-parent; after all, the presence or absence of actual male reproductive organs is irrelevant. Instead this type of decision is based on gender and is driven by the courts' wish to maintain the fictitious link between biological reproduction and the legal construction of family.

While women who co-mother with other women are disadvantaged by the court's insistence on maintaining the two-parent family as heterosexual domain, nonbiological mothers who co-parent with men fare almost as poorly. As this analysis of surrogacy cases makes clear, the court's conflation of sex with gender within the legal fiction requires that nonreproducing women be given a different role in the fictitious reproductive scenario than nonreproducing men. Although nonreproducing women may act in the same way as nonreproducing men in assisted reproductive arrangements—that is, they either consent to or contract for the fertilization of another for the purpose of producing a child they wish to parent—nonreproducing men, especially married men, are given license to direct the reproductive behavior of others, especially their wives, with the result being that their reproductive intent is honored by the courts. At the same time, nonreproducing women, even married women, enjoy no similar protection by the courts, with the possible recent exception of married women who seek to mother children whom the courts have found to be legally free of ties to their biological parents. When taken together, positioning within marriage the legal ability to contract with one's partner to co-parent a child to whom one is not biologically related, restricting legal marriage to couples consisting of male-female pairs only, and employing a biologically bound legal fiction as the sole means of determining "natural" parent status for nonbiological parents work to ensure that the only persons able to initiate the reproduction of a child for the purpose of creating a legally recognizable parenting relationship with that child are heterosexual married men.

Notes

1. I use the terms *nonbiological mother* and *nonbiological parent* throughout the chapter to emphasize the social and psychological relationship these adults developed with the children they were co-parenting. I am aware that in a strict legal sense this terminology is improper because legally these women have been determined by the courts not to be mothers. Still, it is clear from the court records that the women, with the encouragement of the children's biological mothers, functioned as social and psychological mothers while they lived with the children (and in some cases for years after). I use the terminology with the caveat that the reader should keep in mind that I an describing a social and psychological relationship, not necessarily a legal one.

2. Othermothering in African-American communities occurs when women nurture and physically care for children who are biologically not their own. While these women

clearly hold the status of mother within their communities, individuals outside those communities rarely recognize that status as legitimate. For a detailed discussion of "othermothering," see Stack 1974; Collins 1987, 1990; James 1993.

3.   Modell (1998: 159), in writing about Hawaiian culture, identifies women and men who physically and emotionally nurture children in families created outside Western traditional means. Specifically, Modell identifies the cultural practices of *hanai* and *ohana*, which facilitate the "coming together of people who assume responsibility for and loyalty to one another." Among the native people of Hawaii, Modell explains, the cultural practice of *hanai*, an informal adoption in which "one person [gives] a child to another without the necessity of going to court," allows for "a continuity from one generation to another that does not depend on genealogy but on generosity." This practice leads to the creation of families known as *ohana*, "a group of coresiding individuals who consider themselves kin."

4.   Interestingly, it is only after the demise of traditional legitimacy cases, cases in which the birth mother was always assumed to be the legitimate mother, that the legal question of legitimacy for women has arisen.

5.   See, among others, D'Emilio 1983; Benkov 1994; Conrad and Schneider 1992; Weston 1991; Duberman, Vicinus, and Chauncey, Jr. 1989; Jay and Young 1992; and Plummer 1992) for a discussion of the development of lesbian and gay communities over the second half of the twentieth century.

6.   In most limited consent or second parent adoptions the custodial parent (the child's biological mother) agrees to relinquish her right to be the child's sole parent so that her partner may become the child's second parent. Thus she is agreeing to a limited relinquishment. In traditional independent adoptions both biological parents agree to relinquish all rights to the child so that another individual(s) may become the child's legal parents. This is called a full relinquishment. As in stepparent adoptions, in limited consent adoptions the noncustodial parent (usually the biological father) must relinquish all his rights to the child before the custodial parent's partner may be legally added as the second parent.

7.   Because provisions for the limited-consent adoption are not specifically included in California's adoption statutes and no higher court challenges regarding its legality have been heard, the determination as to its legality is made at the superior court level. While many superior court judges have interpreted the adoption statues as allowing for this type of adoption, some have disagreed with this interpretation and refused to grant them.

8.   I do not speak to the issue of gay men in this chapter because there have been no appellate or supreme court cases involving gay men in the state of California.

9.   In 1874 the California legislature passed an amendment to Civil Code 230 adding

that "a child born before wedlock becomes legitimate by the subsequent marriage of its parents."

10.   Civil Code section 193 was first enacted in 1872 (Bancroft and Whitney 1996). It has since been superseded by the Uniform Parentage Act.

11.   The legal right of the nonbiological father over children born to his wife remains intact even in cases where their marriage is later determined to be technically not legal (Bancroft and Whitney 1996).

12.   137 Cal. 298, 301, 70P. 91.

13.   17 Cal. 4th 932, 952 P. 2d 1139, 72 Cal. Rptr 2d 871.

14.   The adoption of Family Code section 4351.5 in 1982 changed this situation slightly by allowing judges to recognize stepparents as parents for the limited purpose of granting visitation awards during divorce proceedings.

15.   My own research suggests that lesbian couples who are of mixed race often seek sperm from donors who are racially similar to the nonbiological mother in an effort to produce children who look like both parents.

16.   The one exception is *Johnson v. Calvert*, in which the surrogate mother was black, the genetic mother was Filipina, and the biological father was white.

17.   222 Cal. App. 3d 1597, 1600, 272 Cal. Rptr. 520.

18.   228 Cal. App. 3d 831, 279 Cal. Rptr. 212.

19.   This definition of de facto parent is taken from In re B. G. (1974) (11 Cal. 3d 679, 523 P. 2d 244, 144 Cal. Rptr. 444).

20.   228 Cal. App. 2d 820, 39 Cal. Rptr. 820.

21.   53 Cal. App. 3d 837, 126 Cal. Rptr. 38.

22.   In *Valle* the father, Manuel Valle, obtained custody of his five-year-old nephew and one-year-old niece when he and his wife, Lucinda, smuggled them into the United States from Mexico using false birth certificates that listed them as the children's natural parents. When Manuel and Lucinda divorced several years later Lucinda sought to have Manuel declared the children's legal father and ordered to pay child support.

23.   Johnson v. Johnson (1979), 88 Cal. App. 3d 848, 152 Cal. Rptr. 583.

24.   There were at least two other cases heard between 1991 and 1997. These cases, both similar in fact to *Curiale* and *Nancy S.*, broke no new legal ground and thus will not be discussed here.

25.   This case was heard in the superior court and thus the decision was neither published nor available to the general public. I received case materials, including the superior court's decisions, directly from lawyers involved in the case. All direct quotes in this case, unless otherwise noted, come from the court's written decision.

26.   The court further explained that the reasons the nonbiological mother lost "psychological parent" status included "some serious mistakes in her conduct with the

children since the break-up of the parties" including actions that undermined the biological parent's parental authority.

27.   59 Cal. App. 4th 302, 69 Cal. Rptr. 2d 160.

28.   All quotes for this case, unless otherwise noted, come from the pleadings filed with the court. The decision to grant the nonbiological mother visitation was delivered in the form of a minute order containing very little information other than the decision itself.

29.   5 Cal. 4th 84, 98–99, 19 Cal. Rptr. 2d 494, 851P. 2d 776.

30.   This supreme court decision overturned the lower court decision in which Justice Richard Parslow ruled that Johnson was more like a temporary foster mother than a biological mother and thus had no parental rights (Grayson 1998).

31.   As Hartouni (1994) and Grayson (1998) both note, the lower court decision was replete with descriptions of Johnson as nothing more than a temporary caretaker—something like a temporary foster mother.

32.   The trial court originally ruled that Anna Johnson was not a mother to this child and thus had no right to either custody or visitation. This decision prevented Johnson from developing a parenting relationship with the child (Grayson 1998).

33.   Family Code section 7613 specifically protects the presumed parental status of sterile husbands whose wives, with their consent, conceive a child via physician-assisted artificial insemination.

34.   25 Cal. App. 4th 1218, 1224–1226, 30 Cal. Rptr. 2d 893.

35.   61 Cal. App. 4th 1410, 72 Cal. Rptr. 2d 280.

36.   In support of this point the court cites *Sorensen,* where the high court ruled that a "reasonable man who . . . actively participates and consents to his wife's artificial insemination in the hope that a child will be produced whom they will treat as their own, knows that such behavior carries with it the legal responsibilities of fatherhood and criminal responsibility for nonsupport" (>Id. at p. 285, 66 Cal. Rptr. P. 2d 495).

8

Uno hace cualquier cosa por los hijos

Motherwork and Politics in Sandinista Nicaragua

Diana Mulinari

What are the consequences of a political discourse that relies upon the image of the suffering and powerful mother? The answer to this question is historically specific. This chapter has two aims. The first one is to explore how the political equation of maternal work and politics that undermined the Somoza dictatorship and supported the Sandinista revolution also contributed to the Sandinista electoral failure in 1990. The second is to highlight the political significance of maternal work during revolutionary struggles. I suggest that within Latin American patriarchal ideology, motherhood is reified at the same time that the practices of mothers are devalued. It is in this space between a discourse that idealizes motherhood and a devaluation of real maternal work that women carve an expanded definition of the political.

Feminist theory has come under sustained criticism for its universalistic, homogenized, and ethnocentric assumptions about women.[1] Alison Bailey (1995) suggests that attempts to understand maternal practices as something all women have in common have not only silenced the diversity of maternal practices but marginalized theoretical questions that emerge from differences among mothers. U.S. black feminist scholarship has challenged the traditional definitions of mothering that derive from white middle-class perspectives aiming to place the maternal experience of African-American women at the center of feminist analysis and research.

Patricia Hill Collins (1994) conceptualizes the field of reproduction and the experience of mothering for ethnic women as a space for survival, identity, and empowerment. Collins asserts that, in contrast to white middle-class children, the survival of racial/ethnic children cannot be taken for granted. One major task confronting U.S. black mothers is that of mediating on their children's behalf in a hostile white-dominated society. Mother-work means helping children to develop meaningful identities within a society that devalues their history and culture. Like those women in Latin America who lack racial and class privileges, African-American mothers in the United States must find ways to fulfill their children's needs for growth and survival in a context of struggle.

Feminist research has sought to make visible women's central role in reconceptualizing the political sphere. Recent social action by women in Latin America has taken a variety of forms and had a number of objectives, ranging from their participation in guerrilla movements, church-linked women's groups, and human rights movements to protest over public services.[2] Since the 1980s a number of texts have placed gender firmly in the center of the Latin American studies research agenda. Several themes have emerged in this literature: the politicization of the private sphere, the development of a gendered citizenship emerging from women's political participation in social movements, and the creation of new rituals of resistance, among others. Sheryll Lutiens (1995) suggests that feminist theorizing in the region has raised new questions about women, problematizing bodies, identities, and agency while asking repeatedly and in innovative ways about the gendered dynamics of global capitalism, states, and domestic and international politics.[3]

Maternal Work and Motherwork

Nancy Naples (1992) reveals the power and continuity of community work performed by women in low-income neighborhoods in the United States. Through the voices of the African-American and Latino women in her study we learn that activist mothering is transmitted from mother to daughter, weaving a cross-generational network. For these mothers good mothering includes social activism to address the needs of the children and the community. Her research shows the centrality of class and "race" in shaping maternal practices and different forms of political activism.

Maternalism has been one way through which Latin American women explain political actions that expand their traditional roles as mothers to the public sphere. Elsa Chaney (1979) focuses on the political activity of upper- and middle-class women in Peru and Chile and argues that it is the ideology of motherhood that compels women to justify their political involvement in terms of an extension of mothering, as an extrapolation of femininity to public life. She suggests that because policies on care and reproduction are devalued in our society, women who situate themselves in the realm of the familial in politics are actually removed from central decisions in policy making. Chaney's material invites further interpretation, inasmuch as men are not conceptualized as entering politics as fathers. By contrast, women as mothers can be and have been called upon to sacrifice themselves for the collective.

Throughout the history of women's political participation maternalism has been one of the most common ways through which women themselves explain their actions—as an expansion of their traditional roles as mothers into the public sphere. Feminist researchers have shown that women's participation in maternalist movements has been central in the establishment of welfare states in Western societies.[4] Maternalist claims have also drawn feminists into alliances with racist and nationalist agendas.[5]

The experience of the so-called Madwomen of the Plaza de Mayo in Buenos Aires—a group of women that began to meet every Thursday at noon because each one had a family member missing—and of the Mothers of El Salvador and Guatemala clearly shows the powerful ways through which the feminist slogan "the personal is political" has been re-created in the Latin American context.[6] Maria del Carmen Feijoó (1989), reflecting on the Argentinean experience, argues that while subsequent events proved everywhere in Latin America that the notion that women as mothers were safer from repression was a myth, motherhood allowed at least a symbolic refuge as a basis for political action. According to June Nash (1990), the capitalist economic crisis in the 1990s has threatened the sphere of reproduction in Latin America by breaking down the subsistence sectors. The author suggests that a shift has taken place from struggles against exploitation in the place of work to a struggle for survival in the community. She further argues that it is mostly women's commitment to families and communities that create this new political arena where women often raise the issue of the right to survival rather than the issue of exploitation in the labor market as their basic political goal. Struggles have been focused on collectivizing and (politicizing) survival.

Women in Nicaragua

Any discussion of women in Nicaragua during the Sandinista revolution (1979–1989) must start with an understanding of their history of poverty and marginalization. Nicaragua was one of the poorest countries in Latin America, and women in Nicaragua, as elsewhere, bore a disproportionate share of these hardships. In 1967 the life expectancy in Nicaragua was fifty-seven years.[7] Poor urban women suffered from poverty-related diseases, and houses lacked both sanitary facilities and clean water supplies. Two out of three children under five years old were undernourished.[8]

Gender ideology within Somozaist discourses emphasized traditional Catholicism with a man as the master of the home exerting authority over dutiful and caring women. Machismo promoted the view that having many children with different women was a proof of virility. Men say: *"Me tiene tres hijos"* (they have three of my children).[9] Somoza's legal system institutionalized discrimination against women. As the head of the family, the husband had the right to collect his wife's salary and exercise total control over their legally acknowledged children. While divorce laws allowed a man to end a marriage because of his wife's adultery, a man's infidelity was not penalized. Nicaraguan feminist researchers have explored the impact of the Sandinista revolution on women's lives, suggesting that despite its shortcomings, the Sandinistas' programs in certain key areas such as work, health, housing, and education have been a major accomplishment in a poor, war-torn Latin American country.[10]

What made the Nicaraguan experience unique was the visibility, presence, and influence of women demanding the inclusion of gender issues within the revolutionary agenda. This is not an automatic product of national liberation struggles. For example, feminism did not emerge from Cuba as a grassroots movement. The fact that Nicaragua's grassroots sectors, particularly urban working-class and rural women, took a significant leadership role in defining a gender agenda is unique in the Latin American experience.

According to Helen Collinson (1990: 152), AMNLAE, the Sandinista women's organization, has undergone several changes largely as a response to the challenges and the pressures of several women's groups. [11] This process of reorganization resulted in six hundred public meetings with more than forty thousand women during April and May 1985. Women gathered to generate proposals and discussed sexuality, reproductive rights, workplace discrimination, and domestic violence. Norma Chinchilla (1990) suggests that Nicaraguan feminists have succeeded in their efforts to articulate class, gender, and national sovereignty into what she defines as a broader and democratic revolutionary popular feminism.

Research Setting

My research experience has been guided by feminist efforts to develop reflexive methodologies.[12] It grows out of my location as a Latin American mother and daughter as well as from my experience as an Argentinean woman forced into exile.[13] My research is framed in a specific historical period and in a specific urban setting, and it focuses on a specific group of women. The knowledge I claim to possess has developed from two central sources: my dialogue with women leaders of the grassroots organizations, on one hand, and hours and hours of conversation with politically engaged Nicaraguan women from an urban working-class neighborhood, on the other.[14]

Urban poor Nicaraguan women were far more prominent in the defense of the revolution than in the counterrevolution, the popular barrios and the grassroots Sandinista organizations being the engendered landscape of their political practice.[15] I used participant observation while living with a family in a Managua barrio, first in 1988 and then in 1989 to complete four months of data collection.

Women's lives in the barrio cannot be understood without an analysis that explores the interrelation of class and gender. The women of my neighborhood had seldom relied on a male breadwinner.[16] A Nicaraguan popular saying bears witness to this: "A mother for a hundred children and a father for none." But they were not alone. On the contrary, the barrio's households were extended webs of kin relationships whose axis is a mother, her daughters and sons, her sisters and brothers, and all their children.[17] The three hundred houses that constituted my neighborhood had an economy based on a broad range of income-generating activities. Most women in the barrio were engaged in different forms of self-employment covering a range of legal, quasi-legal, and illegal activities, the exception being factory workers and those who worked for the Sandinista state.[18] Four of five households had children under eighteen. Women headed two of five households.[19] In four of five houses in my neighborhood the residents had what they conceptualized as a kin member living nearby.[20] This barrio economy, though quite invisible to the outsider, places a strong emphasis on mutual aid and reciprocity, and is fundamental to the production and reproduction of life. It is also the location of women's maternal work. It is from the space of the barrio that women constitute themselves as political subjects, organizing themselves in the struggle for the rights of everyday life. Throughout Latin America, popular neighborhoods are at the core of a gender experience of citizenship.[21]

Mothers, War, and Militarization

In 1982 Nicaragua became militarized; the war effort dominated Sandinista policies and pervaded public and private life. The contra army operated from military camps in neighboring Honduras, mounting low-intensity warfare against the Sandinista state. In 1986 war damages amounted to 60 percent of Nicaragua's export earnings, and defense spending took up half the national budget.[22] The country suffered from a U.S. embargo beginning in 1985. Casualties mounted, and forty-six thousand lives were lost between 1982 and 1987. The direct losses to the national economy were estimated at U.S. $3 billion. According to official statistics, a quarter of a million people were displaced.[23]

Two groups, the Patriotic Front of Mothers and Relatives and the Mothers of Heroes and Martyrs brought together the women whose children had been killed in action. According to the women's organization data, over eleven thousand women in Managua are mothers of children killed or "disappeared" in the war. One of those groups of women met weekly in front of the archbishop's house to request his assistance in locating relatives kidnapped by the contras. Every family mourned a member, neighbor, or friend. Listen to Sandra, a member of the women's organization responsible for political work among the mothers:

> The damage caused by the war is terrible. Fifty thousand people are affected by the war if one includes the disabled and the women who have been raped. I know a rural woman from Chontales who had four [young] children and now has four disabled children. We have to give political attention to the mothers. Sometimes we don't do it, and there is the danger that the right uses the pain of the mothers. Then we have got the issue of the disappeared. The dead are dead . . . and a mother may pray her nine days and at last accepts that he is not there anymore. . . . But the disappeared. I know a rural woman who went to the contras' camps in Honduras to look for a missing son. She was raped during the journey. All this hurts very much.

Sandinistas launched policies both to channel the support of mothers of the soldiers and to win political support of the mothers for the SPM (patriotic military service—two years of obligatory service for all men over eighteen). Daniel Ortega, as president and one of the Sandinistas' leadership, considered that it was AMNLAE's responsibility to "strengthen the consciousness of the mothers who in a very egoistic way oppose the need of the defense and hinder the integration of their sons in the revolutionary work."[24]

Gladys Baez, a Sandinista leader, explained why women, who had made up more than 38 percent of the guerrilla fighters, were not included or were included in very few numbers in the regular army (EPS): "Women have proved themselves to be heroic, combative, courageous and able. But we are not so tough, we march slower and above all we have children. You cannot have a regular army ready for instant mobilization based on a floating population."[25] Doris Tejerino supports her, explaining that the reason is not that women are incapable of performing military tasks but rather that women give motherhood a higher priority than their military responsibilities. Their assertion mirrors the Sandinista's shift from a revolutionary guerrilla group to a state ruling party, the shift from revolutionary struggle to war. To the extent that war was a predominantly male phenomenon and war heroes were primarily male, the society came to give its highest praise to skills and areas associated almost exclusively with men. Women's skills were praised, too, though—specifically their capacity for nurturing and self-sacrifice and their role in armed defense of the neighborhoods.

The *mamas,* as they called themselves, constituted a central element of the Sandinista revolution during the war period. There was in fact a striking official rhetoric praising the role of women as "Sandinista mothers." In practice this referred not to all mothers, not to women with small children, but to older women, grandmothers, who have always had a strong position within Nicaraguan culture. Sandinista discourse on mothers was woven within a class discourse. Sandinista mothers are women from the popular sectors who have lost their children during the insurrection or in the contra war. These mothers experienced a transformation of status after the death of their son or daughter. Their contribution to the revolution was acknowledged in terms of their "sacrifice." They were provided with a minimal extra amount of material resources, and their channels to the Sandinista leadership were broader compared to those of other women. They were also provided with economic support because of the loss of their son or daughter.

In Sandinista discourse, mothers are represented as altruistic and self-sacrificing. Sandinistas usually speak of *el dolor de una madre* (a mother's pain). Some of the organized mothers functioned also as guardians of "revolutionary morality," for example, ensuring that young women remained faithful to their fiancés while the young men were in the military service. The fact that they were acknowledged as the bearers of revolutionary ethos provided them with a claim to a monopoly on the truth, a claim that was often contested by younger women.[26]

Discourses of Sandinista motherhood were reinforced by the contra war. Sandinistas had a pronatalist discourse—legitimated by the war—in which women were praised as reproducers; *"bendita la panza que parió un Sandinista"* (holy the womb that gave birth to a Sandinista) was a slogan painted on one of Managua's walls. This slogan was actually expressing Sandinista rhetoric, insofar as it was officially asserted that women's duty was to replace the great losses of the war. Women's high fertility rates were given a new, "revolutionary" meaning.

The power of the Catholic Church and its opposition to reproductive rights is an important factor in explaining why this has been an area virtually ignored by Sandinista policy; however, it is not enough. In addition to the religious opposition to birth control and abortion, there existed without doubt a strong pro-birth lobby in Nicaragua even among the Sandinista leadership. Lois Wessel (1991) suggests that while the shortages of contraceptives cannot be blamed on an anti-choice policy, the absence of public education is harder to justify. While equal rights for women and men were established in the 1987 constitution, contraceptives and sex education were only minimally promoted.

In September 1987, at a meeting called to mark the tenth anniversary of the founding of AMNLAE, more than a thousand women gathered in Managua. President Ortega claimed that in the context of U.S. military aggression "one way of depleting our youth is to promote the sterilization of women in Nicaragua ... or to promote a policy of abortion." He also claimed that some women who were "aspiring to be liberated" had decided not to bear children, but he argued that such a woman negated her own role in ensuring "the continuity of the human species."[27] Nicaraguan feminists that I have interviewed often speak of this event. Ortega also claimed that the demand for abortion emanated from privileged middle-class Managuans; he was manipulating this sensitive issue during the war against the contras in order to demobilize Sandinista feminists who were campaigning together with unionized working-class and rural women for reproductive rights.

In the meetings of the Sandinista women workers association, it was a common practice for women to present themselves as the mother of a child killed in the insurrection or in the contra war: "I have given the revolution two sons, one who died in the insurrection and the other killed by the contras." These women were active in the revolution in different ways. However, they tended to emphasize their role as mothers; the sacrifice of their children represented their most valued political credential, particularly inasmuch as it allowed them to make demands of the Sandinista government. Maternal sacrifice is a strong political symbol, a symbol that for most Nicaraguans concentrates the suffering of the Nicaraguan people.

The equation of women as mothers with the mothers of the country is full of contradictions. What is the other side of the glorification of maternal sacrifice? The ways women have been valorized in their reproductive functions cannot be separated from the needs of war, revealing experiences similar to those of other societies during war. Nicaraguans were not an exception to this pattern.[28] Judy Kimble and Elaine Unterhalter (1982), discussing the South African experience, argue that to interpret women's reinforcement of traditional roles in postrevolutionary societies as a sign of subordination is an ethnocentric perspective. According to them, in such climates women's work and contributions are for the first time acknowledged. Through social programs the Sandinistas did try to ease the burden of women's mothering and recognize their importance for the revolution.

Many women I met discussed the gains of the revolution in terms of their mothering: access to higher education, better health care, and improved housing for their children.

However, I would like to differentiate the pain I have witnessed in Managuan barrios from the construction of a patriotic motherhood. The leaders of the revolution appeared together with the mothers in an alliance where motherwork and political activity were appropriated by a political class dominated by Sandinista men.

In 1984 women's resistance to their sons' mandatory military service increased. Dora María Tellez, one of the Sandinista representatives in Managua, asserted that she understood the feelings of the mothers, and compared them to the feeling her mother had when she became involved in the struggle.[29] Clara Murguialday (1990) argues that the same strength and cultural tradition that made mothers struggle against the dictatorship to protect their children was now manipulated by the Catholic Church and the political right in relation to the war effort.

I think that from the standpoint of mothers the context was different. While women relying on the ideology of motherhood had engaged as active and autonomous subjects in the struggle against Somoza, they were now being asked to remain passive and obedient, suffering in silence, while their children were sent to war.

Abuela, Tell Me a Story

In discussing what Nicaraguan mothers call "just talking women's talk," I draw on Antonio Gramsci's (1971) concept of cultural hegemony and on feminist historians' notions of oral narratives.[30] The use of narratives has a long tradition in political science, history, anthropology, and sociology. However, due to social science conceptions of what counts as true, narratives are understood in terms of an epistemological Other and in contrast to the hegemonic voice of the researcher. In this hierarchical division of labor, the informants provide the narratives and social science provides the explanations. According to Margaret Somers (1994), a shift has taken place in the way scholars think about narratives; instead of conceptualizing them as forms of representation (telling historical stories), now researchers see social life as storied and the narrative as an ontological condition of social life.

In my research, narratives (both personal and collective) provided a discourse from marginal locations that challenged the powerful Western discourses through which the third world is seen as advancing when its representations are similar to those of the center. Let's listen to Doña Adelina, a Sandinista grandmother:

> It was during the good time, the time of the health campaign.... We got a *chele* who was going to work with our CDS [the Sandinista neighborhood committee]. [31] There he comes, dressed as for the mountain with military boots [laugh] to the meeting we [the mothers] were holding at Doña María's place. He had a black notebook and said that we had to do things right from the beginning [laugh]. So he said. The same afternoon at the hour of the soap opera [*telenovela*] [laugh] he went from house to house and asked the one who opened the door how many adults and children were living in the house. And poor devil [*pobrecito*] he found himself listening to Doña Ana [laugh] who told him the whole story of Alberto [Doña Juana's husband, who had another household in another city and sometimes was in Managua and sometimes not], of La Gladys and her three kids who were living with her now that she at last had left her husband, La Lorena who normally did not live with her but was now living with her because her husband was in the mountains. And then the young children. One was in Cuba but his fiancée who was pregnant was living with Ana [laugh]. The poor *chele* was getting crazy. We had told him from the beginning that we better take all the vaccines with us and give them to everybody in the house. He was a good guy, a revolutionary. He worked very hard afterwards. The *cheles pobrecitos* they are so accustomed to living alone that they do not understand that here in Nicaragua we help each other. We live together [*hechos un bollo*].

One of the most powerful aspects of these narratives is the self-presentation of women as knowing their own communities and society. Another is their active refusal to portray themselves as passive victims. Revolutionary leader Omar Cabezas (1989: 3) tells us that the first time he saw the name of Sandino on one of the walls of the city, his first reaction was to turn to his grandmother, who told the children the story of how her family had lost everything they owned because they supported Sandino. Ten years later his grandmother's stories would become Nicaraguan history. Many women of my neighborhood enjoyed telling stories about their participation and that of the whole neighborhood in the revolution. Doña Rosaura and other Nicaraguan mothers I met in the barrio also told their family histories again and again. She always began with: "Do not forget that we are poor but we are decent and we do not bow down" (*no agachamos la cabeza*).

The women I knew identified themselves as authoritative voices to tell the unwritten story of their communities. While they often began their personal narratives with the phrase "this is not a story to pass on," a story not worth sharing with others, they also claimed that asking the men about the family or the neighborhood was a *babosada* (a very stupid thing to do) because men did not keep things, did not remember the dead as women do.

Due to their central role in the family, urban poor women in Managua are central links in the political culture of the young generation. Many Latin Americans received their first political lessons in the kitchens. Describing and analyzing hidden forms of resistance and struggle has been the concern of a small number of Latin Americanists. Roger Lancaster (1988), in his discussion of religion, class consciousness, and revolutionary processes in Nicaragua, asserts that in the doxa of the people there already are preexisting conditions of self-reflective self-consciousness, which erupt in gossip about the ruling classes. William Rowe and Vivien Schelling (1991) illustrate how popular culture throughout Latin and Central America managed to keep alive traditions and conditions of resistance under conditions of oppression, and they argue that these are central in the articulation of political projects under conditions of rebellion. This hidden knowledge, this subversive way of constructing collective memories was alive in many kitchens in my Managuan barrio.[32]

In the Managuan kitchens I found the same kind of talk. Stories were told with irony, imagination, and skill. I do not assert that these stories are the "truth" about Nicaraguan women. Nor do I claim that these stories go beyond representation to provide the "real" or "authentic" voices of the revolution. I do, however, suggest that the women of my research, in their locations as mothers, both create and re-create collective memories while contesting the male unifying narratives and seeking to reshape social memory from their particular position. Urban working-class mothers' personal and collective narratives constitute part of the politics of resistance.[33]

Mothers against the Dictatorship

The disintegration and collapse of the Somoza system began in the early 1970s. According to John Booth (1982), two major events accelerated the process of popular disaffection. The first was the Christmas earthquake of 1972, which almost destroyed the city of Managua. Relief aid was largely pocketed by the Somoza family, and opposition steadily grew. The second event was the murder of Pedro Joaquin Chamorro, a respected journalist and a member of what was considered the bourgeois opposition to the dictatorship.

The Frente Sandinista de Liberación Nacional (FLSN), formed in 1961, was, despite its guerrilla activities, not politically relevant until 1977, when the name *Sandinista* became visible in the political arena. The Sandinistas did not lead the urban rebellions that broke out at regular intervals. Carlos Vilas (1986) and Carlos Nuñez (1980) have suggested that the fall of the Somoza dictatorship was not the fruit of an FSLN-planned political struggle. Rather, it was the product of different experiences of organization and struggle of the popular sectors, which the Sandinistas brought together in the last year of the insurrection.

The massive participation of Nicaraguan women cannot be understood as a sudden break that carried women into the realm of the political. Women were active and visible in all forms of resistance to the Somoza dictatorship. In 1970 market vendors from León confronted the Guardia (national guard) in order to reach the cathedral; students and workers went on hunger strikes to demand an end to the torture and repression in the rural areas. In response to the assassination of Chamorro, the mothers of prisoners and the "disappeared" occupied the United Nations building in Managua. Women themselves defended the building for twelve days. On January 30 six hundred women gathered in front of the building. Mothers also organized a campaign through anonymous letters sent to the wives of members of the Guardia, asking them to convince their men not to use weapons against Nicaraguan youth.[34]

Women going into the military barracks and demanding the release of their children was one of the first visible signs of open resistance in the urban areas. Nearly three-quarters of the people who took to the streets in the popular insurrection were twenty-five, and women supported their children in their clandestine activity and came to their defense when they were threatened and tortured by the Guardia. [35] As the ferocity of the dictatorship increased, the role of mothers assumed a political dimension.

In Nicaragua, the most important festival of the year is La Purisima, the Immaculate Conception of Mary, celebrated in early December. It is one of the biggest holidays, and Mary is honored almost as much as her son, Jesus. Mother's Day is an important day for Nicaraguans, and on this holiday those women who do not have children are honored as potential mothers. In 1978 La Asociación de Mujeres frentes a la Problematica Nacional (AMPRONAC) re-created it as a protest day with the slogan: The best present for a Nicaraguan Mother is a free Nicaragua. The women's organization also understood the actual mothering practice in Nicaragua, in which women are the primary economic providers for the children. The same year, thousands of women demonstrated in the streets of Managua with aprons and pots under the slogan "Our children go hungry." They were violently repressed. It is within this framework of moral authority as mothers that Nicaraguans women marched to the jails of the dictatorship and demanded of the soldiers, "Listen to the cry of a Nicaraguan mother. Respect the life of your brother."

The campaign launched by AMPRONAC and based on the slogan "Is it a crime to be young? Nicaraguan mothers, let us fight for the respect of the life of our children" engaged thousands of women in Managua. The women's organization gave voice to a sense of injustice against a state that made motherwork—through repression and economic crisis—impossible to continue, and opened the way to engagement in the broader political struggle.

Stories from the Barrio

"Aguero [a conservative politician who opposed Somoza] said that we should answer to the dictatorship as men." Nora, one of my best friends, was speaking to a small audience composed of her daughters and myself. "Well . . . we answered as women."

The earthquake is a metaphor many women use to explain to outsiders the brutality of the system. Said Nora: "We lost our home and Muriel and Osvaldo could not even walk. We had to eat on the floor like dogs. Somoza even stole the blood sent from abroad." The earthquake seems to be a turning point in women's personal political stories. Feelings of rage and anger are related to the earthquake, as in the case of Amanda, who is sixty and belongs to a "Sandinista family." She makes a living cooking food that her daughter sells in the market. Her story is typical of many women's experiences:

> I am not going to lie to you. During that time I prayed to God that Somoza would die and be sent to hell. What he did to us is not the work of a Christian. I could not take care of Silvio, who was a baby. The children lived among stones and wood and without a roof. And what he did with the blood . . .

Memories of the earthquake are so powerful that they cannot be added to the list of the injustices constructing the background of the engagement in revolutionary struggle. Sonia, forty-eight years old, with four children, had worked all her life as a market seller, and had recently found a man who could take care of her and her children. She remembered the earthquake in the following words:

> Well, we have always been poor here, but never been short of food. I always kept the house cleaned and tidy. During the earthquake we lost everything. We had to put the children to sleep on the floor. Now everybody is a *comandante*, a leader of the revolution, but in 1972 I could have killed him [Somoza] with my own hands.

Her reflection is worth discussing, because I repeatedly encountered women who as mothers could do (and did) what as women they never could think of doing. While the equation of women and violence was problematic, mothers' use of violence to defend themselves and their children from the assault of the Guardia was acceptable—and expected. Ruth Roach Pierson (1987) argues that in the Nicaraguan case the main sources of a distinct women's position on war and peace were motherhood and powerlessness, and that these led to women's active participation in violent action for the revolutionary cause.

In the first months after the earthquake women experienced a deeply gendered awareness of the injustice of the system. Somoza's response to the earthquake threatened women's ability to care for others; it also ruined many houses, the geographical location of women's power and the locus of years of patient effort. After the earthquake women's voices in the buses and the marketplaces were difficult to silence. Moreover, women were the ones who transmitted stories about the earthquake and Somoza's role to the children. Many of these children who were nurtured by their mothers' anger were *muchachos* of 1979.

The Muchachos and the Guardia

The *muchachos* designation not only described the biological age of the largest proportion of the Sandinistas but also explained how they were defined within the barrio: as "part of us," as "our children." I shall quote two reflections in order to illustrate my point. The first is made by Melba, a fifty-six-year-old factory worker with four children, active in the Sandinista workers union.

> I kneeled and prayed and prayed so that the *muchachos* would not be caught by the Guardia. Here, at home, they met. They were more than fifteen sometimes. This house was a safe house for the Sandinista front. What a pretty thing all that was. . . . We had to hide the *muchachos*. We had to protect them. . . . Poor things.

The second story is told by Luisa, who is thirty-four years old, has two children, and is sick and economically dependent on her family:

> It was not enough for them to put the *muchachos* in jail. No. Those beasts tortured them. You know Javier. He is so fragile and thin. They had him eight days without eating. The *muchachos* went to my mother's house and I cooked for them. . . . Poor things . . . nothing to eat, and sometimes they were also wet. We made them coffee. These stories are funny sometimes."

While in fact the Sandinistas confronted and defeated the Guardia more than once, the women tended to underline the innocence and the impotence of the *muchachos* against the cruelty and brutality of the Guardia. Their first relation with the Sandinistas was structured within women's praxis of caring for others. Women in the barrio mothered the Sandinistas through the insurrectional period.

"Do you remember when we hid Lauro in the garage and you told the Guardia that they could not come in there because a *señorita* was taking a bath?" Alejandra asked her mother, Nora. But Alejandra herself could not really remember; she was ten years old when the insurrection occurred. However, she "remembered" together with her mother. Everybody loved these stories, especially the ones in which the Guardia was deceived. Each family has two or three stories of their own. In the family with which I lived, the children loved to listen to the grandmother, Doña Rosaura, when she told about her "conversation" with the Guardia:

> They came to tell me that Martin [her son-in-law] was an agitator, an enemy of the state, a communist. And I answered, "Oh ... I did not know," and so on, speaking and speaking, making conversation with the Guardia with the baby in my arms. Then Martin, who was sleeping, woke up and called me from the kitchen. I got paralyzed. But the Guardia told me: "Go now, woman, and take care of your husband."

Even before the end of the story, the whole family laughed.

Mothers and Children

The women of my barrio went through countless sleepless nights. Not only did they know the injustices of the Somoza dictatorship, they had transmitted this knowledge to their children. Most of them also knew the price people paid for confronting the dictatorship. What happened, then, that made them engage in the revolution?

The women I talked to defined themselves as "from Sandinista families," with many of their own kin engaged in the struggle. Others had lived in "safe houses" throughout the resistance to the dictatorship.[36] Women told about these experiences with pride in their voices, but as a fact: "We have always been Sandinista." However, the same women expressed their personal commitment as a process, a moral dilemma in which they had to balance fear for their own lives and those of their children against their hatred of the dictatorship. Doña Rosaura's account, given above, is a description of some of the dilemmas that political participation entails.

Doña Rosaura's daughter, Muriel, remembered her mother during the first days of the struggle this way:

> [Speaking to her mother] Mother as for you ... It is better if you do not tell her [me, the author] anything.... [Speaking to me] My

mother, she has always hated Somoza. She raised us with this hate. When the Sandinistas made an action, she used to say, "God forgive me, but the Somozistas have been asking for this." But when my sisters began to get involved, to get together with the *muchachos,* you wouldn't imagine how she turned out to be. It looked as if she had begun to like Somoza a little bit.

Women had given their children the first lessons in politics, but women also bear the collective memory of defeat and repression, of the uselessness of confronting the dictatorship. When Muriel left, her mother picked up the conversation:

I am going to be sincere with you. I am not as courageous as the others. I thought, "They are going to kill them. They are going to kill her. They are crazy." But do you think that they listened to me? It was not that I did not have revolutionary consciousness [*conciencia revolucionaria*], it was that I was so afraid for them.

To support the children in the revolutionary struggle implied a transgression of one of the fundamental laws in the practice of mothering: never to risk the life of the child. For these women it meant the difficult moral decision of allowing their children to risk their lives. Many women eventually decided that the best way to protect the lives of their children was to support them in the struggle. In the words of Doña Adelina, the mother of one Sandinista woman and Doña Rosaura 's *comadre* (the word means "close friend" or "member of the female network"): "Considering what was happening, we had no other choice than to support them. As a mother I felt that pain and tried to support [my daughter]."

Several women I met shifted from a position of supporting revolutionary men to one of active political participation through their children. The young in the community (both men and women) recorded their mothers as their first political teachers, and many of them tried to show their mothers that politics was about what they have taught them. Josefina, a Sandinista mother, put it succinctly:

> You know, all these years, we have been fighting together with my
> *compañero*. . . . He never spoke to me about the revolution. . . . The
> children did. They talked to me about the revolution. My children
> always tell me that I [laughs] made them revolutionary. . . . They say
> that I have taught them to be Christians, to share with others even
> when we did not have enough ourselves [*aunque no tuvieramos para
> tortilla*]. It is me, they say, that made them Sandinistas.

Women's political action was embedded in their personal relations, particularly in their affective ties to Sandinism as part of the family and kinship tradition of stories and experiences and in their knowledge of the bitter life history of many of those they cared about most. The women of my neighborhood expressed their concerns and acted politically only in the context of these relationships, which were fundamental for their lives. They participated in the struggle in the spirit of the dreams about social justice that they shared with their menfolks. However, their participation was from a different social position than men's. It was both the repression and the brutality of the Somoza regime threatening their children and the economic situation that made their maternal work impossible that provided the basis for their participation in politics.

Gender Struggle and Maternal Work

Most of the narratives of this second period, when women had decided to support the children, ended with "A mother must defend her children" or "A mother who does not defend her children when they are in danger is not a mother." For these mothers, good mothering comprised all kinds of actions, including violent social protest to secure the growth of their children.[37]

Women explained their political actions, particularly those where traditional gender boundaries were crossed (being away, traveling, changing the domestic routine in order to go to meetings), in terms of their moral duties as mothers. Women in my neighborhood did underline and defend their reputation as "good mothers." Moreover, they strongly argued that "good mothering" required women's political participation. Their need to defend their mothering must be understood in the light of men's claims that women's political activity implied a deterioration of their motherwork.[38] Maternal work was a field for gender struggle in the neighborhood. Women were often confronted with male resistance (for example, encountering a drunken husband when coming home from a meeting), and many men often characterized female political activism as simply a way for women to abandon the home in search of sexual adventures.

Listen to Laura, who is thirty-five years old and responsible for the health brigade activities in the community. She has five children.

> To organize myself . . . he was the issue. Before the insurrection he did not say anything. On the contrary, he spoke a lot with his *compañeros* about how much he supported me [*se vanagloriaba*]. But he complained and fought all the time because he did not have his clothes and the supper. I got up at four o'clock in the morning and did all the housework so that he could not say anything.

In short, women organized their political activities so that they could still meet the expectations of maternal work. This fact is central to women's relationship to the field of the political. Men's time agenda changes radically because of their political activities. Women's remains the same despite their political activities. It is in the context of the gender struggle within the neighborhood that one must understand Sandinista women's assertion that staying at home was a proof of bad mothering. A woman who did not participate in the community's activities was not a "bad Sandinista"; she was a "bad mother."[39]

Doña Rosaura, when discussing her trip outside Managua to meet her daughter who was working in the Literary Crusade after the triumph of the revolution, asserted:

> I thought that if my daughter can do it, I can too. And there we went, old as we were, you should have seen us . . . if somebody could

have seen us they probably thought we were crazy . . . but we were doing it for our children . . . you know . . . you are a mother, you understand how it is. A mother does whatever she has to do to support her children.

This statement expressed an ambiguity I frequently encountered in the stories told about women's political participation. The joy and the empowerment women experienced were often silenced, and the stories were often phrased in terms of maternal sacrifice.

Well it was . . . you go out of the house, meet a lot of friends, keep up with one another. . . . After all these years of suffering . . .With this thing, the Crusade, I got a lot of new friends [*nuevas comadres*]. Then when they asked me if I wanted to be responsible for some of the political things in the barrio, I said yes. Even if it is more sacrifice, I had to do these things, it is good for the children and the neighborhood.

The centrality of maternal suffering in women's representation of self within Latin American culture has been linked to the influence of the Catholic Church and its Marian symbolism. Feminist social anthropologist Ruth Behar (1993), who has translated the life story of Esperanza, a Mexican woman, suggests that Esperanza experiences her life as worthy of being told because of her notion of being inspired by the Christian narrative, in which suffering (and particularly bodily suffering) is linked to redemption. Discussing childbirth, Doña Rosaura concluded with the following phrase: "Men may have courage, but no man can suffer as a woman." But discourses on maternal suffering are not related to a subordinated, passive waiting for the decisions of God. Women often use metaphors of maternal suffering to illuminate their ability of active survival, locating their claims to know in their lived experience as suffering mothers. The *mamas* of the neighborhood often told me: "You understand, Diana, you have children . . . you have also suffered." The best way to criticize another women was to assert (as Nora once did) that "she has never suffered . . . she knows nothing." However, not all women phrased rights and political concerns in the language of maternal suffering. Nora was both angry and concerned when she said to her mother:

> You have suffered, I have suffered too. But I do not want my daughter to suffer. Take away from your head all this thing about suffering. I want them to have rights [*que tengan derechos y que no sufran mas*].

I think that I can understand (and support) Nora's analysis. A language of maternal suffering has been used in the neighborhood as a gendered language of resistance under hard conditions of oppression; however, a different language is needed if the aim is not to resist but to subvert gender relations.

Women and War: The Neighborhood

Said Doña Rosaura of her own neighborhood:

> Only in this block, for example, each house, each family had some member killed. Marina had two sons killed during the underground struggle in 1977. Catalina has lost three children: two sons and a daughter who died during the insurrection. The woman who owns the kiosk had two sons killed in the military service, and it seems that Luisita's husband has been kidnapped by the contras.

Mothering implied a different practice in a Nicaragua at war than after the revolution. It was a practice constrained by the Sandinistas' discourses on patriotic motherhood. The *muchachos* had turned into an army; women had to send their children to war. While both young men and women of the barrio participated in the insurrectional period and shared the literacy campaign and the first years of the revolution, *la guerra* (as the war against the contras is commonly called) reinforced old patterns and hierarchies of gender.

In my first visit to Nicaragua in 1988 I met soldiers who were ten years old when the revolution triumphed in 1979. They had grown up in the barrio playing baseball under the shadow of the air defense batteries. I also met mothers who confirmed my feelings that the context was very different. Doña Adelina was very proud of her son who had been killed when he was seventeen years old:

> He was really growing up and you know . . . the dictatorship . . . I always thought that my children were going to grow up fine even if we were poor. He always told me, "I know that you are going to support me, you are a Christian mother and you like to pray, but for us the Christianity we practice is different." . . . My son . . . ask in the neighborhood. Everybody loved him.

She speaks of her son as a person who chose to engage in a political struggle. However, she shifts to the passive voice when she refers to the son who is now in the army: "They are going to send him to the mountains. . . . It is because the contras just won't stop."

Women did not speak of their children's future as soldiers with the same pride as they did when they spoke of what the children were going to do after they finished military service. "He is so intelligent, he is going to be an engineer. Well, that is, after he has been in the army." That their children were going to continue studying—the first in most families to have access to higher education—was something of which maternal hearts were proud, and it was a daily subject of conversation. Military service was not; rather, it was something children must go through. Who would be at home the next year when I came back was discussed loudly in the summer of 1988. "Augusto and Elvin, they will be leaving for the mountains, and then next year Roger and Martin. But then, then we have sent all of them. . . . Then if God helps us they are going to the university," Luisa concluded.

Many women expressed views similar to Luisa's: "I want my son to be a good revolutionary, I want him to study, to work and to be useful to the revolution." To study and to work—no mention of soldiers and heroic battles."[40] Other voices in the barrio taught me that the two years in the army was not only an emotional problem. The domestic economy was endangered when three or four sons were enrolled in the army. In the words of Elsa, a widow and petty vendor, "What I want to say is that one son must stay in the city. I feel very uncomfortable because I am poor.... It is not that I am reactionary.... This problem must be contemplated ... one must think of the mothers that have only one son."

Sofia, a woman who had been engaged in the insurrection and in the first years of the revolution, claimed that "it is not the sons of the Sandinistas who are sent to the mountains." Another woman explained to me why she supported the Sandinistas: "I support the Sandinistas ... everything to the Sandinistas ... so that all this might end once and for all.... I do not want to send my grandchildren to the mountains."

Most of the women I met expressed a feeling of resignation and powerlessness around this issue. Very few blame the Sandinistas for the war. Most of them hate the contras and U.S. intervention. But children in the barrio were not raised to be soldiers. Women raised them for the promise of the revolution they struggled for, not for war.

The Sandinista revolution was not defeated overnight. When visiting Nicaragua in 1988 I heard in the neighborhood where I carried out my fieldwork many comments that began with, "Of course I am Sandinist, but ..." These were the voices of Sandinista women who were reacting to the constraints of an economy of war—"We only eat rice and beans"—or to compulsory military service—"I have two sons in the mountains—I do not want to send my last son." The feeling was very well expressed by Angela's comment when she arrived home from the market and was then asked to participate in a meeting that would take place in the afternoon: "You know that I am a Sandinista, but I am so tired."

Several explanations have been given for the Sandinistas' defeat in the 1990 elections, among them U.S. pressure, the impact of the war on the Nicaraguan economy and the politics of redistribution, and the FSLN itself, with its tendency toward bureaucratization. From the point of view of the women of my neighborhood who had been politically active and supported the Sandinistas, a vote for the Sandinistas was seen as a vote for the continuation of the war. Violeta Chamorro, who represented the UNO coalition, appealed for votes in the name of the maternal, underlining her capacity for reconciliation, for putting an end to the war.[41]

Conclusion

My research also reveals the shift in the experience of maternal work that took place between the insurrection period and the first years of the revolution compared with the period of the contra war. Maternal work was redefined as women's duty to produce soldiers for the nation. I suggest that it is important for feminist theorists to avoid the pitfalls of essentialism and to differentiate between political conditions in which women struggle to redefine the terms of maternal work and political conditions in which maternalist discourses are appropriated by the patriarchal state apparatus.

Privileged notions of motherhood as sacred and of women as fragile and in need of protection and dependence were denied and disrupted for the women I interviewed in Nicaragua. For the women of my neighborhood, valuing and privileging maternal work was a way to resist forms of domination that constrained women's possibilities of mothering and represented poor women as "bad mothers." Nicaraguan women's mothering practices evolved within a discourse that glorified motherhood, on one hand, and undervalued mothers, on the other. The politicization of motherwork must be understood as the explosive response to relations of dominance that disempowered women in their ability to nurture.

My research revealed that there are tensions between women's rights as mothers and their rights as workers, and serious contradictions between women's status as powerful mothers and their status as disempowered citizens. But my research also suggests that during the revolution women employed maternal ideologies in order to engage in practices that they would not engage in simply as women. Undoubtedly, the women of the neighborhood grounded their claims on the powerful traditional notions of mothering found within Nicaraguan culture. These ideologies both protected women and legitimated their involvement in the eyes of their men, other women, and the state. Through their maternal practices women contested hegemonic definitions of mothering and created a landscape where struggles over the meaning and conditions of mothering took place.

Notes

The Spanish phrase in the title of this essay means "One does whatever one must for the children."

1. For further discussion, see Mohanty 1991 and Kaplan 1994.

2. For research on women's participation in guerrilla movements in Latin America, see Lobao 1990. For women's participation in the new social movements, see Nash and Safa 1986; Alvarez 1990; Westwood and Radcliffe 1993.

3. For an overview, see Acosta and Bose 1993.

4. For cross-cultural comparisons of maternal politics and the construction of the welfare state, see Koven and Michel 1993. For further discussion on mothering, see Bassin, Honey, and Kaplan 1994; and Glenn, Chang, and Forcey 1994.

5. For an analysis of the connection between motherhood and Nazism, see Koonz 1987.

6. For further discussion, see Fisher 1989.

7. See *La mujer en Cifras. Docuentos de la Mujer* (Managua: May–Nov. 1987).

8. Figures extracted from Helen Collinson, ed., *Women and Revolution in Nicaragua* (London: Zed Books, 1990), 97.

9. For further discussion, see Stephens 1988.

10. During the time of the revolution, an explosion of Nicaraguan feminist research took place. See, among others, Ana Criquillón, "La rebeldía de las mujeres Nicaraguenses: semillero de una nueva democracia," in *La Construcción de la democracia en Nicaragua* (Managua: Escuela de Sociología, Universidad Centroamericana, 1989); Amalia Chamorro, "La mujer: Logros y limites en 10 años de revolución," in *Cuadernos de Sociología* [Managua] 10 (1989).

11. The full name of this group is Asociación de Mujeres Nicaraguenses "Luisa Amanda Espinosa." The association is named after the first woman to be killed in combat.

12. See Behar and Gordon 1995, among others.

13. For further discussion of the dynamics of fieldwork, see Mulinari 1996.

14. I conducted interviews with women leaders of the different Sandinista grassroots organizations and with leaders of Sandinista feminist organizations. I interviewed women from AMNLAE (the Sandinista women's organization), the CST (Sandinista Worker Federation), the ATC (Association of Rural Workers), the JS (Sandinista Youth), and the Mothers of Heroes and Martyrs. I also interviewed Sandinista women implementing social policy toward women in the OGM (Women's Governmental Office) and the OLM (Women's Legal Office) as well as in more autonomous Sandinista feminist groups.

15. Most researchers focusing on the situation of women in Nicaragua share the view that a high percentage of Managuan women from the popular sectors were active in the Sandinista political project. See Murguialday 1990, and Molineux 1985.

16.   Some scholars argue that the boom of agrarian capitalism relying on migrant labor produced the breakdown of the peasant family units and created a Nicaraguan family pattern in which the woman was the head of the family. Others maintain that the increase of single-mother-headed households was an indirect result of peasant strategies to resist proletarization via the urban migration of daughters. For further discussion, see Gould 1990.

17.   For an analysis of different family patterns in relation to urbanization, ehtnicity, age, and class, see Fauné 1994.

18.   Based on an informal sample in four *andenes* in the neighborhood. For an analysis of the popular classes' survival strategies in Managua, see Garcia 1986.

19.   In 1970 48 percent of Nicaraguan families were headed by women (Maier 1985).

20.   For a discussion of popular habitat and gender, see Feijoó and Herzer 1991.

21.   See Jelin 1990.

22.   Source: Instituto Histórico Nacional, Managua.

23.   For a discussion of the impact of the war, see Marchetti and Perez 1988.

24.   Extracted from *Somos,* the women's organization's magazine, October l984.

25.   Quoted in Helen Collinson, ed., *Women and Revolution in Nicaragua* (London: Zed Books, 1990).

26.   For an analysis of the Mothers of the Plaza in Argentina, see Jelin 1994.

27.   Speech reported in *The Militant,* Nov. 19, 1987.

28.   See Macdonald 1987. For an analysis of the impact of the war in women's lives, see Harris 1988.

29.   *Barricada* (newspaper), Sept. 24, 1984.

30.   For further discussion on feminist narratives, see Gluck and Patai 1991.

31.   The concept of *chele* is used in Nicaragua to name whiteness. To describe another Nicaraguan in the neighborhood as *chele* is to describe somebody (who has with blond hair and blue eyes) not only as "white" but as beautiful. The concept is also used to name white North Americans or Europeans. Managuans differentiate sharply between the use of the term *gringo* or *Yankee,* which was used to name U.S. politics in the country, and the term *chele,* which was used to name, among others, U.S. citizens.

32.   See Buker 1987.

33.   For a similar argument, see Behar 1993.

34.   See Maier 1985.

35.   Vilas 1984.

36.   Safe houses, or *casas de seguridad,* were houses used by Sandinistas to provide a safe place for the guerrillas within the city.

37.   The ways the mother-child relationship was politicized in Argentina and Chile during the 1970s and 1980s are discussed in Agosin 1987, among others.

38.   For an analysis of the politics of masculinity within the Sandinista revolution, see Lancaster 1992.

39.   Ladd-Taylor and Umanski 1998.

40.   For a feminist reflection on the link between motherhood and peace, see Ruddick 1989.

41.   For further discussion, see Dolan 1990.

9

Mythical Mothers and Dichotomies of Good and Evil

Homeless Mothers in the United States

Deborah Connolly

How do cultural norms that assume middle-class material privilege and a stable heterosexual marriage contribute to the marginalization of poor white homeless mothers whose lives deviate from ideologies of "normative" mothering (Appell 1998; Coontz 1992; Polakow 1993; Kaplan 1997)? How do myths of the sacrificial, devoted, and fulfilled mother resonate for women whose lives are characterized by negotiating such things as adequate housing, personal safety, child care, and government bureaucracies? In effect, dominant standards of the good mother readily become another source of injury for mothers whose finances, education, age, living conditions, marital status, and available strategies of solace and escape render such standards impossible to achieve or counterproductive.

Feminist ethnographers have explored conceptions and practices of mothering in a variety of contexts (Glenn, Chang, and Forcey 1994; Harris 1997; Polakow 1993; Ragoné 1994; Luker 1996; Kaplan 1997; Scheper-Hughes 1992). Some feminist theorists have worked to critically recognize the way ideologies of "proper" maternity regulate women (Fineman and Karpin 1995; Roberts 1991; Mink 1995; Ladd-Taylor and Umansky 1998).

However, many feminist theorists have sought to revalue the traditional characteristics and sentiments associated with mothering (nurturance, care, peace, love) either as innate to women or as cultural predispositions to be cultivated and praised (Chodorow 1978). Whereas the masculine ideal in U.S. culture glorifies mothering practices while striving to render their bearers subordinate, some feminists have provided a counterdiscourse that revels in the importance and beauty of motherhood, giving it respect while trying to unbind it from subordination (Forcey 1994). The paradox of such a counterdiscourse, however, is that it is extremely difficult to lift it out of the framework it resists (Tsing 1990). The glorification of mothering traits threatens to reinscribe the equation of maternity as womanhood with the same force as is the case with those who marginalize the practices of mothering. It both silences and endangers women whose lives are not defined by maternal sentiment or who live in circumstances where its expression is dangerous, exploitative, or undesired.

My analysis draws on field research conducted in 1994 and 1995 in a medium-sized city in the northwestern United States that I call North River.[1] There I conducted ethnographic research, working with homeless mothers at a social service agency, North River Resource (NRR). I selected this population because in many ways it epitomizes some of the external markers used to define unfit motherhood, such as poverty, drug addiction, alcoholism, violence in the home, low education levels, youth, marital status, and lack of stable housing. However, my research with homeless mothers is not intended to expand cultural illustrations of "unfit" or "dangerous" mothers. Instead, it attempts to provide a dense description of the lives of mothers who are often used to illustrate irresponsibility, carelessness, and even monstrosity in the domain of mothering.

I conducted my work in a predominantly white urban community. While much research on homelessness has been conducted in larger, more racially diverse urban centers such as New York City, Washington, D.C., and Los Angeles, less attention has been directed at more homogeneous mid-sized cities.[2] North River is a city where conservative stereotypes about race, homelessness, and welfare collide with recipients who are predominantly white. Poor whites disturb the chain of associations typical in U.S. cultural conceptions of normality, power, and privilege. Such disruptions help prevent my research from being uncritically folded into racist narratives about motherhood, poverty, and welfare (Roberts 1991, 1996).

Whiteness constitutes a silent politics in this study. It is mute because, unlike women of color who face racist exclusions overtly, impoverished white women are able to deny the ways in which, as Frankenberg argues, their lives are "racially structured" (Frankenberg 1993). Furthermore, white women are able to identify with what has been imagined as racial normativity.[3] My work examines the relationships between the lives of the white mothers I studied and cultural norms of mothering. While it is beyond the scope of this essay to explore the differences between white women and women of color in this regard, these narratives of white poverty contribute to the changing landscape in our understandings of racial privilege, racial normativity, and racial identifications in general.

Dichotomies of the moralized poles of the virtuous, caring mother and the evil, neglectful one are carefully maintained in the public imagination and in public policies (Tsing 1990; Fineman and Karpin 1995; Roberts 1991; Mink 1995; Ladd-Taylor and Umansky 1998). For example, consider the Susan Smith case, a case that illustrates this dichotomy. In 1994 Susan Smith, a white South Carolina woman, claimed that a black man carjacked her and abducted her two young sons. She was later found guilty of their murders, having pushed her car with the children in it into a lake. The children both drowned.

The Susan Smith case holds a special fascination when considering this issue because it sparks a debate where the crevice between liberals and conservatives deepens and many from both sides fall into the canyon together, making a host of unlikely companions. When analyzing the media reactions to this case, one cannot fail to note the public horror expressed at the image of two white children victimized by the same person expected to devote her life to them, even sacrifice her own life for theirs. How could anyone be so heartless, cruel, selfish, and calculating? An alternative, if somewhat less common view was, how could someone be so unstable and pathological without being identified as such until after the tragedy occurred?

My goal is not to attempt an explanation of Susan Smith's behavior, nor to contribute to the cultural preoccupation with her punishment. What I am doing is to ponder the role that certain conceptions of motherhood play in portraying Susan Smith either as a monster or as a victim of mental instability. My work with homeless mothers has led me to consider how motherhood is associated with a complex set of traits that are represented as universal (such as nurturing, sacrifice, and nonviolence). The "natural-ness" of motherhood makes any deviation from that identity uniquely abhorrent (see Scheper-Hughes 1992).

Susan Smith was tried not simply as a murderer, but as a white *mother* who killed. White middle-class and upper-class women in the United States are bound more closely to the cult of perfect mothering, while black women are more readily assumed to be deviant mothers and their children are viewed as less socially valuable (Roberts 1995; Solinger 1992). Thus, the transgression of motherhood norms by white women is a particularly rich metaphor for understanding how race politics contributes to the cultural fascination with "bad" mothers (Ladd-Taylor and Umansky 1998; Mink 1995). Mothers who are bad or deemed to be "monsters" (Tsing 1990) or "other" (Polakow 1993) engender the model of the normal mother whose conduct they invert. This process of normalization negates the continuum of behavior that more adequately represents how women live their lives. In effect, the model of normal motherhood is produced and enforced even though it does not adequately represent the experiences of mothers—including those purported to embody the ideal. Thus, a fiction is generated that is potentially destructive to all mothers and children. Furthermore, the model of the normal mother creates a series of intense difficulties and binds for impoverished and unhoused mothers living in circumstances far removed from those implicitly assumed to surround normal mothers.

When Susan Smith was at the center of public attention and hostility she became an icon of antimaternity. And through her representation of all that good motherhood is not, she thereby reinforced in reverse an idealized version of good motherhood. The romanticization of the "good mother" is so pervasive that it impacts women in all social strata, such as women who work and leave their children in the care of others, women who cannot afford or find adequate housing for their children, and women whose lives are so full of pain, violence, sickness, and/or poverty that their children are not at its center.

Consider how the cultural staging of normal motherhood might affect someone like Sally, a thirty-three-year-old white woman and a client at North River Resource (NRR). "I wanted kids ... but I didn't," said Sally, looking over at me from her cramped kitchen table. Behind her there was an American flag on the wall. "But my perfect ideal life was I wanted to be married and have kids." Sally has never been married. She has three boys from three different fathers. The first father ran a nude modeling agency at which she was employed; the second never knew she was pregnant; the last one is now in prison. Sally explains:

> He stabbed some guy several times in the chest and it took the
> other guy's life. If the guy hadn't have died then he wouldn't have
> got so severe [a sentence].... Me and him, we will eventually be
> married.... I've moved with my kids ... to protect my kids, even
> though it might look bad on their school records.... I did it to pro-
> tect my kids 'cause if I'd stayed my kids would have kept getting
> abuse or myself and I was always in fear. At one time I had to give
> my kids up temporarily because I was afraid I was gonna hurt them.
> I was really close to my first breakdown. I had such a breakdown I
> couldn't even remember if I had kids or not.... Like I said, it's
> been extremely hectic, really spastic sometimes, being a single par-
> ent for what I've gone through.... My life or death don't mean
> nothing to me.... I would give my life, whatever, in a heartbeat for
> my kids. No problem.

The distance between "I wanted kids ... but I didn't," and, "I would give my life, whatever, in a heartbeat for my kids" reflects an ambivalence that haunted Sally and, as I have discovered, haunts many other homeless mothers. Sally expressed other maternal ambivalences and contradictions as well:

> Me and my kids have been through so much. And I know they love me with all their heart. And I love them. But . . . I just wish I didn't have the part—what they consider abuse. I'm working on it at least. I'm so afraid of losing my kids and I don't want to lose my kids. They would have to kill me to take my kids, whether I accidentally hurt them or not. . . . I don't care if it's the law or not, nobody will get my kids after what I've encountered and had to go through. That's the one thing I can say is mine. The good Lord gave them to me and he's the only one that's gonna take them from me. I feel like that with all my heart. 'Cause, like I said, at least I did have my kids when we went through what we did. At least I have something that I can say that's part of me.

Sally is defensive about her parenting, warning that even if she hurts her kids "accidentally," she will still not consent to their removal. To Sally, to hurt her children accidentally is to hurt them without explicitly or consciously meaning to. Her language is testimony to the ways in which she feels out of control in her parenting even while feeling protective of her right to parent. Sally stresses her love for her children but also her need for them as witnesses and companionship through tumultuous life events. Yet Sally's children have not just endured tribulations with her; they are part of what she has endured, and therefore "nobody will get my kids after what I've encountered and had to go through."

Even though Sally's own lived experiences of parenting are at odds with the larger cultural model of the "good mother," that is, a woman who is devoted to and who sacrifices for her children, she nonetheless subscribes to this model. Yet it is this model that presses women to erase any ambivalence accompanying their efforts to raise their children under difficult conditions. Sally's self-presentation clearly maintains the tensions between the good mother model drawn from the larger culture and the actual circumstances of her mothering.

One route to thinking about cultural models of motherhood is to explore sites where such norms are produced and enforced. Social service settings are just such arenas. Indeed, social services have taken on the role of regulating mothers for a long time (Ladd-Taylor and Umansky 1998; Appell 1998; Gordon 1994; Skocpol 1992; Mink 1995). As Linda Gordon points out, in the early 1900s the kind of intervention promoted to help poor single mothers changed. Previously the emphasis had been on providing charity and moral reform. However, in the early 1900s single motherhood was recast as a more pressing social problem, and social service agencies were employed not only to provide relief for the impoverished but to bring diverse parenting practices into conformity with middle-class norms of the time (Gordon 1994; Mink 1995).

These paradigms continue to resonate through social service programs today. Indeed, at NRR, the staff takes seriously the job of evaluating families and breaking patterns of violence, abuse, and neglect. While such issues are not limited to low-income people, their lives are so often entwined with social service systems that such labels get attached to them easily (Roberts 1991: 1434). Thus, part of the project of serving families becomes teaching and enforcing particular familial codes to clients. For example, NRR has a "no hitting" policy, which means that while you are in the program you are not allowed to discipline your children harshly. (Subsumed under this policy is a dictate against all other forms of harsh punishment, which includes yelling.) The staff see clients' time in the program as an "opportunity" for them to learn nonabusive disciplinary techniques. As is the case with rules in general, this one is enforced to different degrees, depending on the individual client and case worker.

The program director, Margaret, in explaining the policy, said that staff should not be in the position of distinguishing between what is an "appropriate" spanking and what is child abuse. Therefore they must insist that no physical punishment be used, in order to avoid confusion. While the "no hitting" policy is designed to protect children, it also functions to protect staff. As Margaret admitted to me one day, she just does not want to be around such dynamics. Furthermore, the staff does not want to be held

accountable by other staff or external agencies for not addressing neglectful or abusive behaviors.

The "no hitting" and "no yelling" mandates are challenging for clients
to adhere to, if not impossible for some. They are thrust into new environments (here I refer particularly to the day and night shelters, where these
rules are the easiest to enforce) and surrounded by other families and staff,
all of whom are potentially watching their behavior. Since children tend to
experience high levels of stress in shelters, it often produces disciplinary
issues in an environment where many of the tools the parents have relied on
to control their children are deemed inappropriate and potentially abusive.
Clients also know, partly from street knowledge but also from the many
forms they must sign when they come into the program, that NRR staff are
"mandatory reporters." This means that staff members are obligated to
report any signs or incidents of child abuse to Children's Services Division,
a federal agency that has a reputation of acting inconsistently and sometimes arbitrarily (Appell 1998).

Many clients complained about the policies against hitting and yelling.
They say they need to yell at or spank their children in order to get them to
mind. Many imply, and others outright assert, that since I do not have children, I could not understand the nature of discipline. Michelle, a white
twenty-year-old pregnant mother of one, looked me straight in the eye after
I asked her to lower her voice with her daughter in the day shelter, saying,
"Debbie, sometimes you *have* to yell at your kids or spank them, otherwise
they don't hear you."

While I am sometimes uncomfortable, frustrated, and even indignant
when I witness parents being particularly harsh with their children, it is
worth considering the ways in which agency policies dictate norms of motherhood. Implicit in the "no hitting" policy are certain standards that automatically place mothers at NRR under a cloud of suspicion. The very
existence of the rule suggests to clients, staff, and outsiders a "problem" in
parenting, a need for regulation and control. It also makes mothers feel
that they are being parented themselves.

In a session with a client in which we were discussing discipline I asked this mom if she ever hit her child.

"I don't abuse him, if that's what you mean," she replied, bristling with obvious defensiveness. "I've spanked him before, but I don't *beat* him!" She kept her eyes turned away from me as she said this, the anger in her voice apparent. What this client understood, and took offense at, was that my questioning of her disciplinary practices called into question the very nature of her role as a mother. My query implied to her that I viewed her as a person who was in fact capable of abuse and, furthermore, that I might expose her as such, thereby placing her under additional control.

The mothers I worked with at NRR resented any implication that their "proper" maternity was being called into question. However, simultaneously they had complex and sometimes paradoxical relationships with their children, with their identities as mothers, and with outside representations of motherhood. For example, without any prompting from me, Sally said this about the Susan Smith case, which was receiving heavy media attention at the time of our interviews:

> And then you hear this thing, this lady finally admitted to killing those two boys. And I'm sitting there, man, I just started crying this morning when I heard that. I said, "Man, I hope they throw the book at you, lady." But, yet, I shouldn't feel that because maybe there was—maybe she's got—you know? I try to think of other people, too, but it's just something I just cannot see, you know? And because especially where I've hurt my kids sometimes. Where there's been a couple times where I've lost control with the kids. But I turned myself in and they worked with me.

Sally is horrified by the crime and feels Smith should be punished severely. She wants them to "throw the book at her." In this way Sally distances herself from Smith. Smith lost control completely, committing the ultimate sin. While Sally can look down on Smith with a punitive gaze, she also struggles with a certain identification with Smith. She suggests, not quite finishing her sentences, that "maybe there was [a reason], maybe she's got [a reason]." Sally knows that for her, mothering is a struggle, and she wants that aspect of mothering to be more widely acknowledged. One can imagine that she stutters because she does not want to convey the impression that it is acceptable to let her violent impulses win out, yet simultaneously she recognizes that those impulses do exist.

> I hope and pray to God that I never lose my temper again. And before I feel like I'm gonna do that again, and I hate to say this, I'll get something where I can calm myself completely down. . . . That's part of the reason why I got on a lot of downer drugs, so that way I wouldn't lose it. Because there's been a lot of times when I've thought, "God, I'm gonna kill my kids." That's a horrible thought! It's horrible! But the only way I would not get that out is to pop some downers, drink a bottle of Jack, no problem. I drink that stuff like Kool-Aid. I could drink a couple of fifths or pints in a day. . . . My kids, they think, "Oh wow, mommy, she's not mad." They didn't realize a lot of times it's because I was in my own little world on drugs. . . . But I still managed to do a lot of the motherly things. . . . I didn't know how else to do it. . . . Because a lot of times I just feel like I'm going to lose control completely. I hate feeling that way because I feel helpless when I feel that way.

Sally's relationship to her children is an ambivalent one, a combination of love, resentment, and the sense of being overwhelmed. She also struggles with a terrifying acknowledgment that she is not always in control of herself. She uses desperate strategies to protect her children from herself—strategies that deviate from mainstream standards of positive parenting and which place her own life and the custody of her children in further jeopardy. But, she argues, these strategies keep her children relatively safe nonetheless.

Sally claims to use drugs and alcohol to defuse her anger. She says, "I hate to say this," and then confesses that she would use drugs and alcohol again if she felt she needed to in order to protect her kids from herself. Of course, one should be wary of an addict's claim that drugs and alcohol help her maintain positive parenting. While drug and alcohol use might at times calm a person down, such behaviors are just as likely, if not more so, to promote violence and a sense of being out of control. Furthermore, Sally's own version of why she uses them could provide an excuse for future use.

It may be that drugs and alcohol provide at least a temporary numbing against the hatred inside Sally—hatred that was instilled in her during her own upbringing and which continues to wreak havoc on her life and the lives of her children. Yet these kinds of negotiations among anger, violence, and drug use are precisely what is erased from idealized versions of motherhood. Mythical mothers do not experience rage at their children; they never lose control; they do not use drugs (at least not illicit ones) to keep themselves from lashing out at their family. The erasure of these paradoxes and negotiations from discourses on the normal family pushes to the social margins those unable to fulfill the ideal.[4] It also intensifies support for regulatory and penal systems as the only solutions, leaving mothers like Sally with bleak options.

> I know what I'm capable of doing on a really bad time and that part scares me. I hate myself for that part, but [also] that's the part I hate my stepparents for. I will probably go to hell for the hate I have. And I hope it doesn't end up killing me because I'm not a hateful person really. . . . But the hate, it just gets to me so bad. . . . I mean, that's just how I survive—by lying, stealing, doing drugs. I've done jobs that most women wouldn't even think of doing in their lives—just to survive.

Earlier, when Sally talked about "turning herself in," she was referring to an incident when she beat all of her boys bloody with a switch and then turned herself in to the Children's Services Division. At that time, a time when she describes herself as having a nervous breakdown, she gave her children up to foster care while she tried to address her mental health issues. Perhaps it is this kind of personal experience that prompts Sally to both relate to and distinguish herself from Smith, because unlike Smith, Sally was able to acknowledge that her behavior was dangerous, even life-threatening, and she took steps to contain it. Smith did not—perhaps could not.

The Smith murder and other forms of child abuse or endangerment are intolerable. However, one of the questions that its media coverage poses is how good motherhood is constructed antithetically to "monster mothers" (Tsing 1990). Susan Smith did not just commit the social crime of murder; she revealed, to quote *Newsweek*, just "how much evil can lurk in even a mother's heart" (*Newsweek* 1995: 28). The heart, according to *Newsweek*'s imagery, is the place where maternal love is *supposed* to reside. It is the embodiment of care and nurturance. Yet Susan Smith's heart is instead tainted with "evil," an evil so dark that it can lurk in *even* a mother's heart.

While one could view this statement through the simple lens of media exploitation, I believe it reveals a great deal more about cultural norms. These representations of antimothers, monster mothers, "other" mothers can be understood as one facet of a cultural drive to monitor mothers, regulate them intensively, and steer them toward fictive models of normality. The population most affected by such regulatory trends are women who are already marginalized, those who are already suspect because their poverty, their lack of education, and their immersion in pain render them unable to act out the middle-class ideal.

Homeless mothers must either struggle to achieve impossible norms or risk being placed into the dependent category of the incompetent mother. The good mother and her antithesis are produced together through powerful cultural discourses. Such productions protect the impossible model of the good mother by translating homeless mothers into cultural scapegoats. In this way, poor white mothers join the ranks of poor women of color and lesbian mothers, social categories that are deemed outside of normal motherhood. When you see how these two myths intersect and determine each other, then you see the need to change both.

Mothering Daughters

What does it feel like to grow up in a family that is vastly different from idealized portrayals of family life? Most of us have this experience to some degree. For some that experience is more dramatic. This perceived discrepancy tends to be heightened by the fact that chaotic and abusive childhoods are primarily acknowledged through a cultural ethos that fixes all the blame on particular family members. Such individualized blaming increases the pressures on already burdened identities.

Terry, a nineteen-year-old mixed-race woman (of Dutch and Native American heritage), can remember little about her life before the age of ten. She has a few fleeting memories. She remembers opening a can of beer for her dad, covering him with a blanket on the couch; she recalls being sexually abused by her brother; she recalls smoking cigarettes and pot at the age of eight.

She recounts the following about one of her early memories:

> I woke up one night to my mom screaming bloody murder, just screaming.... I opened my door and my dad has this shotgun, he was trying to kill her. I was just going, "What in the hell?" and I hid in my room. I wasn't coming out.... I don't remember what happened. I just remember we were in the car and we were running. And my mom's telling me if my dad finds us, he's gonna rape me and he's gonna kill my brother and he's gonna kill her.... A week ago my dad was perfect and now he's this horrible man that's gonna kill us and rape me.... We ran.... He wasn't supposed to know where we were, it was this big hiding secret. Then my mom went back to him and everything was "great" again.

Terry was ten years old at the time. In retrospect at least, Terry recognizes that things were not actually "great" when they returned. The smooth surface of the family was always a cover for more troubled dynamics stirring underneath. These dynamics, one may speculate, could account for Terry's memory lapses.

What Terry remembers of her later childhood is characterized by depression, several suicide attempts, drug and alcohol abuse, and an active sexual life in her preteen and early teen years. She was bounced back and forth between her parents after they separated and her mother moved across the country with a new husband. Terry's mother had frequent bouts of depression while Terry lived with her. She recalls her mother this way from when she was twelve:

> I felt like I had to be there for them [her mother and stepfather] because my mom, she went through, like, six nervous breakdowns and she wouldn't talk to men, she would only talk to me. So I had to be strong and I wasn't able to tell them about my pain. You know, my mom would just be ... locked in the bathroom, rocking herself. I was the only one that [she would] let in and I would rock her and I would hold her. "It's okay, Mom, it's okay, it's okay, Mom, we'll make it through, we'll make it through it." And she would try to kill herself and I would dig the medicine out of her mouth and say, "No, you're gonna live." ... I had to be the psychiatrist there. I had to be the strong one. I couldn't tell them about my pain.... So I didn't want to die but I couldn't handle that. I just kind of wanted to go away for a while so that I could get a break and start fresh.... So I overdosed.... I kept saying, "Just let me go to hell, just let me go to hell."

Terry portrays herself as a strong and capable woman, capable of saving her mother. But she also acknowledges that these family dynamics overwhelmed her and that her own pain and confusion were at times too much for her to take. In her attempts to mother her mother, a role that she says had to be adopted because of her gender (her mother "wouldn't talk to men"), Terry sacrificed her own needs and well-being. She is the good mother, sacrificial and devoted. While Terry expresses a certain pride in her strength, it does not make her feel worthy—recall that she imagines herself descending to "hell."

After her suicide attempt, Terry moved back across the country to her California hometown to live with her father and brother. She says her dad was rarely around; he was "constantly partying." And she describes her own life at thirteen as a "big party." She was not attending school, was using alcohol and drugs extensively, and was sexually "promiscuous."

I had a problem with sexual promiscuity. I was either always having sex with someone or I was being sexually abused, constantly. . . . You name it—people at stores, people I was dating, people I had never met, people walking down the street trying to drag me into a car, you just name it and it was happening. That was my life, sex was my whole life. . . . [Then] I said, "I can't do this no more," and I gave myself a promise. I said, "All right, I'm not gonna have sex with anybody anymore, not unless I decide to be in a relationship." And I did.

Terry's sexual self-identification as promiscuous and out of control might not be surprising. Recall her earliest memories. Her father had said that he would murder the others, but Terry he will rape. So from an early age Terry understands herself as a potentially sexualized victim. Terry also identified herself as a victim of early sexual abuse by her older brother.

Shortly after thirteen-year-old Terry decided to abstain from sex until she was in a committed relationship, she met seventeen-year-old Carlos.

I kind of took him under my wing and I saw him as something I could shape and something I could take care of, you know? I saw him as like my little child. . . . I always had this need to take care of something, you know? If it wasn't a cat, it was an adult, and I took care of my dad very well, too. I was my dad's mom basically, too. Well, I was the mother of everybody . . . but this person especially I could mother him and I liked that. It made me feel needed and it made me feel wanted.

Terry feels the weight of responsibility to care for those around her, including those much older and those who would traditionally care for her. Her parents, her brother, her boyfriend, even stray cats are seen as her responsibility. Like many children who grow up with alcoholic or drug-addicted parents, Terry has become a parentified child. She is the surrogate mother figure.

Terry's story offers a glimpse into the ways in which young girls and women from an early age mimic the traditional mothering roles that women are expected to embody (Chodorow 1978). Terry's desire to feel and act indispensable toward her mother, to protect her father, and to be needed and wanted by her boyfriend are presented through the rubric of maternity. Yet Terry's embodiment of maternal expression unsettles the very core of motherhood ideals. Her relationships are influenced by cultural ideals but are set in conditions that are radically at odds with them.

For other homeless women, mothering daughters challenges their ability to adhere to cultural models of mother love. Consider Hannah, a twenty-five-year-old white woman and mother of three. Here she discusses her relationship with her five-year-old daughter, Amber.

> After I had her, it's like Joe [Amber's father] took care of her. I just wouldn't go near her or nothing. . . . I guess 'cause he was paying a lot of attention to her and he pushed me and Bobby [her oldest son, of a different father] to the back burner after she was born, 'cause it was his first daughter and all. . . . I still get mad about it. . . . I guess, more I'd say, jealous—because she gets a lot of attention from him and he pushes everyone else aside. So I just get frustrated, not knowing what to do. So I kind of like, push her aside every once in a while. I mean, I didn't want to but I've caught myself even saying I hated her. . . . I love her to a point but . . . it's not like I *hate her* hate her, but I guess it's just frustrating not knowing where you stand.

Hannah acknowledges that Amber has heard her say that she hates her. She says her daughter reminds her of her own little sister, of whom she was always jealous. So Hannah ends up trying to get back at her sister through rejecting her daughter, as well as displacing her own feelings of rejection from her husband onto her daughter.

Hannah's behavior does not fit the ideal of mother love. On the contrary, she exposes the ambivalent emotions of a mother struggling to raise a child whose place in her life is highly ambiguous. Hannah clearly has concerns about her relationship to her daughter ("I don't *hate her* hate her") but she acknowledges only loving Amber "to a point." Hannah's relationship to her daughter has to do with her own experiences as a child as well as the gendered competition for her husband. These are not dynamics traditionally accepted or acknowledged in cultural characterizations of mother love. Yet Hannah is aware of the social norms about mother love. She believes that jealousy, resentment, and ambivalence are not acceptable reasons to reject a child. And so she later provides a more socially acceptable gloss on her relationship with Amber. "I guess I expect too much from her. . . . I want her to have a better life than I did. I guess I'm harder on her for that."

Hannah's ambivalence engenders uncertain sentiments in me. On one hand, I feel myself wanting to protect Amber. I see her in my mind's eye, building a highway out of blocks with her younger brother on the floor of the day shelter, her hand reaching up to push her overgrown blond bangs out of her eyes every few minutes as they pursue the project. I wonder what it means for her to grow up with a mom who hates her but doesn't *hate her* hate her. The unfairness of it unsettles me. But I am also aware that ambivalences usually accompany all expressions of mothering, even in the most favorable circumstances. Maternal love does not magically begin at conception, at birth, or at any other fixed moment. Mothers relate to their children and to the perplexities of parenting in diverse ways, even though most are haunted by a univocal model of mothering. The production of multiple models adjusted to different contexts could serve both Hannah and her daughter. It might alleviate the immense pressure on their relationship; it might produce several possibilities and places for nurturance and love.

In her research on parenting practices in an impoverished community in northeastern Brazil, Nancy Scheper-Hughes recognizes the need to reinterpret mothering, parental love, and responsibility. Her work denaturalizes mother love through interpreting women's "neglect" of their children to be a consequence of larger cultural and socioeconomic constraints. Thus her analysis reframes interpretations that blame mothers for rational decision making under conditions of extreme poverty.

Contemporary theories of maternal sentiment—of mother love as
we know and understand it—are the product of a very specific historical context. The invention of mother love corresponds not only
with the rise of the modern bourgeois nuclear family . . . but also
with the demographic transition: the precipitous decline in infant
mortality and female fertility. My argument is a materialist one:
mother love as defined in the psychological, social-historical, and
sociological literatures is far from universal or innate and represents instead an ideological, symbolic representation grounded in
the basic material conditions that define women's reproductive
lives. (Scheper-Hughes 1992: 401)

Scheper-Hughes de-essentializes mother love by arguing that parental practices and affections occur in specific economic and cultural contexts. This
allows for the consideration of diverse responses to parenthood as something more complex than an expression of individual pathology. Once
mother love is taken out of the realm of the natural, we can examine how
the ideal of good motherhood is itself culturally produced. And we can shift
away from those entrenched dichotomies of good and evil that discipline so
many mothers in difficult circumstances.

Sally's volatile temper, Terry's mother's need to be saved by her daughter, and Hannah's ambivalence toward her daughter are too easily incorporated into a single story of motherhood gone awry (Polakow 1993;
Ladd-Taylor and Umansky 1998). This serves to reinforce a single model of
motherhood and to treat deviations from the model as individual failures.
Such a perspective directs our attention away from understanding the social
and historical circumstances and from diversifying our models. It encour-
ages us to ask "what went wrong" within a particular family or with an individual woman rather than try to understand the race, class, and gender
dynamics in these scenarios.

To hold individuals solely responsible for their actions omits the wider
social milieu. However, it remains politically unpopular to look at mother-

ing through this lens. If we continue to locate the blame, the problem, the deviance, and the pathology solely within the individual, then we must conclude that only the individual needs fixing or, more accurately, punishing. But if we begin to view this problem from a larger social, cultural, and historical perspective, the issue appears more complex, more diffuse, and more costly to repair. Unfortunately, try as we may, the fact is that Susan Smith, Sally, Terry, and Hannah are not unique. Their behavior suggests certain patterns that, rather than creating public hysteria and a backlash that seeks to stigmatize and regulate women, could instead result in social measures that would support and protect families.

Beyond Conception

If ambivalence and complexity often accompany mothering practices, they also participate in the stories women tell about their pregnancies. Unplanned pregnancies, and sometimes even the ones women think they plan for, can produce anxiety, fear, frustration, confusion, and resentment.

Consider Terry, who earlier in this essay became involved with Carlos when she was a teenager. Terry's menstrual period had always been irregular, which she attributes to her drug use (cocaine, marijuana, methamphetamines or "crank," LSD, and alcohol). She never used birth control because her period was so infrequent. Terry got a pregnancy test when she was two and half months pregnant and was "already showing." Terry and Carlos went to an "impersonal clinic" and there she tested positive for pregnancy.

> I tell Carlos I'm pregnant in the doctor's office and he picks me up
> and twirls me around with a big ol' smile. He says, "We're gonna do
> it, Terry!"

Carlos found, at least initially, a thrill in the prospect of a child. On the other hand, Terry was worried and overwhelmed by the news of this unplanned pregnancy and felt a kind of disbelief at Carlos's enthusiasm. She exclaims:

And I'm going, "Oh my God, you're crazy, you're crazy! I'm fifteen years old. I just turned fifteen, you're crazy!" You know, I probably got pregnant on my birthday. I'm doing all these drugs. That's where I panicked, was the drugs.

Another client, Michelle, a white twenty-year-old woman, described telling her then-sixteen-year-old boyfriend that she was pregnant.

Tony [the boyfriend] goes, "I'm gonna be a daddy," and he was, like, all excited. And I was, like, "Oh, my God." I was bawling. I mean, I was really unhappy that I was pregnant. And he was like, "Michelle, we're gonna be parents." And I'm like, "Whatever!"

The contrasting reactions between these two teenage girls and their partners to the news of unplanned pregnancies is revealing. Michelle's and Terry's fears are based on a premonition of the responsibilities that they now face. Their lives have been permanently altered. Male partners did not necessarily face a new permanent responsibility in their life once a pregnancy occurred.[5] Individual men cannot be held entirely responsible for their lack of provision for families in the face of systems that set up poor families for failure and that deter the existence of two-parent families (Bourgois 1995; Gordon 1994). Still, there is an irony in Carlos's "big ol' smile" when one considers his behavior shortly after their son, Braley, was born.

I would be breast-feeding Braley and he [Carlos] would throw plates and everything at me. And I would have to shelter Braley. I would be turning on my side like this and my whole side would be bruised from stuff. And I'm sheltering Braley. . . .

Carlos's enthusiasm toward the idea of fatherhood did not translate into an ability to nurture his family (see Bourgois 1995). Instead, the added responsibility may have increased his tendency toward violence, and Terry's increased dependency heightened her vulnerability to being his victim.

Both Terry and Michelle expressed hesitations about their pregnancies. Both women were uncertain about whether or not they wanted to be parents at this point in their lives. However, both considered adoption more seriously than they considered abortion, which is indicative of a national trend (Luker 1996). While abortion is the more common decision for middle-class white women, it less accessible for poor women. As Kristin Luker points out, abortion tends to be the choice of women who believe that they will have other opportunities available to them in the future if they postpone childbearing, such as a good education, a solid marriage, and/or a career. Women estranged from those middle-class aspirations may feel less compelled to choose abortion. Instead, for some, childbearing offers something that they *can* do with their lives, and offers the possibility of love and hope that is absent in other aspects of their lives (Kaplan 1997; Ladner 1971; Luker 1996). Furthermore, as I will discuss in more detail later, the antiabortion movement has had a profound impact on many impoverished women, framing abortion as a selfish and barbaric decision.

Adoption, on the other hand, may be experienced—at least initially—as something women can do for their children. Adoption is wrapped in maternal ideologies of giving—giving a good home to the child, and giving a good couple a child they desire.[6] Even more currently, Helena Ragoné has discussed the cultural narrative propagated by agencies and internalized by surrogate mothers of choosing to devote themselves to bearing a child for a couple as an ultimate act of gift giving. This may allow women to maintain a self-image more aligned with ideals of good motherhood than abortion does. However, adoption, while often considered by women facing unplanned pregnancies, is less often actualized as a choice than it used to be.[7] For example, Michelle describes her considerations of adoption here:

> Yeah, I was gonna give her up for adoption. That went through my mind a lot. And I brought it to Tony's attention and he got kind of hurt and upset, 'cause he wanted Marissa [their now-three-year-old daughter]. I mean ... if I woulda said, "Tony, I want to get pregnant," he probably would have said, "No way." But because I was

pregnant, you know, he's like, "I want to be a dad, you know, that's pretty cool. We're gonna have a baby." He was real excited. And I hit, like, five months and reality hit me in the face that I was pregnant and really gonna have a baby. I felt Marissa move and I was like, "Oh, my baby's moving," and I got to like it and I couldn't wait to see it.... And I was really excited then. And it got closer and closer and I got more excited and she was born and I was really happy.

Jane, a white twenty-seven-year-old client, also thought about putting her second child up for adoption:

Adoption came through my mind. I was scared, you know. He [her boyfriend] was still using [drugs] off and on and I had fallen down some stairs and hurt myself. And I was without a job and I was scared. I didn't think that I could give the better home. And then I started thinking, well, what if they couldn't give her the better home? It doesn't mean they're better people, it means they have more money. Doesn't mean they'd love her more. And I can have more money and I know that I could love her. So I made the right choice.

As Jane points out, the social pressure to give a child up for adoption is often bound up with cultural ideals about what makes a good home and who makes good parents. While Jane initially felt she should relinquish her child since she does not meet those ideals, she then moved toward challenging them, calling into question the equation that greater affluence equals greater love and a better life for a child.

As Solinger has chronicled, just a few decades ago young unmarried white women were coerced into relinquishing their children and giving them up for adoption (1992). During that era pregnancy for women out of wedlock became pathologized, and women were under immense social pressure to give their babies up to "normal" and "healthy" two-parent middle-class couples. Unmarried black women, on the other hand, were much more likely to keep their children, as they were alienated from the adoption market because of the lack of parents willing to adopt black infants (Solinger 1992). And some have suggested that black communities were by and large more willing to support and accommodate young mothers and infants in a way that middle-class white communities were not (Solinger 1992; Stack 1974). More recent studies, however, suggest that while this may have been true several decades ago, the notion that black communities provide social support for single mothers is no longer the case (Kaplan 1997). Furthermore, the myth that black communities implicitly support single motherhood as a choice has served to further pathologize those communities as integrally deviant and as antithetical to mainstream ideologies about the family (Kaplan 1997).

One factor that may contribute to the decisions of women of color to keep their babies is their long history of having children taken away from them by state intervention (Dorris 1989; Roberts 1991; Gordon 1994). The relationship between child welfare workers and marginalized mothers remains tense today partly for this reason. Marginalized women (poor women, women of color, disabled women, and lesbians) sometimes fear forced sterilization, a fear not unfounded, given past practices with vestiges remaining today (Hartouni 1997: 105).[8] Such histories may promote more community tolerance for "nontraditional" childbearing as well as contribute to women's decisions to bear and raise children outside of the "traditional" nuclear family (Solinger 1992).

The stigma of maternal incompetence experienced by marginalized women may prompt some of them to want to prove their social worth as good mothers. In some cases, pending motherhood may be a prod for women to reorganize their lives and to try to conform more closely to middle-class standards of stability. As Terry explains:

> I was planning on adoption much stronger than abortion. I had paperwork and everything. And I couldn't do it. . . . I became determined that I was going to straighten out my life and I was going to

raise this baby. And I was going to give this baby everything that anybody else could. And I was prepared to do it alone at this point. . . .
I wanted to give this a baby a good life. A clean start.

The cultural contradictions experienced by Terry, Michelle, and Jane
perhaps exemplify a cultural transition. First they experience the cultural
ideology that says that one *should* give one's baby to a more stable "traditional" family. But then they find the cultural window that has been tentatively opened in more recent times and which suggests that birth mothers
love their children uniquely and should raise them no matter what.

Actually, both the logic that glorifies biological motherhood and the
logic that advocates adoption in particular circumstances are weighted with
pressures and discriminations. Neither logic helps women make decisions
that address the complexities of their own lives. Either women are defined
as unfit based on various cultural criteria and pressed to release babies in
order to adhere to social norms, or they are revered as birth mothers
and pressed into a paradigm of mothering that speaks poorly to their actual
circumstances.

After abortion was legalized in 1973 the social terrain in which illegitimate pregnancies occurred changed drastically. Fewer women chose adoption as a way of handling an unplanned pregnancy. And yet abortion was
rarely discussed by my clients as an option they entertained seriously. It may
be that abortion is more widely considered prior to birth even if it is not
openly discussed after birth (Luker 1996). Perhaps once you've had the
child, having contemplated abortion is uncomfortable to admit. Even to
mention it as an option you considered before giving birth may suggest
ambivalence about your child now.

Among clients at NRR there is a marked prolife sentiment. Perhaps in
some cases they react to their marginal social positions by asserting their
right to have and raise children. This may be even more pronounced given
their histories of denial of this right. Indeed, for some, abortion may feel
more like a social pressure than a freedom to choose. For example, consider
the welfare reform measure in some states that dictates that benefits no

longer be increased for families if a new child is born while the parent is already receiving aid (Piven 1996). This policy is allegedly meant to deter those "baby factory" recipients who, the story goes, bear numerous children to gain the few extra dollars a month allotted for new family members. Thus, some women feel pressured into abortion either because they do not have adequate financial means to parent or because of social anger that continues to burgeon against welfare recipients who become pregnant "irresponsibly."

Given these social pressures, the language of choice embraced by proponents of abortion rights may be more problematic and inadequate for homeless women than it first appears. As Solinger notes, the idea of childbearing as a personal choice emphasizes the individual while deemphasizing the social, political, and economic contexts in which that individual is set (1998). One is assumed to be choosing freely and unconstrainedly, and thus is fully responsible for the outcomes of one's choice. So what may be missed in feminist preoccupations with protecting women's right to choose is the inextricable link between choice and consequence (Luker 1996). Women who choose to bear children under difficult conditions can then be berated as having made the "wrong choice," while the circumstances in which they had to choose continue to be unacknowledged (Solinger 1998).

As Luker notes, ideologies of choice tend to support cultural conceptions of individual blame (1996). Young mothers who are poor, uneducated, and struggling to stay above water are treated as if they chose those conditions. Luker suggests that contemporary public rhetoric blames young mothers for their own poverty, advising that these women would not be poor if they had merely postponed childbearing, as their affluent counterparts are doing. She then, however, demonstrates that most of the women so characterized were already poor when they became pregnant. Their poverty is a result not of ill-reasoned choices but of a host of socioeconomic conditions that serve to promote both early childbearing and the difficulties that follow from it (Luker 1996).

Feminists cannot afford to have abortion turn into a moral imperative for some women who are poor, of color, and young while maintaining it as a choice for others who are affluent, white, and mature. The political right has kept feminists and their supporters focused on protecting abortion rights, so much so that they may have lost sight of the need to protect women's rights not only to terminate an unwanted pregnancy but to give birth to and raise children in healthy and safe environments. A less flattering interpretation is that some feminists share the class and race privilege and biases of political conservatives. In general, feminists have failed to adequately address the needs of homeless mothers as they continue to characterize abortion solely in the language of choice—a language that denies the complex circumstances of homeless mothers (see Solinger 1998). Unless feminists provide more active support and backing for women trying to mother under difficult circumstances, we will continue to estrange marginal women who often see some aspects of their lives as appreciated more fully by conservatives. For instance, some homeless mothers may feel that antiabortion conservatives who express care for each and every fetus sympathize with them more. These expressions play on the real fear that homeless individuals and their children might otherwise be treated as disposable beings.

Many clients described relations with social service workers or other professionals in which they felt they were being discouraged from carrying a pregnancy to term because of some type of social status (such as age, race, income, and so on). For example, consider Jane's experience at a clinic during her second pregnancy.

> I was embarrassed to go to my doctor and have a pregnancy test so I went to Planned Parenthood and it was positive. And do you know that they gave me the information on abortions and told me that the State medical card would take care of it? But they didn't tell me that if you plan to keep your child, you should get prenatal care and that your card will also pay for that. They just gave me one option, and I was very upset about that. . . . I think they did it because I had a medical card. I really do. . . . I feel that if I went in there and paid for my visit and had money that maybe they wouldn't think the same way. And that's kind of sad because I was still working, and I

just qualified for the medical card anyway because I wasn't making
enough money. But I was still working.

Jane felt she was discriminated against, judged as unfit to be a parent
because of her financial status. She does not feel empowered by the right
to choose, the right to control her body. Instead she felt pressured not to
have her baby; she felt that others were trying to dictate her choices. She
says, "They just gave me one option, and I was very upset about that."
Hence, it should not be surprising that Jane feels alienated from abortion
rights proponents and instead allies herself with the pro-life movement, a
movement that appears to support and validate her decision to have and
keep a child she wants.

> I just have a hard time with that [abortion]. I think from the minute
> she has a little tiny heart that she's alive. And I really have a hard
> time making the decision to terminate her life. And now even more
> so, now that she's a little girl. And I look at her and think, "How
> would I have the right to terminate her life before she had a
> chance? Who am I to give her life and then to take it away? That's
> not my choice." And she knows about abortion, and she knows that
> was my choice, that I, of course, had that option. And she said she's
> glad that I didn't make that choice. . . . It could be just that I think
> that God doesn't make mistakes and that when people become
> pregnant . . . we are not the ones to take it away. . . . I feel that way.
> And I guess I just have enough faith that, you know, things are
> gonna work out and that my children will be provided for. . . .
> Angela [her daughter] hasn't had to sleep outside yet and she's not
> gonna have to.

Part of the difficulty is that the prolife movement has effectively produced confusion, remorse, guilt, and despair around abortion and then
given women a way to avoid such potential turmoil (Hartouni 1991).

Women can "save" their babies; they are offered the moral high ground. This leaves prochoice proponents in either of two positions. One, of obscuring the complexity of how pregnancy is experienced by women and thus alienating women who expect abortion to be "just another option" but then find it complicated and sometimes disturbing, or two, of addressing the complexities and running the risk of providing even more power to the right wing. A feminism alert to the distinctive life situations of diverse women will maintain abortion as a legal and safe option but will also respect and support women who do not choose that option.

The notions of choice and consequence in current understandings of reproduction tie into middle-class conceptions of family planning. Here I refer to "family planning" not in its unexamined usage as a shorthand for birth control but as an ideology of individual strategizing for future success. The very notion of "planning" suggests a kind of self-control, self-assurance, and reflection that is the emblem of the proper middle class. To plan is to be forward-thinking, to take responsibility for your future. Accidents, irretrievable mistakes, and unexpected responsibilities are reserved mostly for those who are irresponsible, out of control, and unreflective—those who are contained by the immediacy of their lives rather than able to look toward the future.

While clients I worked with generally did not "plan" their lives in the manner idealized by middle-class norms, the notion of planning and making conscious decisions did exist. However, it tended to have a rather different slant than the popular conception of a "planned" family. For example, consider Melanie, a thirty-six-year-old white woman. Melanie met her first husband, Jeff, when she was nineteen years old and he was sixteen. He had just gotten out of juvenile detention hall. He had been sentenced for stealing cars and other forms of burglary. Not long after they started going out, Jeff was caught stealing cars again and was sentenced to five years in prison.

Melanie moved to the city where the prison was so she could be near him and visit him regularly. He pressured her to sneak drugs in to him, which she did, although she never "felt good about it." She never got caught. While he was in prison, he asked Melanie to marry him. She said she wanted to wait until he was released, but he told her it was "now or never." Melanie was twenty-two years old when they were married in the prison visiting room.

> They just set up the date and I got the license. . . . They clear out all the chairs in the visiting room and they have the guy . . . the minister or whatever he is. I rented him [Jeff] a tux and got me a nice dress and we had to have two witnesses and of course there's the guards and stuff. But he's not shackled or anything like that. And we just had the wedding or whatever you call it. And then we get to sit for fifteen minutes and talk and that's it [laughs]. That's the wedding right there. But after that he was doing better and got in the release center and got passes. And that's how I got pregnant with Andrew, which we planned, I planned, we both planned. It wasn't by accident. We wanted to have a son, and it ended up being a boy, too.

Melanie's pregnancy was planned in the sense that it "wasn't an accident." It was not planned as part of a middle-class strategy of home ownership and job security. It also did not turn out the way she expected. During her pregnancy, her new husband began to get out on three-day passes. He returned to burglarizing, heavy partying, and drug use during these releases. He implicated her by both dealing drugs out of the house and storing stolen goods there. When she was four or five months pregnant, Jeff was arrested again during one of his visits and sentenced to additional jail time. Although there was some evidence against Melanie as well, she was not charged.

So Melanie's husband was still in jail when it was time for her to deliver. Clearly this was not part of the plan.

> I came up there [the prison]. . . . I was almost ready to have Andrew and I shouldn't even have rode up there on the bus . . . but I wanted to see him and he wanted to see me. I got up there and he told me he didn't want anything to do with me anymore. He wanted a

divorce. He couldn't handle the whole thing. . . . I couldn't believe it. I was in shock. I was just totally upset bad. And I knew it wasn't good for the baby.

Melanie stopped communicating with Jeff for a while, even though he called her and denied ever having said those things to her. Two months after her son was born she filed for divorce. However, three months after that, before the divorce proceedings had really gotten under way, she came home to find her window broken and Jeff sitting in her front room. He had been released from jail unexpectedly.

Melanie tried to maintain her marriage with him, even after she found out that he was seeing two other girls, who were thirteen and fourteen years old. Jeff became more violent:

> He liked to wrestle around a lot and he'd get mad at me and he'd choke me, but I could usually get his arm away from me. . . . But once he got into jail he pumped, he lifted weights, and was real strong and big. He started throwing things at me after he got out of jail. . . . He'd always miss but he started, like, punching me and stuff in the arm. . . . This is at the same time he was getting into crack, so that probably didn't help matters any . . . and I started doing it too.

It is tempting to treat Melanie's "planned pregnancy" as a mistake. She got pregnant at the wrong time, with the wrong person, under unfavorable circumstances. However, such a judgment presupposes that Melanie had the option of raising children under middle-class conditions; it assumes that the idealized version of a "planned" life might someday be available to her. To say that her pregnancy was a mistake not only disparages Melanie and denigrates her child but projects illusory conditions into the background of her life. Should Melanie take all the blame in this scenario? Is it just a poor decision on the part of an individual woman? Or are women in poverty more susceptible to relationships that become unstable and violent because of the circumstances in which they live?

The circumstances of Melanie's life exist in the details, in the particular accidents and specific pressures she faces within a larger horizon that make it unrealistic for her to project radical changes in those circumstances. We must attend to the details without forgetting the horizon, as those details vary from individual to individual. The clients I worked with do not allow for the glorification of poverty; their stories do not romanticize the "hard yet simple" life. Rather, they press us to consider how specific and variable the conditions of motherhood are, and how general conditions intersect with individual experience, pressure, and accidents to create specific outcomes.

Marginalized mothers are not simply victims or demons. They struggle within and against uncertain social positions that render stability precarious, foresight an ambiguous good, and responsibility a costly enterprise. We need portrayals of these women that do not sanitize their lives, because in an era of punitive characterizations and policies toward marginal sectors, sanitized presentations mostly open the door for others to represent the unseemly stuff even more dramatically. Close attention to the complexity and ambiguity of concrete lives might enable us to effectively counter regulatory trends, challenging the basis of stark formulaic contrasts that divide individuals into absolute categories: deserving/undeserving, innocent/guilty, good/bad, independent/dependent. Furthermore, such considerations may suggest public policies that can address the basic needs of mothers and their children while allowing for self-esteem, personal growth, and empowerment rather than the punitive and regulatory practices currently in vogue.

Notes

1. I have changed the names of all people and places referred to in this essay, to protect the anonymity of those involved.

2. According to the 1990 government census the total population of North River is 424,834. North River's population is approximately 85 percent white, 7 percent black, 5 percent Asian or Pacific Islander, 2 percent Native American, Eskimo, or Aleut, and 1 percent other.

3. As Matt Wray and Annalee Newitz elucidate in the introduction to their collection of essays on "white trash," the concept of "white trash" is "good to think with" when it comes to issues of race and class in the United States because the term foregrounds whiteness and working-class or underclass poverty, two social attributes that usually stand far apart in the minds of many Americans, especially American social and cultural theorists. (1997: 4).

4. For a further discussion of idealized portrayals of family life and corresponding repercussions on contemporary families in the United States, see Coontz 1992.

5. Only 16 percent of the families I worked with at NRR had a biological father present in the family. This picture mirrors the national situation, where the overwhelming majority of homeless families are headed by single mothers (Homes for the Homeless and Columbia University 1998).

6. Giving the "gift of life" is a notion that has been used in a variety of ideologies about maternity and reproduction. Rickie Solinger discusses how between 1945 and 1965 white teens were indoctrinated into the idea that they did not have the right to their illegitimate children, and social service agencies, in alignment with wider cultural ideologies, pressured them to believe that they wanted to give their children up in retribution for their own "mistake" of getting pregnant. In return, supposedly, these girls get the "gift" of a second chance at normal middle-class life. Furthermore, antiabortion activists have dramatized the "miracle of life," effectively casting women as having the responsibility to provide the "gift of life" to their unborn fetuses (Solinger 1992).

7. Luker (1996) emphasizes that adoption rates have gone down significantly in the last forty years. She notes that between 1965 and 1972 20 percent of all white babies and 2 percent of all black babies were given up for adoption. However, between 1982 and 1988 the figures were 3 percent and 1 percent respectively.

8. For more detailed accounts of abuses such as forced sterilization and their impacts on particular communities see A. Davis 1981; S. Davis 1988; Roberts 1991; Collins 1994; Solinger 1994. Additionally, for contemporary discussions about legislation designed to regulate women's childbearing by such means as mandating the implant of the contraceptive Norplant, see Hartouni 1997.

Afterword

Kristin Luker

A colleague of mine, one of the founding mothers of feminist scholarship, swears that this story is true. She was in an airplane with a host of young men, brawny members of a men's college football team. Suddenly the plane hit turbulence and hurtled toward what seemed oblivion. The oxygen masks deployed, and in that second before everything turned out to be all right, my colleague swears that every one of these macho young men on the plane shrieked some variation on the theme of "Mom!" I'm inclined to believe this story, because the one and only time my father shared his war memories with me, he told me the same thing, that every dying man calls for his mother. (No one has ever told me, by the way, what women say in the face of imminent death.)

But there you have it. In motherhood, feminist scholars confront one of the most challenging and perplexing of all social institutions. On one hand, as the essays in this volume make clear, motherhood is constructed. As the scholars in this book introduce us to what the editors call "mothers on the fault lines"—homeless mothers, gestational mothers, lesbian mothers, mothers of transracial children, and all of the other mothers who don't fit the mold—we begin to see how socially and culturally shaped motherhood really is. Once extolled as an essential category across time and space, motherhood turns out to be an institution that incorporates the sexual, racial, and class regimes in which it is situated.

But as those men on the airplane or the battlefield make clear, motherhood is not only that. One of the most recurrent themes in this book is that while motherhood is often venerated, actual mothers are often devalued because they don't live up to the ideal. Whether in the political world of Nicaragua, where women use the discourse of motherhood to challenge the status quo, or in Britain, where white mothers of multiracial children are viewed with suspicion, the very potency of the mother-child relationship seems to be belied by its mixed status.

What this volume makes clear is that for all that motherhood is constructed in a particular time and place and by particular agencies (the law, technology, culture), it comes to take on a life of its own. What is wonderful about this book is that it plays out all of the complexities of the institution it studies. Again and again in the preceding pages, we see real mothers underneath the analyses of how the experience of motherhood is shaped. When an adoptive mother tells Christine Gailey, "The real work with that child had to be done on the inside and that's where we got down to business. She needed to know that she belonged somewhere, and that somewhere was us," we know in our bones the courage that took. When Susan Dalton examines the changing legal strategies that lesbian mothers have used to claim rights to their children, we sense the anguish and longing behind the dry legal prose of claims and statutes and arguments. And when a homeless mother tells Deborah Connolly, "They would have to kill me to take my kids, whether I accidentally hurt them or not," we feel the ache of that ambivalence.

Sometimes the mothers in this book are "failed" mothers—the infertile women in Egypt studied by Marcia Inhorn, the women whose children die or are not "perfect" studied by Linda Layne and Gail Landsman.

And sometimes the mothers that we see are the researchers themselves, showing us their other selves in footnotes or passing mentions. While men researching men rarely feel the need to note how and where they connect with those they are studying, we know that Linda Layne has faced the pain of miscarriage herself and that Gail Landsman's child has a mild disability. The experience of motherhood in this book, in the lives of the writers as in the lives of those written about, refuses to stay in the backstage area of "private" life.

And it's a good thing, too. It remains to be seen if this generation or any other will be able to write about motherhood in ways that capture both its political dimensions and its emotional ones, but it's something we have to try to do. That oldest and most potent relationship (a relationship that is then sometimes extended to a new generation) feels so real, so much as if it could not be any other way, that to understand it as socially located is a real breakthrough. To get a handle on its political and social character in the special locations studied in this book is a powerful first step. Now all we need to do is understand the full depth and range of the lived experiences of motherhood in these and other settings.

Bibliography

Aboulghar, M. A., G. I. Serour, and R. Mansour. 1990. Some Ethical and Legal Aspects of Medically Assisted Reproduction in Egypt. *International Journal of Bioethics* 1: 265–68.

Acosta, Belén Edna, and Christine E. Bose, eds. 1993. *Researching Women in Latin America and the Caribbean.* Boulder: Westview Press.

Agosin, Majorie. 1987. *Scraps of Life: Chilean Arpilleras.* London: Zed Books.

Altstein, Howard, and Rita Simon, eds. 1991. *Intercountry Adoption: A Multinational Perspective.* New York: Free Press.

Alvarez, Sonia. 1990. Women in the New Social Movements of Urban Brazil. In *Engendering Democracy in Brazil.* Princeton: Princeton University Press.

Andrews, Lori B. 1996. Chapter 14: Alternative Reproduction and the Law of Adoption. In *Adoption Law and Practice,* edited by J. H. Hollinger. New York: Matthew Bender.

Appadurai, Arjun. 1986. Introduction: Commodities and the Politics of Value. In Arjun Appadurai, ed., *The Social Life of Things: Commodities in Cultural Perspective.* Cambridge, U.K.: Cambridge University Press.

Appell, Annette R. 1998. On Fixing "Bad" Mothers and Saving Their Children. In Molly Ladd-Taylor and Lauri Umansky, eds., *Bad Mothers: The Politics of Blame in Twentieth Century America.* New York: New York University Press.

Ariès, Philippe. 1962. *Centuries of Childhood: A Social History of Family Life.* Trans. Robert Baldick. New York: Vintage.

———. 1970. *Centuries of Childhood: A Social History of Family Life.* New York: Knopf.

———. 1974. *Western Attitudes toward Death from the Middle Ages to the Present.* Baltimore: Johns Hopkins University Press.

———. 1985. *Images of Man and Death.* Cambridge, Mass.: Harvard University Press.

Arnup, Katherine, and Susan Boyd. 1995. Familial Disputes? Sperm Donors, Lesbian Mothers and Legal Parenthood. In Didi Herman and Carl Stychin, eds., *Legal Inversions: Lesbians, Gay Men and the Politics of Law.* Philadelphia: Temple University Press.

Arriola, Elvia Rosales. 1992. Sexual Identity and the Constitution: Homosexual Persons as a Discrete and Insular Minority. *Women's Rights Law Reporter* 14: 263–96.

Ashbaker, Susan S. 1993. Small White Box. *Unite Notes* 12, 2: 1.

———. 1994. What Will You Look Like in Heaven? *Unite Notes* 12, 3: 5.

Association for Recognizing the Life of Stillborns. 1992. Recognition of Life Certificates. *SHARE Newsletter* 1, 5: 5.

Badran, Margot. 1993. Independent Women: More than a Century of Feminism in Egypt. In Judith E. Tucker, ed., *Arab Women: Old Boundaries, New Frontiers*. Bloomington: Indiana University Press.

Bagley, Christopher, and Loretta Young. 1979. The Identity, Adjustment, and Achievement of Transracially Adopted Children: A Review and Empirical Report. In Gajendra Verma and Christopher Bagley, eds., *Race, Education, and Identity*. New York: St. Martin's Press.

Bagley, Christopher, Loretta Young, and Anne Scully. 1993. *International and Transracial Adoptions: A Mental Health Perspective*. Brookfield, Vt.: Avebury Press.

Bailey, Alison. 1995. Mothering, Diversity and Peace Politics. *Hypatia* 9, 2: 189–98.

Baker, Elena. 1992. Our Special Baby. *Unite Notes* 11, 2: 4.

Baldwin, Paula. 1994. Christmas 1994. *SHARE Newsletter* 3, 6: 5.

Bancroft and Whitney. 1996. Family Code—Annotated—of the State of California. *Deering's California Codes*. San Francisco: Bancroft and Whitney.

Barth, Richard. 1988. Disruption in Older Child Adoptions. *Public Welfare* 46: 23–29.

———. 1993. Fiscal Issues and Stability in Special-Needs Adoptions: Adoption Assistance Payments Should Help Children Get Adopted and Stay Adopted. *Public Welfare* 51: 21–28.

Barth, Richard, and Marianne Berry. 1988. *Adoption and Disruption: Rates, Risks, and Response*. New York: Aldine de Gruyter.

Barthes, Roland. 1983. *The Fashion System*. Trans. Matthew Ward and Richard Howard. New York: Hill and Wang.

Bartholet, Elizabeth. 1993. *Family Bonds: Adoption and the Politics of Parenting*. Boston: Houghton Mifflin.

Basch, Norma. 1992. Invisible Women: The Legal Fiction of Marital Unity in Nineteenth-Century America. In N. F. Cott, ed., *History of Women in the United States*. vol. 3: *Domestic Relations and Law*. Munich: K. G. Saur.

Bassin, Donna, Margaret Honey, and Meryle Kaplan, eds. 1994. *Representation of Motherhood*. New Haven: Yale University Press.

Bates, J. Douglas. 1993. *Gift Children: A Story of Race, Family, and Adoption in a Divided America*. New York: Ticknor and Fields.

Baudrillard, Jean. 1983. *Simulations*. New York: Semiotext(e).

Becker, Gay. 1994. Metaphors in Disrupted Lives: Infertility and Cultural Constructions of Continuity. *Medical Anthropology Quarterly* 8, 4: 383–410.

Bedevian, Armenag K. 1936. *Illustrated Polyglottic Dictionary of Plant Names in Latin, Arabic, Armenian, English, French, German, Italian and Turkish Languages Including Economic, Medicinal, Poisonous and Ornamental Plants and Common Weeds*. Cairo: Argus and Papazian.

Behar, Ruth. 1993. *Translated Woman: Crossing the Border with Esperanza's Story*. Boston: Beacon Press.

Behar, Ruth, and Deborah Gordon, eds. 1995. *Women Writing Culture*. Berkeley: University of California Press.

Benjamin, Walter. 1989. The Work of Art in the Age of Mechanical Reproduction. In David H. Richter, ed., *The Critical Tradition.* New York: St. Martin's Press.

Benkov, Laura. 1994. *Reinventing the Family: The Emerging Story of Lesbian and Gay Parents.* New York: Crown.

Benson, Susan. 1981. *Ambiguous Ethnicity: Interracial Families in London.* Cambridge, U.K.: Cambridge University Press.

Betteridge, Anne H. 1992. Specialists in Miraculous Action: Some Shrines in Shiraz. In A. Morinis, ed., *Sacred Journeys: The Anthropology of Pilgrimage.* Westport, Conn.: Greenwood Press.

Blair, Lynne. 1990. An Empty Room. *Unite Notes* 9, 2: 2.

Blake, William. 1970. Auguries of Innocence. In *A Choice of Blake's Verse,* ed. Kathleen Raine. London: Faber and Faber.

Blank, Robert. 1990. *Regulating Reproduction.* New York: Columbia University Press.

Blee, Kathleen. 1991. *Women of the Klan: Gender and Racism in the 1920s.* Berkeley: University of California Press.

———. 1997. Mothers in Race-Hate Movements. In Alexis Jetter, Annelise Orleck, and Diana Taylor, eds., *The Politics of Motherhood: Activist Voices from Left to Right.* Hanover, N.H.: University Press of New England.

Bongaarts, John, and Robert G. Potter. 1983. *Fertility, Biology and Behavior: An Analysis of the Proximate Determinants.* New York: Academic Press.

Booth, John. 1982. *The End of the Begining. The Nicaraguan Revolution.* Boulder: Westview.

Booth, Wayne C. 1974. *A Rhetoric of Irony.* Chicago: University of Chicago Press.

Bouhdiba, Abdelwahab. 1985. *Sexuality in Islam.* London: Routledge and Kegan Paul.

Bourdieu, Pierre. 1984. *Distinction: A Social Critique of the Judgement of Taste.* Trans. Richard Nice. Cambridge, Mass.: Harvard University Press.

Bourgois, Philippe. 1995. *In Search of Respect: Selling Crack in El Barrio.* Cambridge, U.K.: Cambridge University Press.

Boyette, Kathy. 1996. No Vacation. *SHARE Newsletter* 5, 3: 15.

Boyne, J., L. Denby, J. R. Kettening, and W. Wheeler. 1984. *The Shadow of Success: A Statistical Analysis of Outcomes of Adoptions of Hard-to-Place Children.* Westfield, Conn.: Spaulding for Children.

Brady, Ivan. 1976. *Transactions in Kinship: Adoption and Fosterage in Oceania.* Honolulu: University Press of Hawai'i.

Brown, Carol. 1981. Mothers, Fathers, and Children: From Private to Public Patriarchy. In L. Sargent, ed., *Women and Revolution: A Discussion of the Unhappy Marriage of Marxism and Feminism.* Boston: South End Press.

Brown, Jacqueline. 1998. Black Liverpool, Black America, and the Gendering of Diasporic Space, *Cultural Anthropology* 13, 3: 291–325.

Browne, Ray B. 1981. Introduction. In Ray B. Browne, ed., *Objects of Special Devotion: Fetishism in Popular Culture.* Bowling Green: Bowling Green University Popular Press.

Browner, Carole, and Nancy Press, eds. 1997. The Production of Authoritative Knowledge in American Prenatal Care. In Robbie Davis-Floyd and Carolyn Sargent, eds., *Childbirth and Authoritative Knowledge*. Berkeley: University of California Press.

Buckley, Thomas, and Alma Gottlieb. 1988. *Blood Magic: The Anthropology of Menstruation.* Berkeley: University of California Press.

Buck-Morss, Susan. 1989. *The Dialectics of Seeing: Walter Benjamin and the Arcades Project.* Cambridge, Mass.: MIT Press.

Buker, Eloise. 1987. Storytelling Power: Personal Narratives and Political Analysis. *Women and Politics* 7, 3: 29–47.

Burlingham-Brown, Barbara. 1994. *"Why Didn't She Keep Me?" Answers to the Question Every Adopted Child Asks.* South Bend: Langford Books.

Byrne, Jeffrey S. 1993. Affirmative Action for Lesbians and Gay Men: A Proposal for True Equality of Opportunity and Workforce Diversity. *Yale Law and Policy Review* 11: 47.

Cabezas, Omar. 1989. *Canción de amor para los hombres.* Managua: Editorial Nueva Nicaragua.

Cahn, Katherine, and Paul Johnson, eds. 1993. *Children Can't Wait: Reducing Delays for Children in Foster Care.* New York: Child Welfare League of America.

Calhoun, Craig. 1995. *Critical Social Theory.* Oxford: Basil Blackwell.

Campbell, Hannah D. 1990. The Green Lollipop. *Unite Notes* 9, 3: 3.

———. 1991a. Is My Baby Dead? *Unite Notes* 10, 4: 2–3.

———. 1991b. On Top of Our Tree at Christmastime. *Unite Notes* 10, 4: 3.

———. 1992. The Picnic Basket. *Unite Notes* 11, 1: 5.

———. 1995–96. An Aunt's Grief. *Unite Notes* 14, 3: 2.

Caplow, Theodore. 1982. Christmas Gifts and Kin Networks. *American Sociological Review* 47: 383–92.

Caroll, Vernon, ed. 1970. *Adoption in Eastern Oceania.* Honolulu: University of Hawai'i Press.

Carr, Bruce R., and Richard E. Blackwell, eds. 1993. *Textbook of Reproductive Medicine.* Norwalk, Conn.: Appleton and Lange.

Cashmore, E. Ellis. 1987. *The Logic of Racism.* London: Allen and Unwin.

Casper, Monica. 1998. *The Making of the Unborn Patient: A Social Anatomy of Fetal Surgery.* New Brunswick, N.J.: Rutgers University Press.

Chaidez. 1985. In Pat Schwiebert and Paul Kirk, eds., *When Hello Means Goodbye: A Guide for Parents Whose Child Dies before Birth, at Birth or Shortly after Birth.* Portland, Ore.: Perinatal Loss.

Chamorro, Amalia. 1989. La mujer: Logros y limites en 10 años de revolución. *Cuadernos de Sociologia* 10.

Chaney, Elsa. 1979. *Supermadre: Women in Politics in Latin America.* Austin: University of Texas Press.

Chesler, Phyllis. 1991. *Mothers on Trial: The Battle for Children and Custody.* San Diego: Harcourt Brace Jovanovich.

Chiffens, Michell. 1991. I'm Here, Daddy. *Unite Notes* 10, 4: 1.

————. 1994. Time for Kindergarten. *Unite Notes* 12, 3: 3.

Chinchilla, Norma. 1990. Revolutionary Popular Feminism: Articulating Class, Gender and National Sovereignty. *Gender and Society* 4, 3: 370–98.

Chodorow, Nancy. 1974. Family Structure and Feminine Personality. In Michelle Rosaldo and Louise Lamphere, eds., *Woman, Culture and Society*. Stanford: Stanford University Press.

————. 1978. *The Reproduction of Mothering: Psychoanalysis and the Sociology of Gender.* Berkeley: University of California Press.

Chused, Richard H. 1992. Married Women's Property Law: 1800–1850. In N. F. Cott, ed., *History of Women in the United States*, vol. 3: *Domestic Relations and Law*. Munich: K. G. Saur.

Ciany, Anne. 1999. I'm a Mother Too. S*haring* 8, 3: 6.

Cline, Foster. 1979. *Understanding and Treating the Severely Disturbed Child.* Evergreen, Colo.: Evergreen Consultants in Human Behavior.

Colen, Shellee. 1986. "With Respect and Feelings": Voices of West Indian Child Care and Domestic Workers in New York City. In J. B. Cole, ed., *All American Women: Lines that Divide, Ties that Bind.* New York: Free Press.

————. 1990. "Housekeeping" for the Green Card: West Indian Household Workers, the State, and Stratified Reproduction in New York. In Roger C. Sanjek and Shellee Colen, eds., *At Work in Homes: Household Workers in World Perspective.* Washington, D.C.: American Anthropological Association.

————. 1995. "Like a Mother to Them": Stratified Reproduction and West Indian Child-care Workers and Employers in New York. In Faye Ginsburg and Rayna Rapp, eds., *Conceiving the New World Order: The Global Politics of Reproduction.* Berkeley: University of California Press.

Collet, M., et al. 1988. Infertility in Central Africa: Infection Is the Cause. *International Journal of Gynecology and Obstetrics* 26: 423–28.

Collier, Jane, and Sylvia Yanagisako, eds. 1987. *Gender and Kinship: Toward a Unified Analysis.* Stanford: Stanford University Press.

Collins, Patricia Hill. 1987. "The Meaning of Motherhood in Black Culture and Black Mother/Daughter Relationships." *SAGE: A Scholarly Journal on Black Women* 4: 2–10.

————. 1990. *Black Feminist Thought: Knowledge, Consciousness and the Politics of Empowerment.* New York: Routledge.

————. 1994. Shifting the Center: Race, Class and Feminist Theorizing about Motherhood. In Evelyn Nakano Glenn, Grace Chang, and Linda Rennie Forcey, eds., *Mothering: Ideology, Experience and Agency.* New York: Routledge.

Collinson, Helen, ed. 1990. *Women and Revolution in Nicaragua.* London: Zed Books.

Comaroff, Jean. 1977. Conflicting Paradigms of Pregnancy: Managing Ambiguity in Ante-Natal Encounters. In Alan Davis and Gordon Horobin, eds., *Medical Encounters: The Experience of Illness and Treatment.* New York: St. Martin's Press.

Commission for Racial Equality. 1981. *Racial Harassment on Local Authority Housing* Estates. London: Commission for Racial Equality.

———. 1987. *Living in Terror: A Report on Racial Violence and Harassment in Housing.* London: Commission for Racial Equality.

———. 1996. *Annual Report.* London: Commission for Racial Equality.

———. 1997. *Annual Report.* London: Commission for Racial Equality.

Condit, Celeste Michelle. 1990. *Decoding Abortion Rhetoric.* Urbana: University of Illinois Press.

Connors, Kathy. 1992. Letters. *Unite Notes* 11, 3: 3–5.

Conrad, Peter, and Joseph W. Schneider. 1992. *Deviance and Medicalization: From Badness to Sickness.* Philadelphia: Temple University Press.

Cook, Daniel. 1998. The Commoditization of Childhood: Personhood, the Children's Wear Industry and the Moral Dimensions of Consumption, 1917–1969. Ph.D. dissertation, Department of Sociology, University of Chicago.

Cooksey, Thomas L. 1992. The Aesthetics of Natural Theology: Charles Bucke and the Sublimities of Nature. Paper presented at the annual meeting of the Society for Literature and Science, Atlanta.

Coontz, Stephanie. 1992. *The Way We Never Were: American Families and the Nostalgia Trap.* New York: Basic Books.

Cordes, Renee. 1993. Natural versus Adoptive Parents' Rights at Center of Georgia Court Battle. *Trial* 29: 34.

Costin, Lela, and Shirley Wattenberg. 1979. Identity in Transracial Adoption: A Study of Parental Dilemmas and Family Experiences. In Gajendra Verma and Christopher Bagley, eds., *Race, Education, and Identity.* New York: St. Martin's Press.

Coulson, Noel, and Doreen Hinchcliffe. 1978. Women and Law Reform in Contemporary Islam. In Lois Beck and Nikki Keddie, eds., *Women in the Muslim World.* Cambridge, Mass.: Harvard University Press.

Crapanzano, Vincent. 1981. Rite of Return: Circumcision in Morocco. In Warner Muensterberger and L. Bryce Boyer, eds., *The Psychoanalytic Study of Society.* New York: Library of Psychological Anthropology.

Criquillón, Ana. 1989. La rebeldía de las mujeres nicarguenses: Semillero de una nueva democracia. In *Construcción de la democracia en Nicaragua.* Managua: Escuela de Sociología, Universidad Centroamericana.

Dalton, Susan E. 1998. When Is a Family Not a Family?: The Myth of Biological Reproduction and the Legal Invisibility of Lesbian and Gay Co-Parents. Ph.D. dissertation, University of California, Santa Barbara.

Davenport, Lisa. 1993. The Shoebox. *SHARE Newsletter* 2, 4: 3.

Davis, Angela Y. 1981. *Women, Race, and Class.* New York: Random House.

———. 1998. Surrogates and Outcast Mothers: Racism and Reproductive Politics in the Nineties. In Annette Dula and Sara Goering, eds., *It Just Ain't Fair: The Ethics of Healthcare for African Americans.* Westport, Conn.: Praeger.

Davis, Susan E., ed. 1988. *Women under Attack: Victories, Backlash, and the Fight for Reproductive Freedom*. Boston: South End Press.

Davis-Floyd, Robbie. 1992. *Birth as an American Rite of Passage*. Berkeley: University of California Press.

Davis-Floyd, Robbie, and Carolyn Sargent, eds. 1997. *Childbirth and Authoritative Knowledge: Cross-Cultural Perspectives*. Berkeley: University of California Press.

de Beauvoir, Simone. 1952. *The Second Sex*. H. M. Parshley, trans. and ed. New York: Knopf. Originally published in 1949.

de Certeau, Michel. 1984. *The Practice of Everyday Life*. Berkeley: University of California Press.

Delaney, Carol. 1991. *The Seed and the Soil: Gender and Cosmology in Turkish Village Society*. Berkeley: University of California Press.

D'Emilio, John. 1983. *Sexual Politics, Sexual Communities: The Making of a Homosexual Minority in the United States, 1940–1970*. Chicago: University of Chicago Press.

Deutsch, Francine. 1983. *Child Services: On Behalf of Children*. Monterey: Brooks-Cole.

DiFabio, Jacqueline Pirrie. 1997. Honor My Babies' Lives. *Sharing* 7, 1: 1–2.

di Leonardo, Micaela. 1987. The Female World of Card and Holidays: Women, Families, and the Work of Kinship. *Signs* 12, 3: 440–53.

Dobie, Sharon L., et al. 1998. Obstetric Care and Payment Source: Do Low-Risk Medicaid Women Get Less Care? *American Journal of Public Health* 88: 51–56.

Doerr, Maribeth Wilder. 1992. Memorializing Our Precious Babies. *Unite Notes* 11, 1: 3.

Doherty, Mary Cushing. 1991. The Keepers of the Flame. *Unite Notes* 10, 3: 1.

Dolan, Maureen. 1990. War, Religion and Gender Ideology: The Politics of Peace Symbols in the Nicaraguan Elections. *Critical Sociology* 17, 2: 103–9.

Dolgin, Janet L. 1997. *Defining the Family: Law, Technology, and Reproduction in an Uneasy Age*. New York and London: New York University Press.

Dorris, Michael. 1989. *The Broken Cord*. New York: Harper and Row.

Douglas, Ann. 1977. *The Feminization of American Culture*. New York: Avon Books.

Douglas, Mary. 1966. *Purity and Danger: An Analysis of the Concepts of Pollution and Taboo*. London: Routledge and Kegan Paul.

Douglas, Mary, and Baron Isherwood. 1979. *The World of Goods*. New York: Basic Books.

Down, Martyn Langdon. 1986. *Some Babies Die: an Exploration of Stillbirth and Neonatal Death*. [Film.] Australia.

Duberman, Martin, Martha Vicinus, and George Chauncey Jr., eds. 1989. *Hidden from History: Reclaiming the Gay and Lesbian Past*. New York: New American Library.

Edin, Kathryn, and Laura Lein. 1997. *Making Ends Meet: How Single Mothers Survive Welfare and Low-Wage Work*. Ithaca: Cornell University Press.

Egyptian Fertility Care Society. 1995. *Community-based Study of the Prevalence of Infertility and Its Etiological Factors in Egypt. (I) The Population-based Study*. Cairo: Egyptian Fertility Care Society, Cairo.

El-Mehairy, Theresa. 1984. *Medical Doctors: A Study of Role Concept and Job Satisfaction, The Egyptian Case.* Leiden: E. J. Brill.

Envio. 1986. Managua's Economic Crisis: How Do the Poor Survive? *Envio* (Managua), December.

Erdrich, Louise. 1995. The Broken Cord. In S. Wadia-Ells, ed., *The Adoption Reader.* Seattle: Seal Press.

Esposito, John L. 1982. *Women in Muslim Family Law.* Syracuse: Syracuse University Press.

———. 1991. *Islam: The Straight Path.* New York: Oxford University Press.

Essed, Philomena. 1990. *Understanding Everyday Racism: Towards an Interdisciplinary Theory.* Newbury Park, Calif.: Sage Publications.

Etienne, Mona. 1979. The Case for Social Maternity: Adoption of Children by Urban Baulé Women. *Dialectical Anthropology* 4: 237–42.

Etter, Jeanne. 1993. Levels of Cooperation and Satisfaction in 56 Open Adoptions. *Child Welfare* 72: 257–67.

Fauné, María Angélica. 1994. Cambios de las familias en Centroamerica. *Isis Internacional* 20: 107–51.

Feigelman, William. 1997. Adopted Adults: Comparisons with Persons Raised in Conventional Families. *Marriage and Family Review* 24: 1–2: 199.

Feijoó, Maria del Carmen. 1989. The Challenge of Constructing Civilian Peace: Women and Democracy in Argentina. In Jane S. Jaquette, ed., *The Women's Movement in Latin America: Feminism and the Transition to Democracy.* Boston: Unwin Hyman.

Feijoó, Maria del Carmen, and Hilda Herzer. 1991. *Las mujeres y la vida en las ciudades.* Buenos Aires: Grupo Editor Latinoamericano.

Fein, Ester B. 1998. For Lost Pregnancies, New Rites of Mourning. *New York Times,* January 25.

Ferguson, Phil. 1996. Mental Retardations Historiography and the Culture of Knowledge. *Disability Studies Quarterly* 16, 3: 18–31.

Fineman, Martha Albertson, and Isabel Karpin. 1995. *Mothers in Law: Feminist Theory and the Legal Regulation of Motherhood.* New York: Columbia University Press.

Fisher, Jo. 1989. *Mothers of the Disappeared.* London: Zed Books.

Flango, Victor. 1990. Agency and Private Adoptions, by State. *Child Welfare* 69: 263–75.

Fonseca, Claudia. 1986. Orphanages, Foundlings, and Foster Mothers: The System of Child Circulation in a Brazilian Squatter Settlement. *Anthropological Quarterly* 59, 1: 15–27.

Forcey, Linda Rennie. 1994. Feminist Perspectives on Mothering and Peace. In Evelyn Nakano Glenn, Grace Chang, and Linda Rennie Forcey, eds., *Mothering: Ideology, Experience, and Agency.* New York: Routledge.

Foster, Cindy. 1985. Baby Things. *SHARE Newsletter* 8, 5: 1.

Foucault, Michel. 1977. *Discipline and Punish: The Birth of the Prison.* Trans. A. Sheridan. New York: Vintage.

Frankenberg, Ruth. 1993. *White Women, Race Matters: The Social Construction of Whiteness.* Minneapolis: University of Minnesota Press.

Franklin, Sarah. 1995. Science as Culture, Cultures of Science. *Annual Review of Anthropology* 24: 163–84.

———. 1997. *Embodied Progress: A Cultural Account of Assisted Conception.* New York: Routledge.

Friedeck, Sue. 1995a. When Remembering Becomes More Sweet than Bitter. *SHARE Newsletter* 4, 4: 1–2.

———. 1995b. Caring for those Special Photos. *SHARE Newsletter* 4, 4: 11.

Fussell, Paul. 1983. *Class.* New York: Ballantine Books.

Gaber, Ivor, and Jane Aldridge, eds. 1994. *In the Best Interests of the Child: Culture, Identity, and Transracial Adoption.* London: Free Association Books.

Gailey, Christine Ward. 1998a. Making Kinship in the Wake of History: Gendered Violence in Older Child Adoption. *Identities* 15.

———. 1998b. The Search for Baby Right: Race, Class, and Gender in U.S. International Adoption. Paper presented at the Wenner-Gren symposium New Directions in Kinship Study: A Core Concept Revisited, Majorca, March 27–April 4.

Gamman, Lorraine, and Merja Makinen. 1994. *Female Fetishism: A New Look.* London: Lawrence and Wishart.

Gana, Kathy. 1986. *Unite Notes* 5, 5: 4.

Garcia, Lauro. 1986. *La estrategia de supervivencia de las clases populares de Managua.* Managua: Escuela de Sociología, Universidad Centroamericana.

Gediman, Judith, and Linda Brown. 1989. *Birthbond: Reunions between Birthparents and Adoptees—What Happens After.* Far Hills, N.J.: New Horizon Press.

Gillis, John R. 1994. Memory and Identity: The History of a Relationship. In John R. Gillis, ed. *Commemoration: The Politics of National Identity.* Princeton: Princeton University Press.

Gilroy, Paul. 1987. *There Ain't No Black in the Union Jack: The Cultural Politics of Race and Nation.* Chicago: University of Chicago Press.

Ginsburg, Faye, and Rayna Rapp. 1991. The Politics of Reproduction. *Annual Review of Anthropology* 20: 311–44.

———. 1995a. *Conceiving the New World Order: The Global Politics of Reproduction.* Berkeley: University of California Press.

———. 1995b. Introduction: Conceiving the New World Order. In Faye Ginsburg and Rayna Rapp, eds., *Conceiving the New World Order: The Global Politics of Reproduction.* Berkeley: University of California Press.

Glenn, Evelyn Nakano, Grace Chang, and Linda Rennie Forcey, eds. 1994. *Mothering: Ideology, Experience and Agency.* New York: Routledge.

Glover, Jonathan. 1990. *Ethics of New Reproductive Technologies: The Glover Report to the European Commission.* DeKalb: Northern Illinois University Press.

Gluck, Sherna Berger, and Daphne Patai, eds. 1990. *Women's Words: The Feminist Practice of Oral History*. New York: Routledge.

Goffman, E. 1963. *Stigma: Notes on the Management of Spoiled Identity*. Englewood Cliffs, N.J.: Prentice-Hall.

Golden, Carol. 1993. Faraway Flower. *Unite Notes* 12, 3: 1.

Gomez, Laura. 1997. *Misconceiving Mothers: Legislators, Prosecutors and the Politics of Prenatal Drug Exposure*. Philadelphia: Temple University Press.

Gonzalez, Kelly. 1995. Birthdays and Anniversaries. *SHARE Newsletter* 4, 5: 8–9.

Good, Mary-Jo DelVecchio. 1980. Of Blood and Babies: The Relationship of Popular Islamic Physiology to Fertility. *Social Science and Medicine* 14B: 147–56.

Gordon, Linda. 1994. *Pitied but Not Entitled: Single Mothers and the History of Welfare*. New York: Free Press.

Gorenstein, Shirley. 1996. Introduction: Material Culture. In "Research in Science and Technology Studies: Material Culture," special issue edited by Shirley Gorenstein. *Knowledge and Society* 10: 1–18. Greenwich, Conn.: JAI Press.

Gould, Jeffrey. 1990. *To Lead as Equals: Rural Protest and Political Consciousness in Chinandega, Nicaragua, 1912–1979*. Chapel Hill: University of North Carolina Press.

Gramsci, Antonio. 1971. *Selections from the Prison Notebooks*. London: Lawrence and Wishart.

Grayson, Deborah R. 1998. Mediating Intimacy: Black Surrogate Mothers and the Law. *Critical Inquiry* 24: 525–46.

Greenwood, Bernard. 1981. Perceiving Systems: Cold or Spirits? Choice and Ambiguity in Morocco's Pluralistic Medical System. *Social Science and Medicine* 15B: 219–35.

Groze, Victor. 1991. Adoption and Single Parents: A Review. *Child Welfare* 70, 3: 321–22.

———. 1996. *Successful Adoptive Families: A Longitudinal Study of Special Needs Adoption*. New York, NY: Praeger.

Groze, Victor, and Daniela Ileana. 1996. A Follow-Up Study of Adopted Children from Romania. *Child and Adolescent Social Work Journal* 13, 6: 543–65.

Groze, Victor, and James A. Rosenthal. 1991a. Single Parents and Their Adopted Children: A Psychological Analysis. *Families in Society: The Journal of Contemporary Human Services* 72, 2: 62–77.

———. 1991b. A Structural Analysis of Families Adopting a Special-Needs Child. *Families in Society: The Journal of Contemporary Human Services* 72, 8: 469–81.

Guenther, Debbie. 1991. Recognition of Life Certificates. *SHARE Newsletter* 14, 1: 7–8.

Guillemin, Jeanne Harley, and Lynda Lytle Holmstrom. 1986. *Mixed Blessings: Intensive Care for Newborns*. Oxford: Oxford University Press.

Hairston, Creasie, and Vicki Williams. 1989. Black Adoptive Parents: How They View Agency Practices. *Social Casework* 33: 543–45.

Handler, Richard. 1988. *Nationalism and the Politics of Culture in Quebec*. Madison: University of Wisconsin Press.

Haraway, Donna. 1989a. *Primate Visions: Gender, Race and Nation in the World of Modern Science.* New York: Routledge.

———. 1989b. The Biopolitics of Postmodern Bodies: Determinations of Self in Immune System Discourse. *Differences* 1, 1: 3–43.

———. 1991. *Simians, Cyborgs, and Women: The Reinvention of Nature.* New York: Routledge.

———. 1997. *Modest_Witness@Second_Millennium.FemaleMan_Meets_OncoMouse^{TM}.* New York: Routledge.

Harris, Hermione. 1988. Women and War: The Case of Nicaragua. In Eva Isaksson, ed., *Women and the Military System.* New York: Harvester Wheatsheaf.

Harris, Kathleen Mullan. 1997. Teen Mothers and the Revolving Welfare Door. Philadelphia: Temple University Press.

Hartigan, Jr., John. 1997. Locating White Detroit. In Ruth Frankenberg, ed., *Displacing Whiteness: Social and Cultural Criticism.* Durham: Duke University Press.

Hartmann, Heide. 1981. The Unhappy Marriage of Marxism and Feminism: Towards a More Progressive Union. In L. Sargent, ed., *Women and Revolution: A Discussion of the Unhappy Marriage of Marxism and Feminism.* Boston: South End Press.

Hartouni, Valerie. 1991. Containing Women: Reproductive Discourse in the 1980s. In Constance Penley and Andrew Ross, eds., *Technoculture.* Minneapolis: University of Minnesota Press.

———. 1994. Breached Birth: Reflections on Race, Gender, and Reproductive Discourse in the 1980s. *Configurations* 1: 73–88.

———. 1997. *Cultural Conceptions: On Reproductive Technologies and the Remaking of Life.* Minneapolis: University of Minnesota Press.

Hatem, Merrat. 1986. The Enduring Alliance of Nationalism and Patriarchy in Muslim Personal Status Laws: The Case of Modern Egypt. *Feminist Issues* 6: 19–43.

Hays, Sharon. 1996. *The Cultural Contradictions of Motherhood.* New Haven, Conn.: Yale University Press.

Hely. 1991. Remember Your Baby.

Herda, D. 1989. Keepsakes. *SHARE Newsletter* 12, 3: 7.

Hollinger, Joan Heifetz. 1996. *Adoption Law and Practice.* New York: Matthew Bender.

Homes for the Homeless and Columbia University. 1998. *Homeless Families Today: Our Challenge Tomorrow, A Report.* New York: Institute for Children and Poverty.

Hopson, Darlene Howell, and Derek S. Hopson. 1990. *Different and Wonderful: Raising Black Children in a Race-Conscious Society.* New York: Fireside Books/Simon and Schuster.

Howe, Ruth-Arlene. 1995. Redefining the Transracial Adoption Controversy. *Duke Journal of Gender Law and Policy* 2, 1: 131–50.

———. 1997. Transracial Adoption: Old Prejudices and Discrimination Float under a New Halo. *Boston University Public Interest Law Journal* 6, 2: 409–30.

Hull, Richard. 1990. Gestational Surrogacy and Surrogate Motherhood. In Richard Hull, ed., *Ethical Issues in the New Reproductive Technologies.* Belmont, Calif.: Wadsworth.

Hyneman, Nanci. 1988. Ideas for Remembrance. *SHARE Newsletter* 11, 3: 6.

Iacono, Linda. 1982. Faith. *Unite Notes* 2, 1: 4–6.

Ingle, Kristen. 1981–82. For Elizabeth at Christmas. *Unite Notes* 1, 2: 1.

Ingraham, Chrys. 1996. The Heterosexual Imaginary: Feminist Sociology and Theories of Gender. In Steven Seidman, ed., *Queer Theory/Sociology*. Cambridge, Mass.: Blackwell.

Inhorn, Marcia. C. 1994a. *Quest for Conception: Gender, Infertility, and Egyptian Medical Traditions*. University of Pennsylvania Press, Philadelphia.

———. 1994b. *Kabsa* (a.k.a. *Mushahara*) and Threatened Fertility in Egypt. *Social Science and Medicine* 39: 487–505.

———. 1996. *Infertility and Patriarchy: The Cultural Politics of Gender and Family Life in Egypt.* Philadelphia: University of Pennsylvania Press.

Inhorn, Marcia C., and Kimberly A. Buss. 1993. Infertility, Infection, and Iatrogenesis in Egypt: The Anthropological Epidemiology of Blocked Tubes. *Medical Anthropology* 15: 1–28.

James, Stanlie M. 1993. Mothering: A Possible Black Feminist Link to Social Transformation? In Stanlie M. James and Abena P. A. Busia, eds., *Theorizing Black Feminisms: The Visionary Pragmatism of Black Women*. London: Routledge.

Jay, Karly, and Allen Young, eds. 1992. *Out of the Closet: Voices of Gay Liberation*. New York: New York University Press.

Jeffries, Lisa M. 1998. We've Lost. *Unite Notes* 17, 2: 1.

Jelin, Elisabeth, ed. 1990. *Women and Social Change in Latin America*. London: Zed Books.

———. 1994. The Politics of Memory: The Human Rights Movement and the Construction of Democracy in Argentina. *Latin American Perspectives* 21, 2: 38–58.

Jensen, P., et al. 1987. Climacteric Symptoms after Oral and Percutaneous Hormone Replacement Therapy. *Maturitas* 9: 207–15.

Jetter, Alexis, Annelise Orleck, and Diana Taylor, eds. 1998. *The Politics of Motherhood: Activist Voices from Left to Right*. Darmouth: University Press of New England.

Jewett, Claudia. 1978. *Adopting the Older Child*. Cambridge, Mass.: Harvard Common Press.

———. 1982. *Helping Children Cope with Grief and Loss*. Cambridge, Mass.: Harvard Common Press.

Johnson, A., and V. Groze. 1993. The Orphaned and Institutionalized Children of Romania. *Journal of Emotional and Behavioral Problems* 2, 4: 49–52.

Jordan, Brigitte. 1993. *Birth in Four Cultures: A Cross-Cultural Investigation of Childbirth in Yucatan, Holland, Sweden, and the United States*. Prospect Heights, Ill.: Waveland Press.

———. 1997. Authoritative Knowledge and Its Construction. In Robbie Davis-Floyd and Carolyn Sargent, eds., *Childbirth and Authoritative Knowledge: Cross-Cultural Perspectives*. Berkeley: University of California Press.

Kadushin, A. 1980. *Child Welfare Services*. New York: Macmillan.

Kaplan, Caren. 1994. The Politics of Location and Transnational Feminism: Critical Practice. In Caren Kaplan and Inderpal Grewal, eds., *Scattered Hegemonies: Postmodernity and Transnational Feminist Practices.* Minneapolis: University of Minnesota Press.

Kaplan, Elaine Bell. 1997. *Not Our Kind of Girl: Unraveling the Myth of Black Teenage Motherhood.* Berkeley: University of California Press.

Kay, Herma Hill. 1965. The Family and Kinship Systems of Illegitimate Children in California. *American Anthropologist* 67: 57–81.

Kelly, Mary, and Emily Apter. 1993. The Smell of Money: Mary Kelly in Conversation with Emily Apter. In Emily Apter and William Pietz, eds., *Fetishism As Cultural Discourse.* Ithaca: Cornell University Press.

Kerns, Virginia, and Judith K. Brown, eds. 1992. *In Her Prime: New Views of Middle-Aged Women.* Urbana: University of Illinois Press.

Kimble, Judy, and Elaine Unterhalter. 1982. We Opened the Road for You, You Must Go Forward: ANC Women's Struggle 1912–1982. *Feminist Review* 12: 11–35.

King, Wilma. 1995. *Stolen Childhood: Slave Youth in Nineteenth-Century America.* Bloomington: Indiana University Press.

Kirk, H. David. 1982. *Shared Fate: A Theory and Method of Adoptive Relationships.* Port Angeles, Wash: Ben-Simon Publications.

———. 1985. *Adoptive Kinship: A Modern Institution in Need of Reform.* Port Angeles, Wash: Ben-Simon Publications.

Kleinman, Arthur, and Joan Kleinman. 1991. Suffering and Its Professional Transformation: Toward an Ethnography of Interpersonal Experience. *Culture, Medicine, and Psychiatry* 15: 275–301.

Kline, Marlee. 1994. Complicating the Ideology of Motherhood: Child Welfare Law and First Nation Women. In Martha Albertson Fine and Isabel Karpin, eds., *Mothers in Law: Feminist Theory and the Legal Regulation of Motherhood.* New York: Columbia University Press.

Koonz, Claudia. 1987. Mothers of the Fatherland. Women, the Family and Nazi Politics. New York: St. Martin's Press.

Koven, Seth, and Sonya Michel, eds. 1993. *Mothers of the New World: Maternalist Politics and the Origins of Welfare States.* London: Routledge.

Kuchner, Jean, and Jane Porcino. 1988. Delayed Motherhood. In *The Different Faces of Motherhood,* B. Birns and D. Hay, eds. New York: Plenum Press.

Kurdek, Lawrence A. 1993. The Allocation of Household Labor in Gay, Lesbian, and Heterosexual Married Couples. *Journal of Social Issues* 49: 127–39.

La mujer en cifras. 1987. Managua: Documentos de la Mujer.

Ladd-Taylor, Molly, and Lauri Umansky, eds. 1998. *Bad Mothers: The Politics of Blame in Twentieth Century America.* New York: New York University Press.

Ladner, Joyce A. 1971. *Tomorrow's Tomorrow: The Black Woman.* New York: Doubleday.

————. 1977. *Mixed Families: Adopting across Racial Boundaries.* Garden City, N.J.: Anchor/ Doubleday.

Lambert, Cathi. 1992. The Christmas Tree. *SHARE Newsletter* 1, 5: 5.

Lancaster, Roger. 1988. *Thanks to God and the Revolution: Popular Religion and Class Consciousness in the New Nicaragua.* New York: Columbia University Press.

————. 1992. *Life Is Hard: Machismo, Danger and the Intimacy of Power in Nicaragua.* Berkeley: University of California Press.

Landsman, Gail. 1999. Does God Give Special Kids to Special Parents? Personhood and the Child with Disabilities as Gift and as Giver. In Linda Layne, ed., *Transformative Mothering: On Giving and Getting in a Consumer Culture.* New York: New York University Press.

Lane, Sandra D., and Robert A. Rubinstein. 1991. The Use of *Fatwas* in the Production of Reproductive Health Policy in Egypt. Paper presented at the annual meeting of the American Anthropological Association, Chicago.

Larson, Erik. 1992. *The Naked Consumer: How Our Private Lives Become Public Commodities.* New York: Henry Holt.

Laux, Jana. 1988a. Baby Pictures Questionnaire—Part I. *SHARE Newsletter* 11, 3: 10–13.

————. 1988b. Baby Pictures Questionnaire—Part II. *SHARE Newsletter* 11, 4: 10–12.

Layne, Linda L. 1988. Review of *Some Babies Die.* A Film by Martyn Langdon Down, 1986. *Visual Anthropology* 1, 3: 491–97.

————. 1990. Motherhood Lost: Cultural Dimensions of Miscarriage and Stillbirth in America. *Women and Health* 16(3): 75–104.

————. 1992. Of Fetuses and Angels: Fragmentation and Integration in Narratives of Pregnancy Loss. In Hess and Layne, eds., *Knowledge and Society.* Hartford, Conn.: JAI Press.

————. 1994. Motherhood and Naturehood in the Late Twentieth Century. Paper presented at the annual meeting of the Society for Social Studies of Science, New Orleans.

————. 1995. "Bad Luck Genes": Fate and (Mis)fortune in Genetic Understandings of Pregnancy Loss. Paper presented at the annual meeting of the Society for Social Studies of Science, Charlottesville.

————. 1996a. "How's the Baby Doing?": Struggling with Narratives of Progress in a Neonatal Intensive Care Unit. *Medical Anthropology Quarterly* 10, 4: 624–56.

————. 1996b. "Never Such Innocence Again": Irony, Nature and Technoscience in Narratives of Pregnancy Loss. In Rosanne Cecil, ed., *Comparative Studies in Pregnancy Loss.* Oxford: Berg.

————. 1997. Breaking the Silence: An Agenda for a Feminist Discourse of Pregnancy Loss. *Feminist Studies* 23, 2: 289–315.

————. 1998. "The Cultural Fix": An Anthropological Contribution to Science and Technology Studies. Paper presented at the annual meeting of the Society for Social Studies of Science, Halifax.

————. 1999a. "I Remember the Day I Shopped for Your Layette": Goods, Fetuses and Feminism in the Context of Pregnancy Loss. In Lynn Morgan and Meridith Michaels, eds., *The Fetal Imperative/Feminist Practices*. Philadelphia: University of Pennsylvania Press.

————. 1999b. "True Gifts from God": Of Motherhood, Sacrifice, and Enrichment in the Context of Pregnancy Loss. In Linda Layne, ed., *Transformative Motherhood*. New York: New York University Press.

————. 1999c. Introduction: New Directions in EuroAmerican Gift Exchange. In Linda Layne, ed., *Transformative Motherhood*. New York: New York University Press.

————. Forthcoming. *Motherhood Lost: The Cultural Construction of Pregnancy Loss in the United States*. New York: Routledge.

Lazarre, Jane. 1996. *Beyond the Whiteness of Whiteness: Memoir of a White Mother of Black Sons*. Durham: Duke University Press.

Leach, Edmund. 1976. *Culture and Communication: The Logic by which Symbols Are Connected*. Cambridge, U.K.: Cambridge University Press.

Leake, Chauncey D. 1952. *The Old Egyptian Medical Papyri*. Lawrence: University of Kansas Press.

Lee, Robert, and Ruth Hall. 1983. Legal, Casework, and Ethical Issues in "Risk Adoption." *Child Welfare* 62.

Leicester City Council. 1996. *Leicester Key Facts: Ethnic Population*. Leicester: Leicester City Council.

Leicester City Council. 1995. *Leicestershire in Europe*.

Leicester City Council. 1993. *Leicester Key Facts: Ethnic Minorities, 1991 Census*.

Lewin, Ellen, and Virginia Olesen, eds. 1985. *Women, Health, and Healing: Toward a New Perspective*. New York: Methuen/Tavistock.

Lewis, Aliene. 1991. Untitled. *SHARE Newsletter* 14, 6: 6.

Lobao, Linda. 1990. Women in Revolutionary Movements: Changing Patterns of Latin America Guerrilla Struggle. In Guida West and Rhoda Lois Blumberg, eds., *Women and Social Protest*. New York: Oxford University Press.

Loehlin, J. C., L. Willerman, and J. M. Horn. 1987. Personality Resemblances in Adoptive Families: A 10-Year Follow-up. *Journal of Personality and Social Psychology* 53, 5: 961–69.

Longmore, Paul. 1997. Conspicuous Contribution and American Cultural Dilemmas: Telethon Rituals of Cleansing and Renewal. In David Mitchell and Sharon Snyder, eds., *The Body and Physical Difference: Discourses of Disability*. Ann Arbor: University of Michigan Press.

Luke, Carmen. 1994. White Women in Interracial Families: Reflections on Hybridization, Feminine Identities and Racialized Othering. *Feminist Issues* 14, 2: 49–72.

Luker, Kristen. 1996. *Dubious Conceptions: The Politics of Teenage Pregnancy*. Cambridge, Mass.: Harvard University Press.

Lutiens, Sheryll. 1995. Introduction. *Latin American Perspectives* 22, 2: 3–12.

MacCauley, Pat. 1982. The Longest Sixteen Days. *Unite Notes* 1, 3: 6–8.

Macdonald, Sharon. 1987. Drawing the Lines: Gender, Peace and War: An Introduction. In Sharon Macdonald, Pat Holden, and Shirley Ardener, eds., *Images of Women in Peace and War*. Houndmills, U.K.: Macmillan.

MacFarlane, Alison, and Miranda Mugford. 1984. *Birth Counts: Statistics of Pregnancy and Childbirth*. London: Her Majesty's Stationery Office.

MacPherson, C. B. 1962. *The Political Theory of Possessive Individualism*. Oxford: Oxford University Press.

Madelyn Company. 1996. Keepsake Pendants. *SHARE* 5, 4: 10.

Maier, Elisabeth. 1985. *Las Sandinistas*. México: Ediciones de Cultura Popular.

Maloney, Michael. 1994. Baby Jessica. *Journal of the American Academy of Child and Adolescent Psychiatry* 33: 430–31.

Manniche, Lise. 1989. *An Ancient Egyptian Herbal*. Austin: University of Texas Press.

Mansfield, Lynda Gianforte, and Christopher Waldman. 1994. *Don't Touch My Heart: Healing the Pain of an Unattached Child*. Colorado Springs: Pinon Press.

March, Karen. 1995a. *The Stranger Who Bore Me: Adoptee–Birth Mother Interactions*. Toronto: University of Toronto Press.

———. 1995b. Perception of Adoption as Social Stigma: Motivation for Search and Reunion. *Journal of Marriage and the Family* 57: 653–60.

Marchetti, Peter, and Cesar Perez. 1988. Democracy and Militarism: War and Development. *IDS Bulletin* 19: 3–12.

Marks, Jonathan. 1995. *Human Biodiversity: Genes, Race, and History*. New York: Aldine de Gruyter.

Martin, Bonita, and David Martin. 1995. When We Cry. *Unite Notes* 14, 1: 3.

Martin, Emily. 1987. *The Woman in the Body: A Cultural Analysis of Reproduction*. Boston: Beacon.

Martinson, Becca, ed. 1993. Special Issue on Adoption and Adoptism. *Pact Press*.

McCandish, Barbara M. 1987. Against All Odds: Lesbian Mother Family Dynamics. In F. W. Bozett, ed., *Gay and Lesbian Parents*. New York: Praeger.

McCracken, Grant. 1988. *Culture and Consumption: New Approaches to the Symbolic Character of Consumer Goods and Activities*. Bloomington: Indiana University Press.

McMurtry, S. L., and G. W. Lie. 1992. Differential Exit Rates of Minority Children in Foster Care. *Social Work Research and Abstracts* 28, 1: 42–48.

McVeigh, Brian. 1996. Commodifying Affection, Authority and Gender in the Everyday Objects of Japan. *Journal of Material Culture* 1, 3: 291–312.

Meezan, William. 1978. *Adoptions without Agencies: A Study of Independent Adoptions*. New York: Child Welfare League of America.

Mellon, Emma. 1992. A Ritual to Grieve Pregnancy Loss. *Unite Notes* 11, 1: 2.

Memories Unlimited. 1994. The Memory Box for Personal Loss. *SHARE Newsletter* 3, 5: 13.

Metropolitan Museum of Art. 1978. *Baby's Journal*. New York: Charles Scribner's Sons.

Michaels, Meredith, and Lynn Morgan. 1998. Introduction. In Meredith Michaels and Lynn M. Morgan, eds., *The Fetal Imperative: Feminist Positions*. Philadelphia: University of Pennsylvania Press.

————, eds. 1999. *Fetal Subjects, Feminist Positions*. Philadelphia: University of Pennsylvania Press.

Michaelson, Karen L., ed. 1988. *Childbirth in America: Anthropological Perspectives*. South Hadley, Mass.: Bergin and Garvey.

Miles, Robert. 1989. *Racism*. London: Routledge.

Millar, Marcia Inhorn, and Sandra D. Lane. 1988. Ethno-ophthalmology in the Egyptian Delta: An Historical Systems Approach to Ethnomedicine in the Middle East. *Social Science and Medicine* 26: 651–57.

Miller, Pamela A. 1981. Hair Jewelry as Fetish. In Ray B. Browne, ed., *Objects of Special Devotion: Fetishism in Popular Culture*. Bowling Green: Bowling Green University Popular Press.

Mills, Gloria. 1988. Baby's Breath Lapel Pin and Pendant. *SHARE Newsletter* 11, 3: 6.

Mink, Gwendolyn. 1995. *The Wages of Motherhood: Inequality in the Welfare State, 1917–1942*. Ithaca: Cornell University Press.

Mitchell, David, and Sharon Snyder. 1997. Introduction: Disability Studies and the Double Bind of Representation. In David Miller and Sharon Snyder, eds., *The Body and Physical Difference: Discourses of Disability*. Ann Arbor: University of Michigan Press.

Mitford, Jessica. 1963. *The American Way of Death*. New York: Simon and Schuster.

Modell, Judith. 1989. Last Chance Babies: Interpretations of Parenthood in an In Vitro Fertilization Program. *Medical Anthropology Quarterly* 3, 2: 124–38.

————. 1994. *Kinship with Strangers: Adoption and Interpretations of Kinship in American Culture*. Berkeley: University of California Press.

————. 1998. Rights to the Children: Foster Care and Social Reproduction in Hawaii. In Sarah Franklin and Helena Ragoné, eds., *Reproducing Reproduction: Kinship, Power, and Technological Innovation*. Philadelphia: University of Pennsylvania Press.

Modood, Tariq, and Richard Berthoud. 1997. *The Fourth National Survey of Ethnic Minorities: Diversity and Disadvantage*. London: Policy Studies Institute.

Mohanty, Chandra. 1991. Cartographies of Struggle: Third World Women and the Politics of Feminism. In Chandra Mohanty, Ann Russo, and Lourdes Torres, eds., *Third World Women and the Politics of Feminism*. Bloomington: Indiana University Press.

Molineux, Maxime. 1985. Women. In Thomas W. Walker, ed., *Nicaragua: The First Five Years*. New York: Praeger.

Morgan, Lynn M. 1996a. Fetal Relationality in Feminist Philosophy: An Anthropological Critique. *Hypatia: A Journal of Feminist Philosophy*.

————. 1996b. When Does Life Begin? A Cross-Cultural Perspective on the Personhood of Fetuses and Young Children. In William A. Haviland and Robert J. Gordon, eds., *Talking about People*. 2nd ed. Mountain View, Calif.: Mayfield.

Morley, John. 1971. *Death, Heaven and the Victorians*. Pittsburgh: Pittsburgh University Press.

Mulinari, Diana. 1996. *Motherwork and Politics in Revolutionary Nicaragua*. Lund: Bokbox Publications.

Murguialday, Clara. 1990. *Nicaragua, Revolución y Feminism, 1977–89*. Madrid: Editorial Revolución.

NABSW (National Association of Black Social Workers). 1991. *Preserving African American Families: Research and Action Beyond the Rhetoric*. Detroit: National Association of Black Social Workers.

———. 1994. *Position Statement: Preserving African-American Families*. Detroit: National Association of Black Social Workers.

NAIC (National Adoption Information Clearinghouse). 1998. Adoption Statistics. Washington, D.C., http://www.calib.com/naic/adoptinfo/research.htm.

Namaste, Ki. 1996. The Politics of Inside/Out: Queer Theory, Poststructuralism, and a Sociological Approach to Sexuality. In Steven Seidman, ed., *Queer Theory/Sociology*. Cambridge, Mass.: Blackwell.

Naples, Nancy. 1992. Activist Mothering: Cross-Generational Continuity in the Community Work of Women from Low-Income Urban Neighborhoods. *Gender and Society* 6, 3: 441–61.

Narayan, Uma. 1995. The "Gift" of a Child: Commercial Surrogacy, Gift Surrogacy and Motherhood. In Patricia Boling, ed., *Expecting Trouble: Surrogacy, Abuse and New Reproductive Technologies*. Boulder: Westview.

Nash, June. 1990. Latin American Women in the World Capitalist Crisis. *Gender and Society* 4, 3: 338–53.

Nash, June, and Helen Safa, eds. 1986. *Women and Change in Latin America: New Directions of Sex and Class*. South Hadley, Mass: Bergin and Garvey.

Newman, Katherine S. 1988. *Falling from Grace: The Experience of Downward Mobility in the American Middle Class*. New York: Random House.

Newman, Lucille. 1969. Folklore of Pregnancy. *Western Folklore* 28: 112–35.

Newsweek. 1995. Condemned to Life: After Hearing Disturbing New Details about Susan Smith's Tangled World, a Jury Votes against Death. *Newsweek,* Aug. 7, p. 19.

Niehoff, Michael L. 1995. Holiday Help for the Bereaved. *SHARE Newsletter* 4, 6: 3.

Ninivaggi, Cynthia. 1997. Adoption Relinquishment Ph.D. dissertation, Department of Anthropology, Temple University.

Nucitelli, Linda. 1997. David's Visit. *Unite Notes* 1.

Nuñez, Carlos. 1980. *El papel de las organizaciones de masas en el proceso revolucionario*. Managua: SENAPEP.

Oaks, Laura M. 1998. Expert and Everyday Perceptions of Pregnant Health Risks: An Ethnography of Cigarette Smoking and Fetal Politics in the U.S. Ph.D. dissertation, Department of Anthropology, Johns Hopkins University.

Ochs, Donovan J. 1993. *Consolatory Rhetoric: Grief, Symbol, and Ritual in the Greco-Roman Era.* Columbia: University of South Carolina Press.

Ochs, Elinor, and Bambi B. Schieffelin. 1984. Language Acquisition and Socialization: Three Developmental Stories and Their Implications. In Richard A. Shweder and Robert A. LeVine, eds., *Culture Theory: Essays on Mind, Self, and Emotion.* Cambridge, U.K.: Cambridge University Press.

OTA (Office of Technology Assessment). 1988. *Infertility: Medical and Social Choices.* Washington, D.C.: Government Printing Office.

Paige, Karen Ericksen, and Jeffery M. Paige. 1981. *The Politics of Reproductive Ritual.* Berkeley: University of California Press.

Paoletti, Jo B., and Carol L. Kregloh. 1989. The Children's Department. In Claudia Brush Kidwell and Valerie Steele, eds., *Men and Women: Dressing the Part.* Washington, D.C.: Smithsonian Institution Press.

Patt, Emily C. 1987–88. Second Parent Adoption: When Crossing the Marital Barrier Is a Child's Best Interest. *Berkeley Women's Law Journal* 3: 96–133.

Patterson, Charlotte J. 1992. Children of Lesbian and Gay Parents. *Child Development* 63: 1025–42.

———. 1994. Children of the Lesbian Baby Boom: Behavioral Adjustment, Self-concepts, and Sex Role Identity. In B. Greene and G. M. Herek, eds., *Lesbian and Gay Psychology: Theory, Research, and Clinical Applications.* Newbury Park, Calif.: Sage.

———. 1995. Families of the Lesbian Baby Boom: Parents' Division of Labor and Children's Adjustment. *Developmental Psychology* 31: 115–23.

Patterson, Joan, et al. 1997. Social Support in Families of Children with Chronic Conditions: Supportive and Nonsupportive Behaviors. *Developmental and Behavioral Pediatrics* 18, 6: 383–91.

Perez Alemán, Paola, and Pamela Diaz. 1986. *Diez años de investigación sobre la mujer en Nicaragua (1976–1986).* Managua: Oficina Legal de la Mujer.

Phillips, Mike, and Trevor Phillips. 1998. *Windrush: The Irresistible Rise of Multi-Racial Britain.* London: HarperCollins.

Phizacklea, Anne, and Robert Miles. 1980. *Labour and Racism.* London: Routledge.

Pierson, Ruth Roach. 1987. Did Your Mother Wear Army Boots? Feminist Theory and Women's Relation to War, Peace and Revolution. In Sharon Macdonald, Pat Holden, and Shirley Ardener, eds., *Images of Women in Peace and War.* Houndmills, U.K.: Macmillan.

Piven, Frances Fox. 1996. Welfare and the Transformation of Electoral Politics. *Dissent,* fall, pp. 61–68.

Plummer, Kenneth, ed. 1992. *Modern Homosexualities: Fragments of Lesbian and Gay Experience.* New York: Routledge.

Pohl, Constance, and Kathy Harris. 1993. *Transracial Adoption: Children and Parents Speak Out.* New York: Franklin Watts.

Polakow, Valerie. 1993. *Lives on the Edge: Single Mothers and Their Children in the Other Amer-ica*. Chicago: University of Chicago Press.

Pollitt, Katha. 1987. The Strange Case of Baby M. *The Nation,* May 23: 681–86, 688.

Press, Nancy, et al. 1997. Provisional Normalcy and "Perfect Babies": Pregnant Women's Attitudes toward Disability in the Context of Prenatal Testing. In Sarah Franklin and Helena Ragoné, eds., *Reproducing Reproduction*. Philadelphia: University of Pennsylvania Press.

Racial Attacks Monitoring Project (RAMP). 1991. *Leicester Racial Attacks Monitoring Project: Report 1990*. Leicester: R.A.M.P. Publications.

Ragoné, Helena. 1994. *Surrogate Motherhood: Conception in the Heart*. Boulder: Westview.

———. 1996. Chasing the Blood Tie: Surrogate Mothers, Adoptive Mothers and Fathers. *American Ethnologist* 23, 2: 352–65.

———. 1998. Incontestable Motivations. In Sarah Franklin and Helena Ragoné, eds., *Reproducing Reproduction: Kinship, Power, and Technological Innovation*. Philadelphia: University of Pennsylvania Press.

Rapp, Rayna. 1987. Moral Pioneers: Women, Men, and Fetuses: A Frontier of Reproductive Technology. *Women and Health* 13: 101–16.

———. 1999. *Testing Women, Testing the Fetus: The Social Impact of Amniocentesis in America*. New York: Routledge.

Reddy, Maureen. 1994. *Crossing the Color Line: Race, Parenting and Culture*. New Brunswick, N.J.: Rutgers University Press.

Register, Cheri. 1991. *"Are Those Kids Yours?": American Families with Children Adopted from Other Countries*. New York: Free Press.

Reinharz, Shulamit. 1988a. Controlling Women's Lives: A Cross-Cultural Interpretation of Miscarriage Accounts. *Research in the Sociology of Health Care* 7: 3–37.

Rhode, Deborah L. 1989. *Justice and Gender*. Cambridge, Mass.: Harvard University Press.

Rich, Adrienne. 1976. *Of Woman Born: Motherhood as an Institution*. New York: W. W. Norton.

Richards, David A. J. 1979. Sexual Autonomy and the Constitutional Right to Privacy: A Case Study in Human Rights and the Unwritten Constitution. *The Hastings Law Journal* 30: 957–1017.

———. 1993. Sexual Preference as a Suspect Classification. In David A. J. Richards, ed., *Conscience and the Constitution: History, Theory, and Law of the Reconstruction Amendments*. Princeton: Princeton University Press.

Riggs, Diane, ed. 1995. *Voices from the Heart: Personal Stories from Adoptive Families*. St. Paul, Minn.: North American Council on Adoptable Children.

Rivera, Rhonda. 1982. Homosexuality and the Law. In William Paul et al., eds., *Homosex-uality: Social, Psychological, and Biological Issues*. Beverly Hills, Calif.: Sage.

Roberts, Dorothy E. 1991. Punishing Drug Addicts Who Have Babies: Women of Color, Equality, and the Right to Privacy. *Harvard Law Review* 104, 7.

———. 1995. Racism and Patriarchy in the Meaning of Motherhood. In Martha Albertson Fineman and Isabel Karpin, eds., *Mothers in Law: Feminist Theory and the Legal Regulation of Motherhood*. New York: Columbia University Press.

———. 1996. The Value of Black Mothers' Work. *Radical America* 26(1).

———. 1997. *Killing the Black Body: Race, Reproduction and the Meaning of Liberty*. New York: Pantheon.

Robson, Ruthann. 1992. *Lesbian (Out)law: Survival under the Rule of Law*. Ithaca, N.Y.: Firebrand Books.

Roles, Patricia. 1989. *Saying Goodbye to a Baby*. Washington, D.C.: Child Welfare League.

Rook, Dennis W. 1985. The Ritual Dimension of Consumer Behavior. *Journal of Consumer Research* 12: 251–63.

Rosenthal, James, and Victor Groze. 1991. Behavior Problems of Special Needs Adopted Children. *Children and Youth Services Review* 13, 5–6: 343–61.

———. 1992. *Special Needs Adoption: A Study of Intact Families*. New York: Praeger.

Rosenthal, James, et al. 1991. Transracial and Inracial Adoption of Special Needs Children. *Journal of Multicultural Social Work* 1, 3: 331–32.

Rosenthal, James, Victor Groze, and H. Curiel. 1990. Race, Social Class, and Special Needs Adoption. *Social Work* 35, 6: 532–39.

Rothman, Barbara Katz. 1989. *Recreating Motherhood: Ideology and Technology in Patriarchal Society*. New York: Norton.

Rowe, William, and Vivian Schelling. 1991. *Memory and Modernity: Popular Culture in Latin America*. London: Verso.

Rubenstein, William B. 1993. *Lesbians, Gay Men, and the Law*. New York: New York University Press.

Rubin, Gayle. 1989. Thinking Sex: Notes for a Radical Theory of the Politics of Sexuality. In C. S. Vance, ed., *Pleasure and Danger*. London: Pandora.

Rubin, Lillian. 1976. *Worlds of Pain: Life in the Working Class Family*. New York: Basic Books.

———. 1995. *Families on the Fault Line: America's Working Class Speaks out about the Family, the Economy, Race, and Ethnicity*. New York: HarperPerennial.

Ruddick, Sara. 1989. *Maternal Thinking: Toward a Politics of Peace*. Boston: Beacon Press.

Sack, W. H., and D. Dale. 1982. Abuse and Deprivation in Failing Adoptions. *Child Abuse and Neglect* 6: 443–51.

Sandelowski, Margarete. 1993. *With Child in Mind: Studies of the Personal Encounter with Infertility*. Philadephia: University of Pennsylvania Press.

Sandelowski, Margarete, Betty G. Harris, and Beth Perry Black. 1992. Relinquishing Infertility: The Work of Pregnancy for Infertile Couples. *Qualitative Health Research* 2: 282–301.

Sawyer, Malinda. 1983. Certificate of Baptism. *SHARE Newsletter* 9, 3: 10.

Scheper-Hughes, Nancy. 1992. *Death without Weeping: The Violence of Everyday Life in Brazil*. Berkeley: University of California Press.

Scheper-Hughes, Nancy, and Carolyn Sargent, eds. 1998. *Small Wars: The Cultural Politics of Childhood*. Berkeley: University of California Press.

Schleifer, Aliah. 1986. *Motherhood in Islam*. Cambridge, U.K.: Islamic Academy.

Schneider, David. 1968. *American Kinship: A Cultural Account*. Englewood Cliffs, N.J.: Prentice Hall.

Schneider, Jane, and Annette B. Weiner. 1989. Introduction. In Annette B. Weiner and Jane Schneider, eds., *Cloth and Human Experience*. Washington, D.C.: Smithsonian Institution Press.

Schneider, Judi (Alexander's Grammy). 1996. Grammy's Grief. *SHARE Newsletter* 5(2): 6–8.

Schorsch, Anita. 1976. *Mourning Becomes America: Mourning Art in the New Nation*. Harrisburg, Penn.: Pennsylvania Historical and Museum Commission.

Scobie, Edward. 1972. *Black Britannia: A History of Blacks in Britain*. Chicago: Johnson Publishing Company.

Seiter, Ellen. 1995. *Sold Separately: Children and Parents in Consumer Culture*. New Brunswick, N.J.: Rutgers University Press.

Sennott, Charles. 1996. Adoption Joy Turns to Nightmare. *Boston Globe*, June 16, p. 1.

Shalev, Carmel. 1989. *Birth Power: The Case for Surrogacy*. New Haven: Yale University Press.

Shapiro, Michael J. 1988. The Political Rhetoric of Photography. In *The Politics of Representation: Writing Practices in Biography, Photography, and Policy Analysis*. Madison: University of Wisconsin Press.

SHARE Newsletter. 1991. Recognition of Life Certificates. SHARE Newsletter 14, 6: 7.

Shaw, Stephanie. 1994. Mothering under Slavery in the Antebellum South. In Evelyn Nakano Glenn, Grace Chang, and Linda Rennie Forcey, eds., *Mothering: Ideology, Experience and Agency*. New York: Routledge.

Sherman, Edmund, and Evelyn S. Newman. 1977. The Meaning of Cherished Personal Possessions for the Elderly. *Journal of Aging and Human Development* 8, 2: 181–92.

Sherrill, Kenneth. 1993. On Gay People as a Politically Powerless Group. In Kenneth Sherrill, ed., *Gays and the Military: Joseph Steffan versus the United States*. Princeton: Princeton University Press.

Sheumaker, Helen. 1997. "This Lock You See": Nineteenth-Century Hair Work as the Commodified Self. *Fashion Theory* 1, 4: 421–46.

Shireman, J., and P. Johnson. 1985. Single-Parent Adoptions: A Longitudinal Study. *Children and Youth Services Review* 7: 321–34.

———. 1986. A Longitudinal Study of Black Adoptions: Single-Parent, Transracial, and Traditional. *Social Work*, May-June, pp. 172–76.

Shore, Cris. 1992. Virgin Births and Sterile Debates: Anthropology and the New Reproductive Technologies. *Current Anthropology* 33: 295–301.

Shultz, Marjorie Maguire. 1990. Reproductive Technology and Intent-Based Parenthood: An Opportunity for Gender Neutrality. *Wisconson Law Review* 2: 297–398.

Silber, Kathleen, and Phyllis Speedlin. 1991. *Dear Birthmother: Thank You for Our Baby.* San Antonio: Corona.

Simmel, Georg. 1950. Adornment. In *The Sociology of Georg Simmel.* Trans. and ed. Kurt H. Wolff. New York: Free Press.

Simon, Rita J., Howard Alstein, and Marygold S. Melli. 1994. *The Case for Transracial Adoption.* Lanham, Md.: University Press of America.

Simonds, Wendy, and Barbara Katz Rothman. 1992. *Centuries of Solace: Expressions of Maternal Grief in Popular Literature.* Philadelphia: Temple University Press.

Singer, Milton. 1978. For a Semiotic Anthropology. In Thomas A. Sebeok, ed., *Sight, Sound, and Sense.* Bloomington: Indiana University Press.

Skocpol, Theda. 1992. *Protecting Soldiers and Mothers: The Political Origins of Social Policy in the United States.* Cambridge, Mass.: Harvard University Press.

Smart, Carol. 1991. The Legal and Moral Ordering of Child Custody. *Journal of Law and Society* 18: 485–500.

Smart, Carol, and Selma Sevenhuijsen. 1989. *Child Custody and the Politics of Gender.* London: Routledge.

Smith, Dorothy, and Laurie Nehis Sherwen. 1983. *Mothers and Their Adoptive Children: The Bonding Process.* New York: Tiresias Press.

Smith, Pam. 1988. Suggested Keepsake for Bereaved Parents. . . . *SHARE Newsletter* 11 (3): 6.

Smith, S. L., and J. A. Howard. 1991. A Comparative Study of Successful and Disrupted Adoptions. *Journal of Social Service Review* 65: 248–65.

Smock, Audrey Chapman, and Nadia Haggag Youssef. 1977. Egypt: From Seclusion to Limited Participation. In Janet Zollinger Giele and Audrey Chapman Smock, eds., *Women: Roles and Status in Eight Countries.* New York: John Wiley.

Snowden, R., G. Mitchell, and E. Snowden. 1983. *Artificial Reproduction: A Social Investigation.* London: Allen and Unwin.

Solinger, Rickie. 1992. *Wake Up Little Susie: Single Pregnancy and Race before Roe v. Wade.* New York: Routledge.

———. 1994. Race and "Value": Black and White Illegitimate Babies, 1945–1965. In Evelyn Nakano Glenn, Grace Chang, and Linda Rennie Forcey, eds., *Mothering: Ideology, Experience, and Agency.* New York: Routledge.

———. 1998. Poisonous Choice. In Molly Ladd-Taylor and Lauri Umansky, eds., *Bad Mothers: The Politics of Blame in Twentieth Century America.* New York: New York University Press.

Solomos, John. 1993. *Race and Racism in Britain.* 2nd ed. New York: St. Martin's Press.

Somers, Margaret. 1994. From Category to Relation: Narrative and the Social Constitution of Identity. Paper presented at the annual meeting of the American Sociological Association, Pittsburgh.

Sonbol, Amira el Azhary. 1991. *The Creation of a Medical Profession in Egypt, 1800–1922.* Syracuse: Syracuse University Press.

Speert, Harold. 1980. *Obstetrics and Gynecology in America: A History.* Chicago: American College of Obstetricians and Gynecologists.

Spellman, Elizabeth. 1988. *Inessential Woman: Problems of Exclusion in Feminist Thought.* Boston, Mass.: Beacon Press.

Stack, Carol B. 1974. *All Our Kin: Strategies for Survival in a Black Community.* New York: Harper and Row.

Stephens, Beth. 1988. Women in Nicaragua. *Monthly Review* 40, 4: 1–18.

Stephens, Sharon, ed. 1996. *Children and the Politics of Culture.* Princeton: Princeton University Press.

Stivison, David. 1982. Homosexuals and the Constitution. In William Paul et al., eds., *Homosexuality: Social, Psychological, and Biological Issues.* Beverly Hills, Calif.: Sage Publications.

Stolcke, Verena. 1986. New Reproductive Technologies: Same Old Fatherhood. *Critique of Anthropology* 6, 3: 5–31.

Stolley, K. S. 1993. Statistics on Adoption in the United States. In I. Schulman, ed., *The Future of Children.* Los Altos, Calif. Center for the Future of Children.

Strathern, Marilyn. 1992a. *After Nature: English Kinship in the Late Twentieth Century.* Cambridge: Cambridge University Press.

———. 1992b. *Reproducing the Future: Anthropology, Kinship, and the New Reproductive Technologies.* London: Routledge.

———. 1991. "The Pursuit of Certainty: Investigating Kinship in the Late Twentieth Century." Paper presented at the American Anthropological Association Meetings, Chicago.

Stratton, Jon. 1996. *The Desirable Body: Cultural Fetishism and the Erotics of Consumption.* Manchester: Manchester University Press.

Strong, Pauline Turner. 1998. To Forget Their Tongue, Their Name, and Their Whole Relation: The Contest of Kinship in North America. Paper presented at the Wenner-Gren symposium New Directions in Kinship Study: A Core Concept Revisited, Majorca, March 27–April 4.

Susoeff, Steve. 1985. Assessing Children's Best Interests When a Parent Is Gay or Lesbian: Toward a Rational Custody Decision. *UCLA Law Review* 32: 852–903.

Susser, Ida. 1996. The Construction of Poverty and Homelessness in U.S. Cities. *Annual Review of Anthropology* 25: 411–35.

Sutton-Smith, Brian. 1986. *Toys as Culture.* New York: Gardner Press.

Talbot, Margaret. 1998. Attachment Theory: The Ultimate Experiment. *New York Times Magazine,* May 24, pp. 24–31.

Taylor, Emilie. 1993. A Little Flower. *Unite Notes* 12, 2: 1.

Taylor, Janelle S. n.d. An All-Consuming Experience: Obstetrical Ultrasound and the Commodification of Pregnancy.

Taylor, Linda. 1995. Is International Adoption Overtaking U.S. Adoption? *Adoption Advocates Newsletter* 3, 10: 1–3.

Terbush, Cheryl. 1992. Memorial Bricks. *SHARE Newsletter* 1, 5: 7.

Terrell, John, and Judith Modell. 1994. Anthropology and Adoption. *American Anthropologist* 96: 155–61.

Thompson, Becky. 2000. *Mothering without a Compass: White Mother's Love, Black Son's Courage*. Minneapolis: University of Minnesota Press.

Thorne, Barrie, with Marilyn Yalom. 1992. *Rethinking the Family: Some Feminist Questions*. Rev. ed. Boston: Northeastern University Press.

Thorsen, Liv Emma. 1996. Taming Nature with Things. Paper presented at the joint meeting of the Society for Social Studies of Science and the European Association for the Study of Science and Technology, Bielefeld.

Tizard, Barbara. 1977. *Adoption: A Second Chance*. New York: Free Press

Tizard, Barbara, and Ann Phoenix. 1993. *Black, White or Mixed Race? Race and Racism in the Lives of Young People of Mixed Parentage*. New York: Routledge.

Townsend, Rita, and Ann Perkins, eds. 1992. *Bitter Fruit: Women's Experiences of Unplanned Pregnancy, Abortion, and Adoption*. Alameda, Calif.: Hunter House.

Triseliotis, John P. 1972. *In Search of Origins: The Experience of Adopted People*. London: Routledge and Kegan Paul.

———. 1993. Inter-country Adoption: In Whose Best Interest? In Michael Humphrey and Heather Humphrey, eds., *Inter-country Adoption: Practical Experiences*. London: Tavistock/Routledge.

Troyna, Barry, and Richard Hatcher. 1992. *Racism in Children's Lives: A Study of Mainly White Primary Schools*. London: Routledge.

Tsing, Anna Lowenhaupt. 1990. Monster Stories: Women Charged with Perinatal Endangerment. In Faye Ginsburg and Anna Lowenhaupt Tsing, eds., *Uncertain Terms: Negotiating Gender in American Culture*. Boston: Beacon Press.

Twin to Twin Transfusion Syndrome Foundation. 1994. *Compassionate Deliveries: When Loss Occurs in a Multiple Pregnancy*.

Twine, France Winddance. 1996. Brown Skinned White Girls: Class, Culture, and the Construction of White Identity in Suburban Communities. *Gender, Place, and Culture: A Journal of Feminist Geography* 3(2): 200–24.

———. 1998. Managing Everyday Racisms: White Mothers of African-Descent Children in Britain. In Jodi O'Brien and Judith Howard, eds., *Everyday Inequalities: Critical Inquiries*. London: Blackwell.

———. 1999a. Transracial Mothering and Anti-racism: The Case of White Mothers of African-Descent Children in Britain. *Feminist Studies* 25(3): 729–46.

Twine, France Winddance, Jonathan Warren, and Francisco Ferrandiz. 1991. *Just Black? Multiracial Identity*. New York: Filmmakers Library.

U.S. DHHS (United States Department of Health and Human Services). 1996. Statistical Tables on Foster Care and Adoption. http://www.acf.dhhs.gov/programs/cb/stats/afcars/reed96b.htm.

Valdez, Gail, and J. Regis McNamara. 1994. Matching to Prevent Adoption Disruption. *Child and Adolescent Social Work Journal* 11: 391–403.

Van Gennep, Arnold. 1960. *The Rites of Passage*. Chicago: University of Chicago Press.

Van Sant, Dorothy. 1986. Farewell Rituals and Religion. *SHARE Newsletter* 9, 4: 9–10.

Ventura, Stephanie J., et al. 1995. Trends in Pregnancies and Pregnancy Rates: Estimates for the United States, 1980–92. Centers for Disease Control and Prevention/National Center for Health Statistics, *Monthly Vital Statistics Report* 43, 11.

Vick, Carlotte. 1995. Out of Sight, Out of Mind: The Child Welfare Data Collection Problem. *Adoptalk* (NACAC), fall, p. 4.

Vilas, Carlos. 1986. *The Sandinista Revolution*. New York: Monthly Review Press.

———. 1984. *Perfiles de la revolución Sandinista*. Havana: Casa de las Américas.

Voegele, Liz, ed. 1991. Recognition of Life Certificates. *SHARE Newsletter* 14, 6: 7.

Wadia-Ells, Susan, ed. 1995. *The Adoption Reader: Birth Mothers, Adoptive Mothers, and Adopted Daughters Tell Their Stories*. Seattle: Seal Press.

Walker, Thomas, ed. 1993. *Nicaragua: The First Five Years*. New York: Praeger.

Ware, Vron. 1992. *Beyond the Pale: White Women, Racism and History*. London: Verso.

———. 1996. Island Racism: Gender, Place and White Power. *Feminist Review* 54: 65–86.

Warnock, Mary. 1984. *The Warnock Report: Report of the Committee of Inquiry into Human Fertilisation and Embryology*. London: Her Majesty's Stationery Office.

Weitzman, Lenore J. 1985. *The Divorce Revolution: The Unexpected Social and Economic Consequences for Women and Children in America*. New York: Free Press.

Wendell, Susan. 1996. *The Rejected Body: Feminist Philosophical Reflections on Disability*. New York: Routledge.

Wessel, Lois. 1991. Reproductive Rights in Nicaragua: From the Sandinistas to the Government of Violeta Chamorro. *Feminist Studies* 17, 3: 537–49.

Weston, Kath. 1991. *Families We Choose: Lesbian, Gays, Kinship*. New York: Columbia University Press.

Westwood, Sallie, and Sara Radcliffe, eds. 1993. *"Viva": Women and Popular Protest in Latin America*. London: Routledge.

WGBH. 1994. *Adoption: In Whose Interest? Say, Brother!* Documentary.

White, Elizabeth H. 1978. Legal Reform as an Indicator of Women's Status in Muslim Nations. In Lois Beck and Nikki Keddie, eds., *Women in the Muslim World*. Cambridge, Mass.: Harvard University Press.

Whyte, Susan Reynolds, and Benedicte Ingstad. 1992. Disability and Culture: An Overview. In Benedicte Ingstad and Susan Reynolds White, eds., *Disability and Culture*. Berkeley: University of California Press.

Williams, Patricia. 1991. *The Alchemy of Race and Rights: Diary of a Law Professor*. Cambridge, Mass.: Harvard University Press.

Willis, Susan. 1991. *A Primer for Daily Life*. New York: Routledge.

Wilson, Anne. 1981. In Between: The Mother in the Interracial Family. *New Community: Journal of the Commission for Racial Equality* 9, 2: 208–15.

———. 1987. *Mixed Race Children: A Study of Identity.* London: Allen and Unwin.

Wilson, Lawrence A., and Raphael Shannon. 1979. Homosexual Organizations and the Right to Association. *The Hastings Law Journal* 30: 1029–74.

Wolf, Margery. 1972. *Women and the Family in Rural Taiwan.* Stanford: Stanford University Press.

World Health Organization. 1987. Infections, Pregnancies, and Infertility: Perspectives on Prevention. *Fertility and Sterility* 47: 964–68.

Wozniak, Danielle F. 1997. Family Values: The Social and Self Construction of Foster Mothering in the United States. Manuscript.

Wray, Matt, and Annalee Newitz, eds. 1997. *White Trash: Race and Class in America.* New York: Routledge.

Yngvesson, Barbara. 1997. Negotiating Motherhood: Identity and Difference in Open Adoption. *Law and Society Review* 31, 1: 31–80.

Zelizer, Viviana A. 1985. *Pricing the Priceless Child: The Changing Social Value of Children.* New York: Basic Books.

Zerbel, Tom. 1987. Burial Cradle. *SHARE Newsletter* 10, 3: 7.

Zola, Irving. 1993. Self, Identity, and the Naming Question: Reflections on the Language of Disability. *Social Science and Medicine* 36, 2: 167–73.

Zwimpfer, D. M. 1983. Indicators of Adoption Breakdown. *Social Casework* 64: 169–77.

Index

abortion
  and adoption, 58–59, 286–90
  and disability, 185
  poor women and, 283, 286–90
  and pregnancy loss, 118
  Sandinistas on, 242–43
  and surrogacy, 68–70
abused children, 25–26, 35–36, 39–40,
    172, 266–74
AC Controls Ltd., 122
adoption
  and abortion, 58–59, 286–90
  class in, 51–54, 283–87
  cultures where normative, 20–21, 26–27
  divorce following, 28–29
  international, 26–27, 34–35, 42–54
  Islamic prohibition, 166
  and kinship beliefs, 11–13
  limited-consent, 193–94
  open, 26–27, 35–36, 50
  and poverty, 44–45, 54, 283–87
  of premature babies, 184–85
  public-agency, 29, 36–42, 50, 53–54
  and race, 3, 11–54, 58–59
  single-parent, 27–36, 47–48
  through surrogacy, 193
African-Caribbean culture in Britain, 76-
    105
Aiding a Mother Experiencing Neonatal
    Death (AMEND), 129–31

AIDS, 48, 158
American Civil Liberties Union (ACLU),
    59
AMNLAE, Nicaraguan women's group,
    237, 240–42
antiracism, 77, 79, 82, 94–105
Asociación de Mujeres frentes a la
    Problematica Nacional
    (AMPRONAC), 247–48
Association for Recognizing the Life of
    Stillborns, 129–31
attachment disorder, 47
authority, maternal, 6, 263–97

Baby M case, 11–12, 50
Baby's Journal (Metropolitan Museum),
    121
"Baby Things" (Foster), 119–20
"bad" mothers, 17, 24-27, 266–97
Baez, Gladys, 240
baptismal certificate, do-it-yourself,
    129–31
Baulé society, 20
biological determinism, 18
"biopower," 159–60
"birth bond," 14–15, 17
boundaries, mother/child, 31
Britain, multiracial families in, 76–105
Buzzanca, Luanne and John, 223–27
Buzzanca v. Buzzanca, 223–27